Children's Literature

PRENTICE-HALL INTERNATIONAL, INC., *London*
PRENTICE-HALL OF AUSTRALIA, PTY. LTD., *Sydney*
PRENTICE-HALL OF CANADA, LTD., *Toronto*
PRENTICE-HALL OF INDIA PRIVATE LTD., *New Delhi*
PRENTICE-HALL OF JAPAN, INC., *Tokyo* ·

Children's Literature: Strategies of Teaching

ROBERT WHITEHEAD

Sacramento State College

PRENTICE-HALL, INC., ENGLEWOOD CLIFFS, NEW JERSEY

MODERN ELEMENTARY METHODS SERIES

Contents

CHAPTER ONE

A Planned Program in Literature: Introduction

Creating in children a love for literature is a basic part of the educational process. Necessary to the development of that love are good books, a well-defined literature program, and inspired, knowledgeable teachers. Without these essential ingredients, few children will ever reap the rewards of a full and satisfying literary experience: the feeling of pure joy which a fine story brings; sensitivity to and appreciation of the beauty of the English language; a deepened understanding of human behavior, ideals, and spiritual values.

Since a child's appreciation of literature comes partly from exposure to stimulating stories and books, it is reassuring to note that there is available today a wealth of well-written, attractively illustrated, and intensely moving books. The children of today can tap the treasury of the past or draw upon the abundant stream of current literature by visiting their public library or by utilizing the school library.

Equally important to the development of literary appreciation in children is the establishment of a creative, sequential program of literature activities designed as an intrinsic part of the total reading plan. Such a plan views literature as a functional part of the total reading program, making a significant contribution to both reading and the building of an appreciation for literature by: motivating children to read more and better books; helping boys and girls to explore new interests and to tackle new problems; providing youngsters with meaningful, literature-centered reading practice; expos-

1

ing the young reader to the great literary heritage of the past and the present.

But in an exploration of literature in a classroom setting, the teacher is the key, the spark, and the guiding spirit. She is the one person in command of a knowledge of children, the books they read, and the methods and materials for teaching literature. No one is in a better position to know the backgrounds, interests, maturity and reading levels, and values of the pupils than the teacher. The teacher is the builder of programs, the "provider-of-time" to read, the initiator of activities, the sparkplug who shows children by her own enthusiasm that the reading of literature is a joyous and rewarding form of recreation.

Keeping the importance of the teacher in mind this chapter opens with a discussion of some principles necessary to a successful and fruitful literature program. It then proceeds to enumerate the objectives of a literature program, and to examine the scope of children's literature. The chapter explores children's reading preferences by age levels, and closes with a discussion of how a teacher may assess and ascertain the literature interests and tastes of her students.

PRINCIPLES OF A SUCCESSFUL LITERATURE PROGRAM

The basic intent of this book is to describe specific practices which will aid the classroom teacher in planning an attractive and effective program in literature. In order to help formulate and evaluate the procedure as we progress, it seems useful first to list a few basic principles for the teacher:

1. How an instructor approaches the teaching of literature—how she feels about children and books and the literature program—goes a long way in determining children's lifelong attitudes toward reading. If the teacher sincerely understands and appreciates the value of children's books and stories, has a concern for the well-being and education of boys and girls, and is willing and able to provide an exciting, functional program of literature, her students will become more and more enamoured of the reading process. The result is a lifetime habit of good reading. The teacher is the key to children's attitudes.

Those teachers of children's literature who hasten to bring children and fine books together are the ones who found adventure, knowledge, and understanding in stories and poems when they were young. Indeed, I would venture to say such teachers still pick up a juvenile book with fond expectations of pleasure and wonder. Such teachers remain Becky Thatchers or Tom Sawyers; they still enjoy going down into the hole with Alice; they continue to feel a tingle of terror as they listen for the cadenced stomp of Long John Silver's peg leg on the deck of the ship.

Fortunate are the children who have such a teacher. It is this teacher —the one who has felt deeply and appreciated fully—who can stimulate children to truly appreciate their literary heritage.

However, no teacher can "turn herself on" to fill this role. She must truly live it—be it—a teacher of literature. To feign a knowledge of and interest in literature when none is there will never work, and may even do irreparable harm. Children above all others have the capability of seeing through such a facade, and they immediately label the teacher as "phony." It would be better if a teacher who is fearful of recognizing and expressing emotion, kindness, sympathy, and love as expressed in literature does not teach literature at all.

2. The teacher must keep uppermost in her mind the fact that books are to be enjoyed. If there is no fun for the child in reading books and in the accompanying literature activities, there is little learning, little relaxation from daily cares, little resolution of personal problems. The teacher must provide her pupils with opportunities to share the individual joy they have gleaned from their literature experiences. An informal and relaxed atmosphere is indispensable to the attainment of the goal. In short, the teacher and her pupils must find fun and relaxation in literature. This must be one of the primary goals.

3. The teacher must recognize the interests and abilities of each individual child and build upon these interests. She must take the child from where he is, not where the teacher would like him to be. The advancement toward full literary appreciation for each child must be accomplished in an orderly, sequential fashion. Along the way the teacher must ascertain the genuine literary preferences and interests of the child rather than imposing upon him her own perception of what is worthwhile in literature.

4. Methods of instruction should be aimed at assisting students in experiencing what a poem or story has to say. Table 1 graphically illustrates a number of positive procedures—accompanied by their negative counterparts—that tend to strengthen children's interests in literature.

5. The teacher must be acquainted with a wide variety of techniques, activities, devices, and media which will stimulate, develop, and reveal children's interest in and knowledge of literature. A teacher's ability to promote an appreciation for literature will be greatly advanced when she has acquired a knowledge of (a) the characteristics of a stimulating

TABLE 1

DO LET CHILDREN	DON'T REQUIRE CHILDREN TO
Study style and plot if it adds to their enjoyment.	Study style and plot development mechanically.
Discuss, dramatize, and manifest enthusiasm for books through creative endeavors.	Submit to formal tests over story facts.
Recall voluntarily authors and details that have titillated their fancies.	Memorize the names of authors and details of their lives.
Lay up a treasure house of favorite poems *if they like.*	Commit to memory the teacher's favorite poems.
Tell voluntarily of the attitudes, values, and behaviors they have seen developed in books and book characters.	Grasp the moral and theme of all the stories they read.

physical environment, (b) how to build and conduct literature units, (c) techniques of oral and written interpretation, (d) dramatization, (e) construction media and techniques, (f) literature games, and (g) audio-visual resources.

6. The teacher must have a broad knowledge of children's stories and poems. No teacher can teach literature successfully while resting on a few old classics and a brace of new, shiny-faced dollar dreadfuls. Nor will her literature program be balanced until it includes the study of all forms of literature.

It is not possible for a teacher to be familiar with all the new children's books and techniques, but it is imperative that she know of the best books and materials by preparing herself in the following ways:

read children's books. There is no suitable substitute for balancing a new book in your hands, studying the format and illustrations, reading the contents critically, and evaluating the book in terms of the needs and interests of your class or of an individual youngster.

Acquaint yourself with children's books by:

borrowing . . . . from the public and school libraries.
browsing . . . . at the department store exhibits.
visiting . . . . the juvenile literature alcove of a nearby college or university.
buying . . . . an occasional volume for yourself.
sharing . . . . books with children.

read books about books. Such books as May Hill Arbuthnot's *Children and Books* and Charlotte Huck and Dorothy Young's *Children's Literature in the Elementary School* are of inestimable value to a teacher who wishes to acquire a working knowledge of children's literature: its history, standards by which to judge books and stories, and materials and methods in teaching literature to children. These and other professional books are also replete with various bits of information that add color to a storytelling hour or a read-aloud session with children: how the Mother Goose verse "Pussycat, Pussycat" is based upon an incident that occurred in Queen Elizabeth's court; that McCloskey's daughter provided the germ of the idea for his *One Morning in Maine*. A list of other books about books can be found in the bibliography in the back of this book and at the ends of the various chapters.

utilize the anthology. An alert teacher of literature is never far from her anthology. A carefully compiled anthology is the single, best resource a teacher has at her command, containing the cream of the literature stock, past to present. Enabling the regular classroom teacher to produce at a moment's notice a poem or story that will capitalize on the teachable moment, the anthology is also a valuable tool for the substitute teacher who has no home library from which to draw material and for the teacher residing in a remote area where library resources are limited.

comb other publications. Other sources of guidance in the selection of children's reading matter, prepared by specialists in children's literature, are available in many forms. A significant number of these sources are readily accessible to the teacher, including:

. . . children's magazines, many of them of top quality, providing a constant stream of excellent short stories and poetry.

. . . publisher's catalogs, giving helpful information about the subject matter and grade-level suitability of new juvenile publications.

. . . graded booklists, prepared by various governmental and private agencies, as well as by qualified librarians and teachers.

. . . periodicals and newspapers, publishing regular sections and columns devoted to analytical articles and to reviews of juvenile books.

participate. The teacher dedicated to enlarging her fund of information about children's literature will avail herself of the opportunity to enroll in college courses in literature for children. Equally profitable experiences are active participation in regional conferences, local institutes, and workshops on literature, which are fashioned to the needs of teachers.

7. The teacher must plan a continuing program of evaluation in terms of two main purposes: (1) growth in children's knowledge and appreciation of literature and (2) advancement in the area of personal and social understandings. While reading is only one of many influences

upon children's lives, the teacher must be ready to capitalize upon the guidance aspects of literature. Even though they cannot be measured statistically, attitudes are developed, values are changed, and behavior is influenced by the reading of literature. On-going evaluation must be made in terms of these goals.

TEACHER'S OBJECTIVES: A REFLECTION OF ATTITUDE TOWARD CHILDREN'S LITERATURE

A literature program has as its goal the building in children of knowledges and skills as well as attitudes and appreciations. In such a program children are started on a wide range of real and imaginary literary experiences that become a shared heritage through which they learn to better understand and communicate with their fellow men. Along the way they are introduced to the techniques for evaluating the literature they read, so that by the time they leave school they will have the means to understand, enjoy, and appreciate literature and its humanizing values. This last ought to be the primary aim of a program of literature.

The following list of objectives has to do specifically with the goals the teacher has in mind for individual youngsters as they read literature and participate in the activities of the literature program.

1. *To Help the Child Understand Himself and His Present Problems.* The current period of accelerated scientific and social change, which brings confusion and anxiety to individuals within a family, increasingly forces a child to call upon his own resources to solve his problems. The child needs to know that he has many a ready ally in solving his problems in the form of literature characters who have been successful in their encounters with similar problems. In this way the young reader comes to realize that his present struggles in life are no different than those encountered by other boys and girls in and out of literature.

2. *To Provide Opportunities for Escape from Routine.* All children yearn for and deserve escape from routine. Literature provides a haven of retreat and comfort for pressure-weary boys and girls. The miracles and magic of fables and fairy tales, the "just for fun" adventures of MacGregor's *Miss Pickerell* and McCloskey's *Homer Price*, and the animal tales wherein the reader assumes the role of the protector: all are popular with children. This escape is not a retreat from reality. Rather, it is a chance for children to enjoy beautiful writing, to laugh, and to return to their assigned tasks relaxed and with restored spirits.

3. *To Provide a Focus for Leisure-Time Activities.* The children of today are beckoned by a host of possible leisure-time activities. It is the

responsibility of the schools to help children select what is best for them as individuals—what is worthwhile and of lasting quality. The proper introduction of good books should enable children to associate pleasure with literature and help form a fast and lasting bond between a child and the book-reading habit.

4. *To Develop an Appreciation of Country and American Ideals.* An important objective of education in the American society is to implant in children a deep and lasting love for their country. Biographies of courageous Americans, seen in such books as Daugherty's *Daniel Boone* or Beard's *Our Foreign-Born Americans: What They Have Done for America* develop in children an understanding of the historical growth of this country and an appreciation of the men and women who built it. Literature infuses the child with the spirit of the American way of life in a manner that avoids the didactic, formal approach to teaching patriotism.

5. *To Increase the Child's Knowledge and Understanding of the Problems of Others.* Simply, literature helps the child appreciate and understand other people at home and abroad. The homogeneous character of many neighborhoods and communities limits a child's knowledge of others, particularly in the primary grades. Literature provides the means whereby the child can learn about many other cultures and countries. The child comes to see the similarities between his own experiences and those of children elsewhere, and this helps friendships and understandings develop and ripen.

6. *To Discover and Develop Ethical Standards.* The really fine books help develop in children a sense of high ethical standards. The worthwhile books of fiction and biography show characters as they really are, uncovering their weaknesses and strengths, their virtues and vanities as the plots and biogaphies unfold. The wise teacher helps the child to analyze the qualities of the literature characters and leads the child to identify the proper attitudes and decisions. Further, the reader eventually finds the words with which to express his own thoughts and ideals.

7. *To Utilize Literature as a Source for Further Creative Endeavor.* Books serve as the wellsprings of creative effort for many children. A beautiful passage in a story may stimulate one child to write an original poem; a well-illustrated book may challenge another youngster to paint or do sculpturing. Other feelings aroused in books may lead to dancing, the dramatization of stories, and/or singing. Further, children should be given frequent opportunities to share books with their classmates via puppetry, art, music, and the like, avoiding the inhibiting and conventional oral or written book review.

8. *To Promote an Appreciation of the English Language.* Teachers

who read to boys and girls the best of children's literature will, in the process, expose them to the full beauty and flavor of the English language. The teaching need not be overt, for casual references to a particular word or phrase will often do. Indeed, children recognize immediately a particularly melodious, rhythmic, or emotional word or phrase and delight in rolling it about their tongues, often ad nauseum. "Klickitat Street," "jabberwocky," "Godfrey Gordon Gustavus Gore," and thousands of other language elements have been memorized instantly by children. Such phonologically appealing items represent good opportunities for children to "play" with the language. Children's awareness of language will be developed into an appreciation by the ever-alert teacher as she reads aloud good poetry and stories.

SCOPE OF CHILDREN'S READING

When children have pleasant experiences with all types of literature activities, their tastes and knowledges will inevitably be extended. Conversely, minimal exposure to books and creative literature endeavor, or experiences heavily weighted by adult prejudices, tend to limit children's interests. Particular care is warranted when bringing children into initial contacts with biography, dramatization, and poetry, for children often turn away from these in disgust when a teacher's introductions and presentations are vapid and uninspired. The following categories of books suggest the types of reading matter preferred by children at different stages of development.

Adventure

Adventure stories have universal appeal. In a well-written adventure story, a child can travel to strange places like Sollow Sellew, or meet unusual characters like Onion John. Adventure stories are particularly good for emotional release, being a substitute for real-life adventures. Most children love the emotional catharsis they experience when thrust into a book filled with deep and dark mystery and adventure.

Primary children take great delight in books of everyday life adventure. Many authors have a knack of converting everyday living experiences into high adventure, while at the same time giving children insights into people, problems of growing up, and standards of behavior.

Animal Tales

Children of all ages enjoy stories about animals. Whether the books on the library shelf deal with wild or tame animals, real or fanciful ones, the books are well-worn. Such books instill in children a love and respect for animals. At the same time, children learn of the harsh struggles of living things, and of man's sometimes inhumanity toward animals. Small children are eager to personify animals; older boys and girls dearly love the dog and horse books, whether in fact or fiction.

Biography

Children quickly identify themselves with the central character of a biography, and they gladly participate with the principal character as he struggles to attain his life goals. In directing children to biography, teachers must learn to avoid weak books and treatments of individuals that bore children. Children prefer heroes of action (Simon Bolivar) to those of ideas (Thomas Jefferson).

Biographies may be correlated with almost every subject matter area of the curriculum: art, history, music, mathematics, and so on. They often prove to be much more exciting reference material than the encyclopedia or textbook.

Fables, Folk and Fairy Tales

Fables are the briefest types of narrative, their value lying in the fact that a moral is drawn and the philosophies of ancient peoples are revealed. These two characteristics, plus their abstract nature, usually consign fables to the upper elementary grades, where they should be used in limited numbers.

The folk and fairy tales are quite simple narratives, which enable the reader to examine the emotions and cherished ideals of peoples of many cultures. Their simplicity of theme, the wonder and enchantment of the animals who speak, their exaggeration and wit make folk tales an endearing form of literature to young readers.

Humor

Amusing books, poems, and stories—those with a wry twist or a direct pun—find a ready audience with children of all ages. Giggles and guffaws are contagious, providing children with a much-needed release from their school routines, and teachers should deliberately induce such reactions in their classrooms in the daily read-aloud sessions. In this fashion children are led to pick up and to follow again the antics of *The Five Chinese Brothers*, the hilarious adventures of Bartholomew Cubbins, or William Cole's *Humorous Poetry for Children*.

More subtle humor is equally appreciated by children. Fanciful tales with a modern twist, in which supermen and talking animals cavort, make the impossible truly funny to most young people. The present-day orientation to the sciences, reflected in the choices of books that teachers read to children, tends to force children away from the funny, fanciful tales. In her choice of books, the teacher should not allow her children to be swept away on the tide of science-oriented books, thus depriving the youngsters of the wondrous magic of humorous and droll tales which serve as healthy escape from dull routine.

Informational Books

The greatest growth in any area of children's literature, both in the quality and quantity of books produced, is in the category of nonfiction. This growth has occurred for many reasons: the insatiable curiosity of children; the "explosion" of knowledge; the genuine excitement that children feel over aircraft, space, and space travel; and the attractiveness of the books themselves with their brilliant formats and illustrations, accurate subject matter, and vivid, imaginative writing. Children seek out and pore over books on almost any subject imaginable: animal care, cooking, skiing, woodworking. Teachers would do well to reacquaint themselves each new school year with the library collections of informational books they draw upon. If they do not, the children will quickly overwhelm them with the tremendous array of facts and figures they have assembled from these volumes.

Myths

A myth is an involved tale of a god or godlike beings, giving the reader an understanding of the beliefs prevalent in an ancient culture. With children, the attractiveness of a myth lies in the human attributes of the gods and in the dramatic action of the story. Myths are more suited to older children, for the following reasons: the plots are likely to be too complicated or inappropriate in content for younger children; many of the concepts are beyond the children's experiences and understanding; much of the vocabulary may be unfamiliar; and, more often. than not, the sentence structure will be rather complex.

Nursery Rhymes

Practically every type of character, plot, setting, and theme a child will encounter in his later readings is to be found in the nursery rhymes. For this reason, primary teachers should see to it that children are exposed to the full complement of nursery tales. The nursery rhymes have particular qualities which make them appealing to young people: rhythm, vigorous action, humor, pathos. Add to this the variety of subject matter—animals, arithmetic (counting rhymes), dramatization, people, riddles, songs—and it is easy to see why children are so captivated by these appealing verses and sayings.

Books About Other Regions, Lands, Peoples

Technological advancements in transportation and the birth of new nations have produced great curiosity among children about their far and near neighbors. Both the regional stories—about Indians, Quakers, and the like—and the stories of other lands and peoples have found a waiting audience of children. These expertly wrought stories which give a conception of how and why people live in a certain area show how people of other regions are like us in their customs, ideals, and everyday activities.

Poetry

When children listen to poetry presented by one who knows what children like and who reads with meaning and a sense of enjoyment, they turn to it repeatedly as a means of emotional experience.

The teacher remains the key to meaningful poetry experiences for her students. Types of poems to be avoided are those with long, flowery descriptions, complex figures of speech, and poems not of the child's world. Children seek out poems with fine rhythm and melody, and those that paint a recognizable picture and/or tell a story.

Children's tastes and appreciations for poetry will improve as the teacher or a child recites a favorite poem or from sheer pleasure with a rhyme or rhythm recently heard, or during a "teachable moment" (for example, at the rise of an unexpected storm). Positive feelings for poetry are often masked by boys. But the teacher will feel rewarded for her untiring efforts when that first chuckle or other expression of approval bursts through.

LEVELS OF DEVELOPMENT AND CHILDREN'S READING INTERESTS

What children read is determined primarily by who they are, their interests, and the time in which they live. Yet, it is interesting to note that teachers and librarians report little change in the basic reading

TABLE 2

SUBJECT OF FAVORITE STORIES	CHARACTERISTICS OF STORY LINE	BOOK
Age: preschool Animal and nature stories Fairy tales (simple) Familiar people, things, settings Finger play verses Jingles Nursery rhymes Rhythms	Is repetitive in text. Demands some participation, as in touching and naming. Enables child's name to be inserted for real characters. Is quite simple. Introduces poetry.	Is ·colorful, or has bold figures (if done in black and white) on every page. Has an attractive, sturdy cover and large type. Is lap-size. Has occasional "pop-out" quality. Has more pictures than text. Is 24-48 pages in length.
Ages: six through eight Animals (pets and talking beasts) Fairy tales (simple) Familiar environment (family, play, school) Fanciful tales Humor and nonsense (slapstick) Mechanical devices, (cars, tractors, etc.) Real-life stories	Has a real plot (suspense and action). Is fast-paced, with action. Is brief and can be completed in one sitting. Helps reader identify with the character. Is convincing and understandable. Is easy to read, with simple vocabulary, short sentences.	Is eye-catching. Has large, clear type. Has 25 per cent or more of page space given to illustrations. Colored illustrations in preference to black and white. Synchronizes picture and text. Is 50 to 60 pages long, if fiction, less if nonfiction.

tastes of children as compared to those of their parents. Table 2 lists the types of books enjoyed by children today at various stages of development. At the same time the chart notes the characteristics of favorite story lines, and with the preferred formats in books, as seen by the different age groups.

Concurrently, a teacher would do well to keep in mind the following ten ideas about children and the literatures they read:

1. Characters, settings, plots, and themes must be simple and truthful (with the exception of books of fantasy, of course).

TABLE 2 (Cont.)

SUBJECT OF FAVORITE STORIES	CHARACTERISTICS OF STORY LINE	BOOK
Ages: nine through eleven		
Adventure	Has a vivid action plot.	Is 100 pages or more in length.
Animals (wild or tame, real or fanciful; dog stories for boys; horse stories for girls)	Has solid worth and appeal.	Has type that is neither too large nor too small.
Biography	Uses amusing words and names.	Has accurate illustrations that contribute to the book.
Different countries and people	Employs exaggeration and absurdity.	Has uncluttered margins.
History and historical fiction	Begins quickly.	Has open appearance and lively drawings.
Humor	Concentrates on the conversations.	Uses sentences that are not too long nor involved.
Invention	Uses the characters to carry out the plot.	
Mechanics	Has action, atmosphere, and strong characterization.	
Poetry		
Science and science experiments		
Sports and games (boys)		
Tall tales		
Ages: twelve through fourteen		
Adventure and mystery	Is fast moving, and forceful.	Has eye appeal.
American life (pioneer and present)	Helps reader meet his personal problems.	Is brief (a preference of boys).
Biography	Stresses individuality.	Has attractive illustrations (but they are not the primary reason for acceptance or rejection).
Career stories (girls)	Is accurate and detailed, if nonfiction.	Is designed basically to appeal to boys, although many books for girls alone are available.
Fantasy	Has sharply delineated characters.	
History	Has extensive plot and characterization.	
Humor		
Myths, legends, hero tales		
People of other lands		
Romance (girls)		
Science and science fiction (boys)		
Sports (boys)		
World affairs		

2. Most children prefer dialogue to description.

3. Most children prefer real people like Tom Sawyer, not gossamer Cinderellas.

4. Consult boys and girls rather than booklists when determining what children *really* enjoy.

5. Each book in a series should be judged on its own merits.

6. Funny words and expressions in stories titillate the fancy of young readers.

7. Generally, girls will read boys' books, but boys reject girls' books.

8. Generally speaking, humorous literature is the most popular type of reading material among children.

9. Story lines should be borne along by three types of words: concrete, colorful, and imaginative.

10. The first few paragraphs of a successful book or story open with quick action.

ASCERTAINING READING INTERESTS

The teacher of literature will want to utilize all of the various methods that are available to help her determine the reading interests of her boys and girls. The simplest technique is *observing* the daily behavior of students. Observations, play tasks, drawings, and other activities will reveal interests which the teacher may note on anecdotal record cards.

Formal and informal *interviews* with children will uncover their reading likes and dislikes. The most useful interviews will encourage the child to talk freely about his aspirations, favorite books, games, movies, sports, and radio and television programs. A mimeographed outline to guide the formal interview will provide uniformity of procedure and offer a convenient means of recording the information. To be most productive, the use of the interview technique must be on-going, because transitory interests of young children often provide information that is soon outdated.

Very large classes often make anecdotal recording of observations and interviews impractical. In that case *questionnaires* may prove helpful. Interest questionnaires are fundamentally of two types: (1) the interest and activity poll, and (2) the incomplete-sentence inventory. Interest and activity polls—both long and short forms—are usually checklists upon which each child expresses his preferences. These questionnaires may be prepared cooperatively by teachers or purchased commercially, the former having an advantage in that it may be adapted more readily to local conditions.

The advantages of the various activity poll forms, such as the one shown on pp. 15–19, are as follows:

1. Detailed information is provided on the reading likes and dislikes of children.

2. The form may be administered to almost any class group, with the teacher reading each item to children with a reading ability below the fifth grade level.

3. The questionnaire provides its own handy record form for each individual polled.

LEISURE-TIME ACTIVITIES POLL

Student's name .... **Grade** ....

Teacher's name .... **Date** ....

A. HOBBIES

1. What do you like to do in your spare time?

   a. ....   d. ....

   b. ....   e. ....

   c. ....   f. ....

2. List your favorite hobbies and sports.

   a. ....   c. ....

   b. ....   d. ....

B. TELEVISION, MOVIES, AND RADIO

1. Television

   a. About how many hours a day (Monday through Friday) do you spend watching television? .... On Saturday? .... On Sunday? ....

   b. List your favorite television program first, then your second, third and fourth choices.

      (1) ....   (3) ....

      (2) ....   (4) ....

   c. Make an X in front of the kind of television programs that you like to watch.

.... adventure	.... love/romance	.... specials
.... animal/nature	.... movies	.... sports
.... cartoon	.... musical	.... travel
.... comedy	.... mystery/detective	.... war
.... documentary	.... news	.... Western
.... educational	.... science/science fiction	

   d. Who is your favorite male television personality?

   ....

   e. Who is your favorite female television personality?

   ....

2. Movies

   a. About how many times a month do you go to the movies during school time (September 1 to May 31)? ....
   Summer (June 1 to September 1)? ....

   b. Name the two or three best movies you have seen recently.
      (1) ....
      (2) ....
      (3) ....

   c. Make an X in front of the kinds of movies that you like.

.... adventure	.... musical
.... animal/nature	.... mystery/detective
.... cartoon	.... science fiction
.... comedy	.... sports
.... documentary	.... travelogue
.... educational	.... war
.... love/romance	.... Western

   d. Who is your favorite male movie star?
      ....

   e. Who is your favorite female movie star?
      ....

3. Radio

   a. Do you own a transistor radio? Circle one: Yes   No

   b. Do you have a radio in your room at home? Circle one: Yes   No

   c. About how many hours a day do you spend listening to the radio? ....

   d. When do you do most of your listening to the radio?
   Check one or more:
      (1) On weekends ....
      (2) Before school (6 to 8 A.M.) ....
      (3) After school (4 to 6 P.M.) ....
      (4) During the summer ....
      (5) While doing homework ....

   e. Make an X in front of the kinds of radio programs that you like.

.... biographical sketches	.... love/romance stories
.... comedy spots	.... music/disc jockeys
.... commentaries	.... news
.... educational programs	.... sports events

   f. What is your favorite radio program? ....

   g. Who is your favorite radio personality? ....

C. COMICS, MAGAZINES, AND NEWSPAPERS

1. Comics

   a. About how many comic books do you read in a week? ....

b. Name the comic books you like best by giving the title (such as *Little Lulu*) or the type (funny, etc.).

(1) .... (4) ....

(2) .... (5) ....

(3) .... (6) ....

c. Who is your favorite comic book character? ....

2. Magazines

a. To what magazines does your family subscribe (at home)?

(1) .... (3) ....

(2) .... (4) ....

b. Which of the above-mentioned magazines do you read?

(1) .... How often? ....

(2) .... How often? ....

(3) .... How often? ....

c. What magazines do you read when you visit the dentist?

(1) .... (2) ....

d. To what magazines do you wish you could subscribe?

(1) .... (2) ....

3. Newspapers

a. What newspaper(s) do you read?

Check one:

(1) .... Daily? .... Sometimes? ....

(2) .... Daily? .... Sometimes? ....

(3) .... Daily? .... Sometimes? ....

b. Make a D in front of the part of the newspaper that you read daily. Make an S in front of the part of the newspaper that you sometimes read.

.... book reviews .... local news

.... columnists .... movie ads

.... comics/cartoons .... music and records

.... crime news .... pictures

.... fashions .... society page

.... financial page .... sports section

.... front page .... television/radio

.... headlines .... war news

.... letters to editor .... world news

Other: ....

D. BOOKS

1. Books: Specific

a. Name the books that you have read during the past school year:

(1) As a class assignment   (2) Because you wanted to

(a) ....   (a) ....

(b) ....   (b) ....

(c) ....   (c) ....

(d) ....   (d) ....

b. Did you enjoy reading the class-assigned book? Circle one: Yes   No
Why or why not? ....

c. How many books did you read during the past summer? ....

d. From where do you get your suggestions as to which books to read? Mark
them with an X.

.... browsing in libraries   .... mother

.... classroom teachers   .... other books

.... father   .... recommended booklists

.... friends   .... resource teachers

.... librarians   .... visiting bookstores

.... magazines

Other: ....

e. Make an L in front of the kind of books that you like to read:

.... fact   .... fiction

.... adventure   .... mystery/detective

.... animal/nature   .... occupations

.... battle/war   .... people/places

.... biography   .... picture books

.... cowboy   .... poetry

.... fable/folk/myth   .... religion/race

.... funny   .... science

.... historical fiction   .... science fiction

.... history   .... space

.... hobbies   .... sports

.... holidays   .... spy

.... how-to-do-it   .... travel/exploration

.... love/romance

Other: ....

2. Books: General

a. Do you belong to a book club? Circle one: Yes   No
What is the name of the club? ....

b. Do your parents belong to a book club? Circle one: Yes   No
What is the name of the club? ....

c. What has been your "all-time" favorite book? ....
....

d. Why is this book your favorite? ....

....

e. What book have you read that was suggested by a television program?

....

f. What book have you read that was suggested by a movie?

....

Shorter forms of the checklist type and incomplete-sentence inventory are often just as revealing, the children responding with checkmarks or frank responses to open-end questions. Primary-grade forms may provide a space for drawing as well.

A teacher could adapt and expand upon the questionnaires shown below.

FORM I

Name: ....   Date: ....

Check the books you like to read about:

Adventure: .... in other lands

.... outdoors

.... about children like me

History: .... famous people

.... important events

Make-believe:

.... fairy tales

.... funny stories

.... epics, legends, myths

Science: .... discoveries and inventions

.... nature and animals

.... space and space travel

FORM II

My name is ....

My grade is ....

My age is ....

The date is ....

I like to read about ....

I like reading more than ....

I would read more if ....

I don't like to read about ....

Here is a picture from my favorite story:

A teacher may want to take an inventory of the literary backgrounds of her students. The inventory can give the teacher insights into the personalities of the students, as well as a knowledge of their literary background. A carefully constructed inventory of 50 to 75 multiple choice items sampling children's knowledges of the classics, biography, modern fiction, poetry, and the like will suffice. For the busy teacher who needs a ready-made literary measure, write to Scott, Foresman & Company and request the latest copy of the booklet *Taking Inventory of Students' Literary Background* (authored by Charlotte Huck). The inventory is also found in the students' Skillbook for *Dimensions*, the new Grade 7 book in the Scott, Foresman Basic Reading Program.

Free Personal Reading

CHAPTER TWO

Free personal reading is known by many names: free-choice reading, independent personal reading, recreational reading, and library book reading. But whatever its name, a well-thought-out program in literature makes provision for regularly scheduled free personal reading periods.

By the use of the term "free" reading we do not mean to imply that a teacher adopts a hands-off policy. Rather, the program, to be justified, must be firmly in the hands of the teacher and must contribute to the development of both literary appreciations and skills. To achieve these ends, the teacher must give careful consideration to the principles and goals of a free reading plan and must maintain a careful watch on these aims. For it has been shown that even an activity-centered and popular program with poorly conceived aims soon deteriorates and erodes children's interests, eventually yielding little or no growth in the requisite skills and understandings.

In order to help the teacher focus early on some proper goals of a free personal reading program, Chapter 2 opens with a brief discussion of four principles that will help her establish a dynamic free reading program in an elementary school classroom. Following that is a discussion of some general techniques of guiding individuals in their recreational reading. Detailed instructions are given for the establishment of a classroom reading center and book collection, and the roles of children in planning and operating the reading center are outlined.

21

To show that "just reading a book" is not the sole activity of a free reading program, attention is directed to the value and character of student-developed bulletin boards and devices for book recording. Celebrating book week, starting a classroom book club, and sponsoring a school book fair are other natural outgrowths of a program of free reading, and Chapter 2 provides complete instructions on how pupils may be involved in organizing and carrying out plans for these. A brief source list of materials and resources concludes the chapter.

PRINCIPLES AND BELIEFS ABOUT FREE PERSONAL READING

Teachers will need a set of standards to guide them as they work with children in a free personal reading program. Four such standards are offered in the following paragraphs:

1. A program of free personal reading should mean just that: "free" time for the children, "free" from regularly scheduled reading instruction, during which they may select and read a book of their own "free" choice. That is, the child is not to be made dependent upon the teacher for his choice of reading matter. He is to be permitted to make his choice from among the hard or easy, fat or thin, hardbound books or paperbacks. And he is to be allowed to read this book in its entirety, or but a few pages, at his own rate of reading.

2. A wide variety of reading materials is to be made available to the children in the classroom reading center or in the school library. This should include books and magazines on a diversity of subjects, at various reading levels. *How* the books are obtained is up to the teacher. Whenever possible, however, children should be involved in the selection process.

3. Free personal reading time should provide the teacher with opportunities to consult with children regarding the interpretation (and selection, if the children ask for guidance) of materials they are reading. This is one of the ways in which children elevate their skills of general reading, of word analysis, and of comprehension; similarly, children learn to select and evaluate materials against the highest literary standards.

4. The program should be activity-centered and should permit young people to interact with their peers in the pursuit of increased literary knowledges and appreciations. Activities must be fresh, stimulating, and ever-changing. The byword is "participation." To be minimized are the so-called "standard book reports" seen in the two-minute oral book re-

view, the one-page written analysis of plot, and the mimeographed form asking the reader to write about "the funniest or best part" of the story.

GUIDING FREE PERSONAL READING

As has been noted previously, a sound free reading program must make a solid contribution to the entire curriculum. If a program of independent reading cannot be justified on this ground, then it has no place in the curriculum.

What must a teacher do to ensure that her free reading program will lend itself to learning, that reading skills and literature will be promoted, and that attitudes and understanding will be advanced?

First, the establishment of a *regular time* for recreational reading is important. Particular emphasis must be placed on the word "regular," so that children have something to look forward to and so they may make adequate preparations for the period. Do not threaten children with withdrawal of their free reading period privileges for misdemeanors they commit in class. Teachers do not take away children's arithmetic assignments or science textbooks when they misbehave; why is the free reading or library privilege always so used? Loss of this privilege certainly does not set well with children, nor does it help to instill in them the proper attitudes toward reading and literature.

To some teachers a regular free reading period means a daily time allocation of 20 to 30 minutes, the time being apportioned equally between morning and afternoon sessions. Slower readers and young children in particular respond well to this scheme, finding in it a welcome accommodation to their short attention spans, a release from tedium, and a fulfillment of their need for the security of regularly scheduled events.

Many teachers reserve longer blocks of time, but have the class meet less frequently. A 45-minute classroom free reading period on Monday afternoon, plus a like amount of time spent in the school library on Thursday morning—during which the children browse among the books and locate fresh materials—may prove to be just right for a group of older, more able readers who can concentrate longer. Or the children may meet for an hour and a half on a Wednesday morning to participate in a Book Fan Club meeting, watch a film based on a favorite book, or engage in another of the numerous activities which can be the outgrowth of a planned program of free personal reading.

Still other teachers prefer to operate on a more informal schedule. In such a program, children are encouraged to read before class, during unassigned minutes, and upon completion of regular assignments. With respect to this last option, caution must be taken that certain readers—

namely, the less able and an occasional "bookworm"—do not hastily turn to their free reading material and leave the regularly assigned subject matter poorly studied or not consulted at all.

A second concern of the teacher setting up a free reading program is uncovering ways to help readers find interesting and worthwhile books. While it is true that many readers are self-starters, it is equally obvious that others are not. It is the children in this latter group who must be "baited" and there are a number of ways to go about this:

> ... The teacher should bring to class at one- to two-week intervals a special collection of books—above and beyond the regular consignment allocated to her—which she has assembled from the school or public library. As the teacher gathers together this "bucket of books" she should (a) note the chapter headings, (b) spot read the contents, (c) make mental notes of stimulating illustrations, and (d) read the summaries of the stories printed on the book jackets. As she makes mental notes of the stories, the teacher should be matching them with youngsters in her class whom she feels need a little extra push to get them interested in the free reading process.

One teacher brought books and his "reluctant dragons" together by following just such a routine. Each Monday morning, following a Saturday visit to the city library, he displayed his "book bait" on the chalkboard tray at the front of the room. He held up each book, one at a time, pointing out the attractive cover and describing briefly an exciting scene or character from the book. Comments to individual children as, "Margie, I thought of you when I read of Sham in *King of the Wind*," or "Chuck, you will like the racing sequences in Gault's *The Checkered Flag*," are designed to make the particular children eager to get their hands on the specific titles.

Other ways of stimulating children to free read are:

> ... Have them build their own booklist. We are not referring here to the usual teacher-built lists, which are often static and classic-centered, but rather to short bibliographies of interesting titles assembled by the children themselves. For example, an ideal end-of-the-year activity is for a class to make a list of books they recommend for future classes, for example, "Three Best Books for the Third-Graders," or "Five Funny-Bone Ticklers for the Fifth Grade."

> ... Accompany the children on a visit to the school or public library. Although the first visit should be structured to give the librarian time to acquaint the children with library facilities and their use, the most important purpose of that and subsequent visits is to give each child adequate browsing time. Each child should come

away from the library with a book that *he has chosen* because *he could not resist the book.*

Exploring with children the characters, plots, and themes of books they read is a third useful goal of a sound free reading program. But in every instance, the help proffered by the teacher must be informal. McKee emphasizes this point when he notes: "The methods used to help children build an abiding interest in good reading material and a taste for such material must be inherently informal."[1]

As the child-readers approach their instructor with their own questions and comments on the stories they are reading, the teacher may assay what a child is gaining in the way of literary knowledges and appreciations by asking the children a salient question or two about the stories. Or the teacher may pass quietly among the children seated at their stations, stopping here and there to inquire about a picture in a book, to ask about the basic plot of a story, to help an individual focus upon the motives and behavior of characters they are encountering, and to help the children relate the books to their own lives.

Since one of the goals of a free reading program is to make provision for growth in literature appreciation through individual and group questioning, the wise teacher will have at her command a series of searching questions, such as the following, which are designed to expose children to the meanings of book plots, themes, and characters.[2]

1. What was the most important decision that (*name of character*) had to make?
   What was the main problem that (*name of character*) had to face?
2. Where (in what locale) and when (in what time or era) did this story take place?
   How do you know?
3. How did the characters change during the course of the story?
4. How would you meet and solve the same problems as those encountered by the characters in the story?
5. What is the lesson (the moral) this story teaches?
6. Why do you think (*name of character*) behaved as he did?
7. How do you know this story really happened?
8. Can you tell another story, or relate a true experience of your own, in which a similar problem was encountered?
9. What is one new word, fact, or idea that you have learned from reading this book?
10. Would you recommend this book to others?
    To whom?   Why?   Why not?

[1] Paul McKee, *The Teaching of Reading in the Elementary School* (Boston: Houghton Mifflin Company, 1948), p. 568.

[2] Derived principally from Charlotte S. Huck and Doris A. Young, *Children's Literature in the Elementary School* (New York: Holt, Rinehart & Winston, 1961), pp. 266–67.

A word of caution. Whatever answers to the above questions are supplied by children, they should be accepted by the teacher at full value. We must assume that the reader's expressions, reactions, and understandings are derived from his own values and experiences. No teacher has the right to belittle a youngster's replies, nor to impose her own interpretations.

A fourth factor that must be considered in a program of free personal reading is the soft-cover book: the paperback and even the comic book. Imposing in number, inexpensive in price, and relatively attractive to children in format and ease of handling, both paperbacks and comic books are found frequently in the hands of children. And when the teacher says, "This is our free reading period, to read what we like," there will be those boundary-pushers who will want to test the teacher's actions against her words by bringing in a paperback or comic book. The best advice is to accept the presence of the books and to heed the words of Horton in Dr. Suess's *Horton Hatches the Egg*:

> I meant what I said
> And I said what I meant . . .
> An elephant's faithful
> One hundred per cent!

Paperbacks can be a valuable tool in the free personal reading program. They fit nicely into boys' pockets and satisfy their hunger to *own* a book. Attractively displayed and promoted through book clubs and book-club activities, paperbacks often serve as magnets to the reluctant reader, who finds in them an increasing variety of subject matter and that "little something different."

Every month hundreds of different kinds of comic books find their way into the hands of children. Many youngsters pore over them religiously while registering only ill humor when asked to select a library book or read from a basal reader. Filled with action-packed adventures and fast-moving, slangy dialogue, they may be a force with which the teacher has to contend in a free reading program. Even if the problem should not arise then, it is bound to crop up some other place, for the comics throw out a strong web that encompasses most children sometime in their lives.

What should the challenged teacher do if some children want to read comic books during the free reading period? We would recommend the following action:

a. Adopt the philosophy that if you can't beat 'em, join 'em.

b. Help children to develop tastes and appreciations for the best comic books as you do for good books and stories.

c. Have children bring to class and analyze the most popular comic books against the criteria of accuracy, authenticity, quality of illustrations, and general literary merit.

d. Set up a comic book trading post in the classroom with acceptable comic books (usually the classic and humorous comics) being permitted on the shelf as measured by standards developed by the class.

e. Counter the comic book syndrome by surrounding children with a wealth of the best in children's literature.

A fifth way to guide children's free reading is to encourage them to read at home. Soliciting the cooperation of the parents in this matter is an absolute essential. Children react positively when they have parents who remove obstacles to home reading and who provide a proper home environment.

The following list details some ways in which the teacher can invoke the aid of parents in establishing a read-at-home habit for their children:

... Have the class prepare and distribute to their homes a monthly summary of classroom literature activities. This may be in the form of a newsletter or literary magazine which includes book reviews, original stories and poems, and news of other language arts activities.

... Provide parents with lists of read-aloud books for family sharing and enjoyment. Remind mothers and fathers that a book in their hands sets a good example.

... Advise parents that gifts of books and magazine subscriptions, the purchase of reference books, and the establishment of a quiet study center in the home all contribute to good reading and study habits.

... Remind parents through their children that there is fun to be found in a family visit to the local library or the bookmobile.

Finally, the teacher who is determined to guide children through a sound and sensible program of free personal reading will want to keep the following points uppermost in mind:

... Be excited about stories and poetry.

... Be interested in children.

... Be generous with browsing time.

... Be aware of what individual children are reading.

... Be searching when asking questions.

... Be solicitous of the slow reader's needs.

... Be activity-minded.

ESTABLISHING A READING CENTER

One of the first essentials of a good literature program is provision in the classroom of attractive surroundings that will help create an atmos-

phere conducive to enjoyable reading. To this end there should be a
library corner or reading center in every classroom, and it should be the
brightest and most attractive part of the room.

The center should be the most physically suitable, quiet, and easily
accessible spot available to the class and the teacher, yet out of the way
of normal classroom traffic. Further, the plans for the reading center
should be developed as a cooperative venture, with the teacher giving
the pupils a major role in the discussion of the project and with each
pupil being readied to accept a portion of the responsibility for establishing and maintaining the reading center.

CHILDREN'S PARTICIPATION IN
PLANNING THE READING CENTER

Engaging children in the process of creating a classroom reading center
does much to stimulate their enthusiasm for the designing, construction,
continued support, and maintenance of the reading center.

The first step in such a plan is a discussion period during which the
teacher leads the pupils into an examination of the potential advantages
and uses of the proposed center. Children will be quick to see and appreciate the delightful possibilities of a quiet corner where they can go
to relax and enjoy a good book.

Next, space must be selected for the library center. Here again, it is
surprising how resourceful children can be in visualizing the potential
of nooks and crannies. They are quick to uncover places where a reading
center might be located:

... in a space taken up by cabinets or boxes of supplies.

... in a corner now occupied by a piano.

... in an unused anteroom or cloak room adjacent to the classroom.

... between a blank wall and a portable room divider or a moveable
chalkboard.

It is truly amazing how alert and imaginative children become when
their attention is directed to finding and establishing a location for
their reading center. They will find a place for the center if there is
enough desire for it! That desire the teacher must instill in them through
her own enthusiasm for the project.

NEEDED HARDWARE IN THE
READING CENTER

The physical environment to be established can range from the very
simple to the most elaborate. Teachers and children should discuss the

available corner, what it will accommodate, and what will be most functional and practical to put in it. At the outset, flexibility of arrangement should have priority, with books, equipment, and supplies moving in and out of the corner as changes in needs and interests dictate.

The following items of equipment can be considered for placement in the center.

... Comfortable *chairs*, colorfully painted and decorated, will be inviting to children. Easy chairs that have outlived their usefulness in a private home may prove to be just the right thing for the reading center. A rocker or two, or even a striped canvas lawn chair will provide a bright touch. Regular classroom chairs may be used, taking on a more festive air when the children fashion gay chair pads and backs with pictures of clowns and elephants painted on them.

Small portable primary-grade chairs usually fit well in a library corner. A real sofa would add a nice touch to the reading center, but a suitable substitute manufactured from three or four primary chairs fastened together and covered with soft cushions will do also. Less formal chairs may be constructed from orange crates. To build such a chair, stand the crate on its end, leaving in the partition to form the seat. Remove the upper front piece and cut the upper sides in half, making an intriguing "box" chair. The chair may be painted, decorated with drawings, or covered with simple slip covers.

... One or more *tables* of the appropriate size for the children should be placed in the reading center. If a library table is not available, a card table will suffice. Or you may fashion a table by stacking two columns of bricks or standing two boxes on end as supports, and using a plank for the table top. Enameling or painting these in bright colors will add a distinctive touch.

... *Bookshelves* constructed of apple or prune boxes, bricks and boards, and wallboard are commonly found in library corners. To construct a crate bookcase, nail two prune boxes together and stand them on end. The partitions will hold the books in place. Low, open shelves are recommended, particularly for primary grades; a limited number can be designed to hold the taller books used in those grades. The shelves should be varnished or painted in pastel colors or to harmonize with the colors of the walls in the room.

... Other pieces of equipment that often prove functional and add a "homey" touch to the reading center include:

A *file box* for holding reading record cards can be made from a shoebox or cheese box.

Curtains made from unbleached muslin and decorated with children's drawings can be hung around the windows.

Lamps, vases, and *figurines* add to the overall character of the book center. Adequate lighting in the reading center is a must to make it an exciting place to visit. Seasonal flowers arranged in decorative vases made by the children from bottles, jars, and gourds can be used to good effect in decorating a table or bookcase. Figurines constructed and/or dressed to represent various book characters may be hung on a wall or placed on the windowsill.

Decorated *bookends* made from cement poured in paper milk cartons serve as practical book holders.

Easels, small display *cabinets*, and *wall racks* for the display of magazines and books are inviting to the visitor, as are a *fish bowl*, a *terrarium* or *aquarium*, a *map*, a *globe*, and an *atlas*.

A BANG-UP Idea for the reading center: Construct a book-reading booth from a large refrigerator box by cutting a door in the front and a window for ventilation in one side. Build a door latch that will permit a child to close the door from the inside or outside. Drop a well-insulated extension light cord through a hole in the top. The refrigerator reading booth provides a quiet hideaway for one to two readers.

THE CLASSROOM BOOK COLLECTION

The bookshelves and tables in the classroom reading corner should contain a balanced collection of good books at many reading levels and on a wide variety of subjects germane to the activities and interests of the class. What books to include in the collection should be determined by conferences between and among the teacher, the children, and the school librarian if there is one.

Formation of a small group of children to work with the school librarian or teacher in building the collection will prove to be a valuable activity. Experience has shown that when the children have a voice in the selection of the books, they are more apt to read them and to take care of them.

A literature-oriented classroom possesses a substantial library of books and magazines. There is no fixed number for a properly stocked classroom library, for a quality collection of 50 books may prove far superior to a much larger one. However, a collection of 150 books can probably be considered ideal.

The range of difficulty of the books should vary from easy-to-read volumes to books that challenge the more advanced readers, from fiction to nonfiction. Colored tabs of different hues may be used to mark the different levels and to separate fiction from nonfiction.

No collection should be allowed to remain static; rather, titles should move in and out of the collection as needs, interests, and topics of study change in the classrooms. A collection that is fixed fails to hold the interest of the readers. A fluid and continuous supply of fresh materials may originate from:

... the school's central library.
... city and county libraries.
... private collections of children.
... collections of other classes at the same grade level.
... teachers' purchases from their share of the school's trade book fund.
... the bookmobile collection.
... the state library.

Current copies of children's magazines mounted in student-made magazine racks and purchased with allotments from a PTA fund also help to keep reading related to current events.

The classroom collection of books should be displayed attractively on the tables and bookshelves provided. Exciting looking books in reasonably good condition, in attractive, colorful book covers and jackets will arouse the interest of the children.

Some of the books should lie on a low shelf or table, opened to a colorful illustration so that the pictures may serve as an enticement to the readers. As bait, books may be grouped by authors or by subjects to form an attractive display. A "book of the week" can be mounted on a wire book holder in a conspicuous place in the reading center. All in all, the books on display should contribute a sense of "informality with purpose" to the reading center and to the children who use it.

A BANG-UP Idea for buying a book: Early in the school year the teacher can provide each youngster with a jar labeled with his name. Encourage each child to "bank" in the jar his small change. Subsequently, the child will save enough to buy one book—a paperback or a hard-cover edition—by the end of the school year.

CHILDREN IN THE READING CENTER: OPPORTUNITIES AND RESPONSIBILITIES

The children will show a growing appreciation for the book center and the book collection there as they move in and out of the center, as they assume some responsibility for shelving and charging out books, and as they oversee their own general conduct as they use the center.

It is important that the children feel free to move into the library center and utilize its services and materials during their free time. After a regular classroom assignment is completed, and they have a few minutes to spare, they should be allowed as a matter of course to go to the library shelves, select a book, and sit down in a favorite chair. Initially, the teacher will want to instill in the children the idea that browsing in the reading center is to be treated as a distinct privilege, and it is not to be considered a time-killing routine.

At other times—frequently, it is hoped—all the children will be given the opportunity to move into the center, where they may choose a book, after which they can sit down and share their individual enjoyment with their peers.

At the outset, regular periods for primary children might be necessary to show these children how to profit most from the reading center and its resources. In the process they will begin to learn such basic library techniques as caring for books and classifying them. Further, the teacher may employ the reading center to help children build their powers of discrimination. During a discussion she may send the children to the reading center to:

> touch a green book.
> bring back two red books.
> select a long, thick, or thin book.
> put a tall book on the teacher's desk.
> tell the name (title) of a blue book.

An experience story written to reflect the children's visit to a school or public library, or their reaction to the building of their own reading center, is a proven worthwhile educational activity. The experience story written by a first-grade class might include sentences on what materials the children contributed to the building of the center, who was selected as the first child-librarian, and the name chosen for the library. The story could be completed with the children drawing a picture of the library in their room.

Older children will certainly assume the responsibility for the library corner as a spare-time activity. Committees may be formed to assume the various tasks, with different pupils selected to do the jobs on a rotating basis. Among the tasks that the children can ably perform are the following:

... making simple catalog cards, by author and/or title.

Author: Cleary, Beverly	(use shoebox-
Title: Henry Huggins	size cards or
Kind of book: Humor	cut paper forms)

... making sign-out cards for each book.

Author	Cleary, Beverly
Title	Henry Huggins
Due date	Your name
	1.
	2.

... filing the sign-out cards, returning them to the pockets of books, and maintaining other necessary records.

... seeing that books are checked in and out properly.

... changing, maintaining, and arranging books and book displays on tables and shelves.

... labeling shelves and books, the children as a group devising their own *workable* classification system.

A BANG-UP Idea for reading-center workers: At the end of the school year the teacher invites all the children to a "library-center luncheon." Each child brings his own lunch, and the teacher provides the milk and cookies. A few literature games can be played and the teacher may want to take this opportunity to talk about some special books that children can find at the public library for summer reading.

Desirable book-corner citizenship is taught by developing attitudes of courtesy and consideration toward each other, the reading center, and its materials. Each child should be made individually responsible for the general appearance of the library corner, and he should be taught to realize the intrinsic and monetary value of the equipment and books therein. With regard to the value of books, teachers who understand that books *do wear out* will be welcomed by children. Likewise, the teacher who exercises care in handling her own books will do much to lead children to treat books with respect.

Bulletin board posters can be made to remind everyone to be courteous in the library center and to handle the books carefully. With the whole class joining in the discussion, one class made charts of the standards for the care of books and for proper conduct in their library center.

Our Library *Book* Standards

1. We have clean hands before we use our books.
2. We turn pages of books from the upper right hand corner with dry fingers.
3. We don't mark in our books or tear the pages.
4. We don't turn down page corners or use paper clips, rulers, or pencils as book markers.
5. We don't bend our books and break the binding.
6. We don't leave our books on radiators, or carry them in the snow or rain unless they are in a sturdy paper or plastic wrapper.

Our Library *Conduct* Standards

1. We speak and move quietly.
2. We are courteous to the acting librarian.
3. We leave our library-corner chairs and tables in good order.
4. We learn where the books are.
5. We *print* our names neatly on the sign-out cards.
6. We leave our sign-out cards in the file box under the last name of the author.
7. We return our books promptly to the acting librarian when we have finished reading them.

A BANG-UP Idea on book care: When inaugurating a discussion of proper book care in the primary grades, get the children to pretend they are books. Assign each child the title of a favorite, well-known book. Tell the "books" that some children are coming to the library to read them. A friendly elf has given the books the power to talk to the children. The books are to tell the children how they wish to be treated and handled.

A BANG-UP Idea on book care: Have the children cut book-jacket shapes from colored construction paper. Add faces, eyes, arms, and legs to the book shapes. Mount the book shapes on a bulletin board, adding "talk balloons" which allow the book shapes to tell how they wish to be handled by the readers.

BULLETIN BOARDS

The literature bulletin board can be one of the most effective book promotion devices used by the classroom teacher. It helps to further an attractive literature program and to deepen the children's interest in books.

A few guidelines for the general arrangement of bulletin board materials are as follows:

1. The arrangement should be neat, simple, and attractive to the eye.

2. The display should focus on one theme at a time, with themes being changed frequently.

3. Balance, harmony of color and form, and contrasts in colors, shapes, and textures contribute to the attractiveness of the display.

4. An appropriate caption, brief and specific, will point up the meaning of the display.

Various materials should be used for lettering and backing. Letters of many styles can be made: paper, ceramic, pre-cut letters, stencil-cut, or rubber stamped. Backing can be of colored construction paper, corrugated cardboard, or a variety of fabric materials. Colored yarn and pins, "cardboard arrows," pennants, and rotating turntables add to the attractiveness of the bulletin board.

Most schoolrooms today contain bulletin boards, made of cork or some other surface to which pins or adhesive materials may be attached. If more display space is needed it may be improvised from room dividers, free-standing corrugated paper, pegboard, wallboard, or an easel.

Pupils should participate in planning, arranging, and contributing to the bulletin board. The teacher will want to supervise the preparation of the displays to assure that the bulletin board is artistically sound and properly focused upon the current literature topic.

Once the bulletin board has been erected, a brief discussion of the mounted material and its message should take place. A bulletin board committee should be appointed to make a list of the names of all who contribute items to the displays. The committee may want to maintain a file of display materials once the materials have outlived their immediate usefulness. These may be turned over to the teacher for use with subsequent classes.

Suitable materials and approaches for bulletin board displays include:

1. Colorful book jackets, both commercial and pupil-made.

2. Borders of interesting quotations from books, authors, and illustrators, embellished with scroll-like drawings.

3. Lists, by categories, of good books obtainable in the class or school library: seasons, holidays, hobbies, fiction, nonfiction, science, vacation reading, and the like.

4. Book reviews and notices of book events clipped from magazines and newspapers.

5. Children's drawings, posters, and paper sculpture interpretations of characters and scenes from favorite stories, books, and poems.

6. Lists of good reading habits and the proper care of books.

7. Maps showing homes and birthplaces of authors or imaginary characters from books.

8. Time lines showing the position of authors and their books in relation to history.

9. Pictures of book characters, authors, and story settings posted for identification by the pupils.

10. Quizzes, matching authors and characters to book titles.

11. Questions pupils can answer only by reading a certain type of book.

12. Letters from authors and illustrators.

Following are the names and descriptions of some bulletin board ideas that have been used successfully.

bookworm bookshelf.   Book spines (cardboard tubes, halved lengthwise and covered with colored paper) rest on a bookshelf (3 feet of quarterround taped to a bulletin board). Title, author, and reader's name are printed on the spines. Bookends are bookworms fashioned from egg cartons. (Constructed by Maris Bergevin, student, Sacramento State College, California.)

thumb-thing drawing.   A large thumb is constructed from paper and affixed to the bulletin board. Children's drawings of book characters are grouped around it. Title the display "Thumb-thing Drawings."

rendevouz with something new.   Paper rockets with planets and spacemen are the center around which jackets from new books on rockets, space, and interplanetary science fiction are grouped.

famous february heroes.   Pictures of famous February-born Americans—Edison, Lincoln, Washington—are displayed along with book jackets from biographies about these individuals.

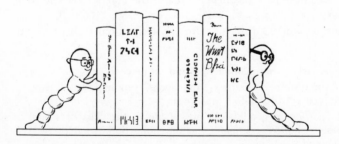

reading 'round the clock. A large paper grandfather clock with many hands points to book jackets grouped around it.

books to laugh over. A large clown face, with cut-out pictures of people laughing, forms the focal point around which are grouped jackets from humorous books.

go flying with a kite—and a book. Colored kites with decorative "book jacket" tails fly across the bulletin board.

basket of books. A large basket made of construction paper is pinned to the bulletin board. Book titles are printed on tall-stemmed paper flowers that extend from the basket.

bullet passes and books. A huge "paper" football player and football may be displayed in early fall along with book jackets from football books.

Other titles for bulletin boards which will lead the imaginative child to other display ideas include *Keys to Successful Reading*; *Note-able Books*; *Stop, then Go, for Books*; *Going Fishing for a Book?*; *A Treasure Chest of Books*; *Skating Along with Books*; and *Book Leaves are Falling.*

TECHNIQUES AND DEVICES FOR BOOK RECORDING

Teachers have developed a variety of book record devices to encourage children to read widely. Generally, these devices may be placed in one of four categories: bulletin board charts, card files and notebooks, reading wheels and ladders, and contracts.

Before passing on to a discussion of these four categories, it is worth enumerating the objections to book recording devices, in order that the teacher may come to recognize and to avoid the pitfalls of using them. In summary, the objections are:

1. Book recording devices often encourage quantity rather than quality reading.

2. Books are chosen for their brevity and simplicity; the child gains credit for mediocre accomplishment.

3. Slow readers become discouraged because they cannot keep up the pace.

4. Reading is for recording (credit) and not for fun.

As we can see from this brief list, the drawbacks are not inherent in the devices themselves, but rather in the way they can be used. The

alert teacher will want to observe carefully to what end the book recording devices are being employed by the children and take appropriate
action.

The bulletin board approach is based on some illustrative display,
around which the child or a class group places a record of the books
that have been read. The most common device makes use of a miniature
book replica on which the child records the author and title of each
book he has read. Each child then mounts the book replicas on his poster
and puts up his poster for others to see.

On another type of basic chart, a child records his reading by placing
a star, a square, or some other symbol on a graph-like poster such as
the one below. Different colors might be used to represent different types
of books read.

Other variations on this basic approach for individual records include
the following:

1. A paper cutout of an Indian head and war bonnet is made by
each child and mounted on the bulletin board. For each book read, the
individual child adds a feather upon which is written the name of the
author and the title of the book.

2. For every book read the child adds to his own paper clown an
additional feature of the clown's costume: gloves, hat, shoes, jacket, and
baggy pants.

3. Each child has a paper vase or tree mounted on the bulletin board.
As soon as the child completes the reading of a book, he adds a paper
flower to the vase or a paper leaf to the tree, upon which are written the
title and author's name. Multicolored flowers or leaves can be used to
represent different types of books.

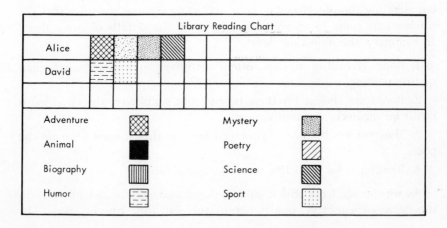

4. An "Astronauts in Space" chart is a huge poster upon which each child has designed a space capsule made from construction paper. Pasted to each capsule is a list of books that the child has read. As additional books are read the capsule is moved upward and thumb-tacked by the reader into outlying orbits designated by colored yarn stretched across the poster at intervals of one inch.

5. Each boy and girl makes a paper parachute with his own silhouette dangling from its shroud lines. For every 50 pages of a book read, the parachute descends an agreed-upon distance registered against a tape measure fastened to the side of the bulletin board. For a successful jump (reading the entire book) a paper airplane is pasted on the parachute and the jumper returns to the top of the bulletin board for another trip down.

6. Caricatures, self-portraits, or photographs provided by individual children are pasted on envelopes which are then mounted on the bulletin board. Slips of paper with the name of the author, the title of the book, and the child's reaction to it are inserted into the envelope.

7. A paper book train, using black yarn for the tracks, has a flat car cut from construction paper for each child. Colored "logs," with titles of books and authors' names written on them, are added each time a book is read.

Class esprit de corps can be heightened by book record charts which emphasize the contribution of the entire class working as one. Such a book chart is the "bookworm." The teacher provides a colored paper reproduction of a worm's head. The children work as a class to lengthen the worm by pinning up paper segments containing the titles of the books they have read. A bookworm may "run" up and down several walls.

A similar group book chart is the baseball diamond. For this activity the class is divided into three or four teams, with nine players to a team. Each team adopts a name, draws a baseball diamond on a large piece of tagboard, and designs a set of cut-out players. The first player who completes a book pins his player on first base. He and subsequent baserunners are advanced when additional books are read by other team members. For example, each book reader already on first base is advanced, in turn, to second, third, and finally to home plate, where a run is scored (a point is given) for his team. The name of each player is kept on a team roster and each child earns a "paper" baseball bat when he reads an entire book.

Another group project employs a large Easter basket which is filled with tongue depressors marked on one side with a child's name. On the reverse side of the stick is the title of the book the child has read.

Children often respond well to the teacher's suggestion to keep a written record of everything they read during their free reading time. Such a record may take the form of an "I Recommend" card signed by each child making a report. Filed alphabetically by title in a community file box, these 5 x 7 cards contain a brief written report on one side and an illustration on the other.

A child might keep an individual notebook in which are listed books, poems, and stories he has read. An extra copy of the list might be sent home at report card time for parents to see.

Children sometimes are inclined to restrict their reading to a single area of literature. To encourage a more balanced reading program, teachers use a reading wheel, a book ladder, or a variation thereof. In his reading, the child plans to cover each of several areas. For those unfamiliar with this type of device, a few illustrations are given below.

With a compass each child draws a large "wheel" on a piece of colored construction paper. From scraps of different colored paper he

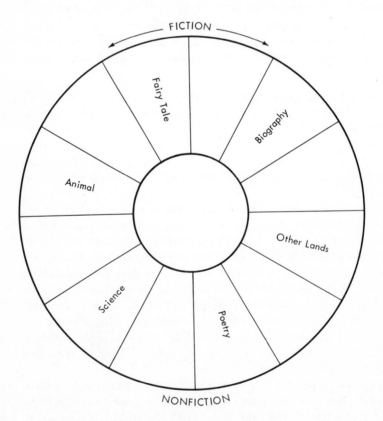

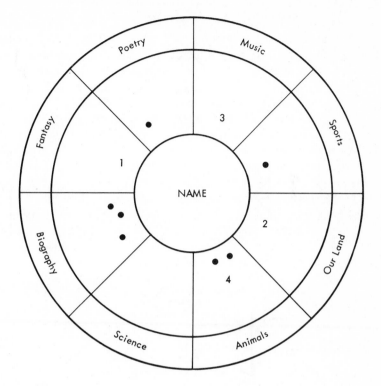

makes "spokes" to fit in his wheel. The spokes are labeled to represent various areas of literature (e.g., biography, history, poetry, etc.). After a library book is read in a particular area, the pupil puts the proper spoke on the wheel, until the wheel has a full complement of spokes. Such a wheel might resemble the one pictured on page 40.

A similar circle chart is divided into pie-shaped wedges, as illustrated above, each wedge representing a different topic. As a child finishes a book he lists it by number on the back of the chart, then records the appropriate number in the proper segment. Or if a number of books are read in each category, these may be acknowledged simply by pasting a small colored piece of paper in the proper wedge.

Two other devices that encourage balanced reading are the book ladder and the baseball diamond. With the former a paper stairway is built, with each riser representing an area of reading. Upon reading a book in the proper category, the child advances a paper shoe up the ladder. The baseball diamond is a device through which the child advances around the bases "by the number", reading a book in the category called for. This latter device is illustrated on page 42.

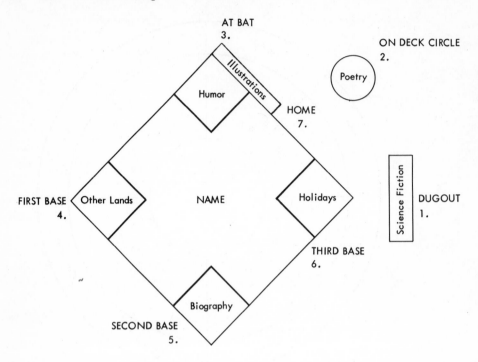

The contract plan of reading can be used profitably in the recreational reading program. A contract between the teacher and each individual child usually takes the form of a booklet, which the child can make from a piece of folded and stapled tagboard or a Manila folder, and ordinary writing paper. The outside cover may be illustrated with a picture from a favorite story. The inside front cover contains the contract, which may read:

> I, (*name of child*), agree to read (*10*) books, one in each of the following categories: adventure, animal, history, (teacher adds others). I agree to record and answer the (*5*) questions (which the teacher devises) for each book read and paste a written copy of my answer sheet in this notebook.

> Date: .... Signed: ....
> (Child's name)

> Witness: ....
> (Teacher's name)

The contract is then inserted into the next page of the booklet; it may take the following form:

```
                        Contract for
Name: .................................................................
Date: .................................................................

.....................................................................................
.....................................................................................

        Title of Book                  Title of Book
1.                          6.
2.                          7.
3.                          8.
4.                          9.
5.                          10.
```

On subsequent pages the child responds to the following questions for each book he reads:

Fiction:

1. The book was about ....
2. The story took place in (setting) ....
3. Some of the people in the book were ....
4. The person I liked best in the book was .... because ....
5. The most exciting adventure this person had was when ....

Nonfiction:

1. The book was about ....
2. One thing I learned from the book was ....
3. Some ways in which the information in this book has helped **people** are ....
4. Here is one problem (about things in my book) which was not **solved:** ....
5. I recommend this book because ....

A BANG-UP Idea for promoting wide reading: Each child is to "eat his way" through a balanced meal by reading, during a school year, a book to match each course of a dinner. As many helpings as desired may be eaten of one course, provided that the boy or girl eats one dish of every type.

	Title	*Author*
hors d'oeuvres: adventure	....	....
soup: animal story	....	....
salad: poetry	....	....
meat: biography	....	....
vegetable: fairy tale	....	....
beverage: science	....	....
dessert: humor	....	....

CELEBRATING BOOK WEEK

National Children's Book Week is observed annually during one week in November. Recognition of this occasion furnishes the teacher with a splendid opportunity to further stimulate and guide children in developing an appreciation of good literature. In the forefront in promotion of Book Week is the Children's Book Council, an organization that supplies

schools with Book Week posters, seals, streamers, bookmarks, mobiles, and other aids on ways to celebrate this event.

Schools and individual classes throughout the country celebrate Book Week in a combination of ways. In addition to incorporating into their Book Week plans some of the activities mentioned elsewhere in this volume, a school and its teachers might make use of the following suggestions:

1. Have a Book Parade, with children dressed as favorite book char-

acters parading from room to room in the school. A quiz might evolve from this, with the children trying to guess who their visitors are.

2. Decorate the cafeteria and hallways with mobiles, posters, and other artistic expressions of favorite book characters and scenes.

3. Conduct an all-school homemade candy sale and an after-school or Saturday waste paper drive to raise money for the purchase of books for the library.

4. Arrange to have an author or illustrator speak at an assembly and display and discuss some of his works. Primary children might better enjoy going on stage themselves and reciting nursery rhymes and showing big paintings of books they have read.

5. Plan a book exchange, wherein children bring books from home to lend each other.

6. Advertise new book arrivals in the library by having a dozen different children thumbtack the jackets of twelve new books to rulers and parade them from room to room telling about the books.

7. Let primary-grade children form a "Story Train," using streamer-decorated wagons. Place an apple box on each wagon, the box being decorated with pictures of famous storybook scenes and dolls representing book characters. Have the children pass from room to room, each telling something about his display and the whole group singing a train song.

8. Conduct a school-wide poll to discover the "Top Ten Book Week Books." Set up a polling booth where for one cent (optional) a child may vote for his favorite book. (The money may be used to buy a book for the library.) Post the results in the entranceway to the school by erecting a huge oaktag poster with ten brightly colored numbers running down one side and the names of the authors and their books, in order of selection, running down the other.

9. Select a special exhibit of books centered around the Book Week theme of the year.

A BANG-UP Idea for Book Week: Issue each child a "gold" pouch (made of paper or cheap leather), and give each boy or girl a "gold nugget" (a navy bean sprayed with gold paint) when he has done each of the following during Book Week:

1. Read all or part of a given book.
2. Read aloud one poem.
3. Written on paper what appears on the title page of a book.
4. Recorded the titles and authors of two books on *(any subject chosen by the teacher)*.
5. (Teacher adds other items.)

STARTING A BOOK CLUB

Greater enthusiasm for reading and books can be generated by having interested children—particularly those in the upper elementary grades—organize and participate in a classroom book club. Very often such a club has its genesis with the children. Or sometimes it is the teacher who initiates the formation of a book club, pointing out how the club will increase the children's interests in reading more and better books.

Membership in a book club should always be presented to the children as a special activity in which they can engage *if they wish.* To establish with children that they may join or refuse to join of their own volition is an important step in forming a book club. When a sufficient number of boys and girls express an interest in forming a book club, the organization of the group may proceed. Officers are elected, usually a president and a secretary; a treasurer is optional. Some clubs charge dues, as little as a penny a week or a nickel a month or semester. In certain communities, charging dues is a questionable practice, for it prohibits some children from joining. In other schools, the collection of such a sum may be altogether proper, and the monies collected may be applied to the purchase of a book for the class reading center.

Each club will probably want to establish a few simple rules relative to frequency and time of meetings, to membership and committee eligibility and responsibility, and to establishment of the purposes and goals of the club. Meetings should be held during school time, particularly in rural and suburban areas, so that children who are bussed home will still have a chance to participate. Meeting for 45 minutes every other Friday afternoon or once a month is a good practice. Consistent attendance should be required of members, but this will come automatically if well-thought-out events are planned by the program committee.

Within the book club, smaller "fan" clubs may be established to exchange information about particular authors (such as the Kjelgaard Kids) or types of books (such as the "Bronco Riders," a club for girls who love horse stories). Other sub-clubs may focus on the classics, prize-winning books, books about the circus, and so on. The use of the fan club idea suggests that the teacher would have to be on guard to prevent the establishment of cliques.

Though the aforementioned book clubs are designed for the average and above-average reader, the formation of a club for primary-grade children and other less-able readers is not precluded. One first-grade teacher rounded up (she called her group "The Reading Round Up" Club) a library of preprimers, primers, first readers, and "easy-to-read" trade books. From among these books each child who joined the club was to select and read a book a week *at home.* Letters were sent to parents explaining the program and its procedures, and a note from the parent was sent to the teacher when the child completed reading each of his books. To encourage the children, the teacher gave each child an inexpensive book when he had read the required minimum of five books.

For slow readers, a special reading club (the "Take Your Time" Club) can be formed. Each week the club members select from a basal reader a story that they have enjoyed. The story is divided into parts and each child prepares a part for oral reading. On a day assigned, the members of the club read their story to another class at the same grade level. Each member of the club wears a paper hat with the club's name and a picture of a clock on it. A chairman introduces the story. After reading their story, the club members return to their own homeroom and discuss techniques of oral reading and incidents.

The greater part of all activities in a typical book-club meeting is devoted to furthering children's appreciation for and knowledge of literature. To this end the children should take part in planning and carrying out the programs in the classroom, either as individuals or as members of a group. At times the members of one club may exchange programs with other reading clubs in the school or school district.

Suggestions for a rich variety of activities have gone before in the book and others will follow later when there is a discussion of book reviews, dramatic interpretation of books, oral presentations, and the like. But at this point a typical book club program is presented for an upper-grade group.

READING FOR FUN CLUB
MEETING NO. 3

A. Topic
1. Sheila Burnford's book, *The Incredible Journey.*
2. Walt Disney's movie of the same name.

B. Planning Committee
1. The "Real Animals" Fan Club.
2. Program to be 50 minutes long.

C. Objectives of the Committee
1. To help club members become better acquainted with a modern classic.
2. To advertise the book, *The Incredible Journey,* either in its hardcover edition or in paperback. (Display copies of the book.)
3. To introduce club members to three wonderful animals.

4. To learn something about the author of the book.

5. To see the differences between the book and the movie.

D. The Program

1. Roll call (led by the secretary): 5 minutes
Each club member is to answer to his name by giving the title and
author's name of a book he is reading at the present time.

2. Announcements (by the president): 1 minute
The Robin Hood Fan Club will be in charge of the next meeting,
to be held on November 14.

3. Miss Hanley, the teacher, introduces the book topic of the day:
10 minutes
   a. Holds up a copy of the book, *The Incredible Journey*, for all
   to see.
   b. Briefly reviews the entire story.
   c. Tells a little about the life of the author, Sheila Burnford, including the fact that the Labrador retriever in the story was her
   own gun dog.
   d. Shows a few pictures of Luath, Bodger, and Tao, the three central figures of the book.
   e. Reads the short excerpt from the story about the encounter of
   Tao and the bears.
   f. Announces that the "Real Animals" Fan Club has worked out
   a skit about *The Incredible Journey*, and that they will present
   it now.

E. The Program, with the "Real Animals" Fan Club: 25 minutes

1. Martha, as mistress of ceremonies, takes her place before a tin-can
microphone placed on a table. She announces, "Today Station
B-O-O-K presents the story, *The Incredible Journey*."

2. "Let me introduce to you, Bob Rogers, who will show and discuss
some selected sketches he has drawn from the book." (Bob does so.)

3. "Next, we will hear from Mr. Longridge, played by Greg Waters,
and his faithful dog, Luath, played by Marcie Phillips. (A boy
and a girl come forward, one wearing a "dog" false-face, the other
carrying a script. The two discuss their life together at the old
stone house.)

4. "Here is Johnny Rivers," says the chairman, "to read us a few
paragraphs from the story." (The boy does so, choosing the scene
where Tao is almost drowned.)

5. (Either individually or in small groups other children may dramatize a scene from the book, tell the story with puppets, use a feltboard, and the like.)

F. Evaluation: 5 minutes

1. At the conclusion, the program is returned to Miss Hanley. She asks, "How many have read the book and seen the movie, too? What differences (of any type) did you see between the story in its two different forms? (A discussion ensues.)

2. The club members evaluate the meeting by asking questions and by commenting on the quality of the presentation by the "Real Animals" Fan Club, both as to its strong and weak features.

G. Closing Exercise: 5 minutes

1. The secretary signs out each member by asking him to relate something new he has learned about the book, *The Incredible Journey*, or its author. Or he may mention the title of another book about dogs or cats that would be good for further reading.

In addition to the "home-grown" book club, millions of children annually receive books as members of commercial book clubs such as the Young Reader's Book Club and the Arrow Book Club. Details on membership, costs of joining, and other useful information may be obtained by contacting the following selected book clubs.

JUVENILE BOOK CLUBS

BOOK CLUB AND ADDRESS	AGE LEVEL	KINDS OF BOOKS	WHEN BOOKS ARE SENT	HOW TO JOIN
Book Plan 921 Washington Ave. Brooklyn, N.Y. 11225	8 months to 18 years	Personalized service, in which books are chosen from files kept on clients	Monthly	By mail to address
Catholic Children's . . . 262 E. Fourth Street St. Paul, Minn. 55101 Picture Book Club: Intermediate Club: Knowledge Builders: Older Girls Club: Older Boys Club:	6-9 9-12 10 up 12-16 12-16	Books on Catholic themes; those stressing character building and wholesome family relationships	Monthly, Sept. through June; or every other month, Sept. through June	By mail to address
Catholic Youth Garden City, N.Y. 11530	9-15	Biographical books on Catholic figures in history	Monthly	By mail to address

BOOK CLUB AND ADDRESS	AGE LEVEL	KINDS OF BOOKS	WHEN BOOKS ARE SENT	HOW TO JOIN
Challenges Education Center Columbus, Ohio 43216	7-12	Fiction and nonfiction	6 times a year	By mail to address
Junior English				
Senior English				
Am. Hist.-Junior				
Am. Hist.-Senior				
Citizenship & Gov't.				
Current Affairs				
Current Science				
Junior Literary Guild Franklin Street Garden City, N.Y. 11530		Fiction and nonfiction of quality	Monthly	By mail to address
Picture Book Club:	5-6			
Easy Reading Club:	7-8			
Intermediate Club:	9-11			
Older Girls Club:	12-16			
Older Boys Club:	12-16			
Parents' Magazine 80 Newbridge Road Bergenfield, N.J. 07621		Fiction	Monthly	By mail to address
Read Aloud Club:	2-6			
Beginning Readers:	5-7			
American Boy:	8-12			
Calling All Girls:	8-12			
Scholastic Books 904 Sylvan Ave. Englewood Cliffs, N.J. 07632		Paperbound reprints and originals of fiction and nonfiction		Through clubs in schools
See-Saw:	5-6		4 times a year	
Lucky:	7-8		6 times a year	
Arrow:	9-11		6 times a year	
Teen Age:	12-14		8 times a year	
Campus:	14-17	Campus club features classics and contemporary books	9 times a year	

BOOK CLUB AND ADDRESS	AGE LEVEL	KINDS OF BOOKS	WHEN BOOKS ARE SENT	HOW TO JOIN
Weekly Reader Children's Education Center Columbus, Ohio 43216		Fiction and nonfiction	6 times a year	By mail to address
Primary Division:	5-8			
Intermediate Div.:	8-10			
Young America:	10-13			
Young Folks Book Club 1376 Coney Island Ave. Brooklyn, N.Y. 11230	5-12	Fiction and nonfiction	Monthly	By mail to address
Young People's Book Club 226 N. Cass Ave. Westmont, Ill. 60559	7-12	Fiction	Monthly	By mail to address
Young Reader's Press Katonah, N.Y.		Fiction and nonfiction	6 times a year	By mail to address
King Cole Club:	6-7			
Willie Whale Club:	8-9			
Falcon Club:	10-12			

SPONSORING A BOOK FAIR

A wonderful experience for a school, a teacher, and the children is the planning of a book fair. Sometimes, a fair is an annual event, co-sponsored by a community agency or the school PTA. The process can be a wearing and trying one, but most rewarding for all concerned.

Besides the obvious fact that a book fair proves to be a delightful experience for the children, it offers other advantages as well:

1. It gives children an opportunity to browse among and discover new books for reading.
2. It strengthens home and school ties as parents visit, contribute to, and possibly buy books to read aloud to children at home or to donate to the school library.
3. It highlights the merchandise and services of local bookstore dealers, who may lend books for display purposes and for sale.

A book fair of the type described here is a one-school, two-to-three-day affair as contrasted to the broader, community-wide book bazaar, which will serve a complete school district and which may run for a month or longer. A fair of the type we are interested in can be conducted by one or two teachers with aid from their classroom groups and interested parents.

A well-run book fair, even one relatively modest in scope, calls for considerable preplanning. One to three months is usually sufficient; therefore, the teacher who begins thinking with her children in September about a book fair can be ready by early November. The November date is often ideal, coinciding with National Children's Book Week and avoiding December which is a busy time of the year for everyone. April and May—between Easter and the closing of the school year are also fine months for spring book fairs.

Other elements of preplanning, which pose relatively minor problems for the planning group but which bear directly upon the ultimate success of the fair, include the following:

1. Gaining the support of the principal, the school and/or public librarian, various supervisors, parents, and local book dealers.

2. Selecting a theme: "Reading-Right through the Year"; "A World of Wonderful Books"; "Fun with Friends and Books."

3. Finding a place and space. Multi-purpose rooms, school gymnasiums, libraries, a vacant room, or a long hallway may be the place. Space for exhibit tables, with ample areas (aisles) for browsing, storage, and special programs (optional) must also be available.

4. Establishing the hours of operation. Every class group in the school should be scheduled into the exhibit area at least once during the regular school hours (twice if books are to be sold, the second visit to be for the express purpose of buying books). After-school and evening hours should be for children accompanied by their parents.

The formation of committees will be necessary, the number of committees being determined by the scope of the fair. Insofar as possible, involve the children in committee work; it is good training and they take great delight in "working at the fair." For example, each class in a school might assume the responsibility for manning and caring for one display area (see the Book Display Categories listed on page 53).

The following people might be part of the listed committees, with the teacher or librarian serving as over-all coordinator and chairman of each:

Teachers/Librarians	*Pupils*	*Parents*
Book selection	Decorations	Finance and sales
Exhibits	Entertainment	Publicity
Scheduling of groups	Hospitality ———→	
into the exhibit ←——	Planning ———	

The number and types of books to be displayed will depend on the space available, on whether single or multiple copies of books are to be displayed (multiple copies will be necessary if books are to be sold at the fair site), on the degree of cooperation obtained from a book dealer, and on the categories of books that are established. If the planning committee wants a single copy of each title, 200 to 600 different books should prove sufficient. If books are to be sold from the display titles, as many as 2,000 to 3,000 books may be needed.

Establishing the categories of books to be displayed is an important step. If the following list does not seem appropriate, the teacher might consult with a librarian or refer to the bibliography at the end of the chapter.

Book Display Categories

1. Animals, both fiction and non-fiction
2. Aviation, space, and space travel
3. Biography
4. "Easy-to-read" books
5. Fairy and folk tales, myths, and legends
6. Humor
7. Miscellaneous: art, hobbies, music, etc.
8. Nature and science
9. Old favorites: classics, etc.
10. Picture books
11. Poetry
12. Prize-winning books: Newbery and Caldecott award winners
13. Second-hand books: old books (from home) for 25¢ and less
14. Science fiction
15. Sports: fiction and nonfiction

An important matter is determining whether books are to be sold or merely displayed. If books are for display only, a school or a library will often be able to supply enough books for the exhibit. A bookstore operator will often loan books for such a worthy cause, although some dealers do not feel they can release from their shelves the large stocks called for. A cooperative venture, with a number of book dealers each being asked to supply books for one or two categories, will often solve this problem.

If books are to be sold—a fund-raising, but limiting factor at a book fair—a local bookstore or wholesale dealer will undoubtedly be willing to cooperate. The teacher should try the local bookstore owner first, then turn to the wholesale jobber if the local dealer cannot help. Librarians and bookstore dealers can supply teachers with the names of district and out-of-town jobbers. A list of nationwide wholesale distributors is also available for ten cents from The Children's Book Council, Inc., 175 Fifth Avenue, New York, N.Y. 10010.

When negotiating with local bookstores and wholesale dealers for consignments of books to be sold, the teacher must have clearly in mind the details on such matters as the discounts to be allowed, services (will

Andersen's Fairy Tales

the bookstore send an agent to the fair?), and the types of books to be consigned.

Again, in the case of books to be sold, it must be decided early if (1) display books will be sold upon demand (if so, how many multiple copies of each book should be ordered?), (2) orders will be taken for delivery later, (3) books on display will be sold on the last day of the fair, or (4) order forms are to be taken by the purchaser to the local dealer, who will credit the discount to the school against its future purchases. The teacher who works with an out-of-town jobber will want to know also if unsold books can be returned, who assumes the shipping costs, and how much time will be required to deliver the order.

As has been suggested before, involving the children in the planning for the book fair is of the utmost importance. Children can provide added fair attractions in the form of displays and performances, a parade of storybook characters, art decorations for the display area, sponsorship of film showings, puppet shows, dioramas, and different colored signs to mark the different exhibit areas. Children also make fine hosts and hostesses, each child "working a shift" during the exhibit period.

Parents fill a vital role, too, not only as visitors to the book fair, but as publicity directors, finance chairmen, and co-hosts with the children and the teachers. One or two mothers and fathers can do wonders: getting spot announcements on radio and television, obtaining newspaper coverage, and securing a speaker for a "Night Out with Books" program in conjunction with the fair. A few eager and responsible parents will gladly assume the responsibility for arranging and displaying the books, making a schedule of volunteer workers, accessioning the books when they arrive, and selling the books.

SELECTED MATERIALS AND RESOURCES FOR THE TEACHER

Book Care

BEGINNING RESPONSIBILITY: BOOKS AND THEIR CARE. Chicago: Coronet Films. Ten-minute film on book care, for grades K-5.

THE BOOK. New York: Young America—McGraw-Hill Book Company, Text-film Department. Film on book care, for grades 6 and up.

DISCOVERING THE LIBRARY. Chicago: Coronet Films. Eleven-minute film on proper procedures in the library.

IT'S FUN TO READ BOOKS. Chicago: Coronet Films. Eleven-minute film.

LET'S BE GOOD CITIZENS AT THE LIBRARY. San Francisco: Gateway Productions. Ten-minute film.

LIBRARIES ARE FOR CHILDREN, BRONX, N.Y.: Fordham Publishing Company. Thirty-two lessons on library skills.

THE LIBRARY—A PLACE FOR DISCOVERY. Chicago: Encyclopaedia Britannica Films, Inc. Sixteen-minute film on how to use the library, for upper elementary and junior high school.

LIBRARY SKILLS. Minneapolis: T. S. Denison & Company, Inc. Workbooks and teaching guides on how to use the library, for grades 4–6.

THE STORY OF A BOOK. Los Angeles: Churchill Films. Eleven-minute film on how a book is made, for grades 4–8.

Book Corner

SPACE, ARRANGEMENT, BEAUTY IN SCHOOL. Washington, D.C.: Association of Childhood Education International, 1958. Pamphlet.

Bulletin Boards

Coplan, Kate, POSTER IDEAS AND BULLETIN BOARD TECHNIQUES: FOR LIBRARIES AND SCHOOLS. Dobbs Ferry, N.Y.: Oceana Publications, 1962. Book.

Egan, Mary J., and Cynthia Amrine, USING YOUR LIBRARY: 32 POSTERS FOR CLASSROOM AND LIBRARY. Dansville, N.Y.: F. A. Owen Publishing Co., 1965. 32 posters.

Jacobsen, Sybil, MAKE FRIENDS WITH BOOKS. New York: The Children's Book Council, Inc., 1949 and later editions. Booklet.

Kelley, Marjorie, CLASSROOM-TESTED BULLETIN BOARDS. San Francisco: Fearon Publishers, 1961. Pamphlet.

Mathre, T. H., CREATIVE BULLETIN BOARDS. Minneapolis: T. S. Denison & Company, Inc., 1962. Booklet.

Randall, Reino, and Edward Haines, BULLETIN BOARDS AND DISPLAY. Worcester, Mass.: Davis Publications, 1961. Booklet.

Ruby, Doris, 4D BULLETIN BOARDS THAT TEACH. San Francisco: Fearon Publishers, 1960. Booklet.

Book Week

Catholic Book Week. Villanova, Penn.: Catholic Library Association. Write for information about a descriptive booklet.

Jewish Book Month. New York: Jewish Book Council of America. Write for information.

National Children's Book Week Order Form. New York: Children's Book Council, Inc., 1968.

National Library Week Promotional Aids Brochure, New York: National Book Committee, 1968.

Book Fairs

BEST BOOKS FOR CHILDREN, INCLUDING BOOKS FOR YOUNG PEOPLE. New York: R.R. Bowker Co., 1968. Booklet.

BIBLIOGRAPHY OF BOOKS FOR CHILDREN. Washington, D.C.: Association of Childhood Education International, 1968. Booklet.

BOOK BAZAARS. New York: Scholastic Teacher. Booklet.

BOOKS FOR THE TEEN AGE. New York: New York Public Library, Public Relations Office, 1968. Booklet.

HOW TO HOLD A SUCCESSFUL SCHOLASTIC PAPERBACK BOOK FAIR. Englewood Cliffs, N.J.: Scholastic Book Services, 1966. Pamphlet.

LET'S READ TOGETHER: BOOKS FOR FAMILY ENJOYMENT. Chicago: American Library Association, 1964. Booklet.

LISTS OF DEALERS SUPPLYING EXHIBITS OF CHILDREN'S BOOKS. New York: Children's Book Council, Inc., 1964. Pamphlet.

RECIPE FOR A BOOK FAIR. New York: Children's Book Council, Inc., 1962. Booklet.

SEVEN ALA CRITERIA FOR BOOK FAIRS. Chicago: American Library Association, 1963. Booklet.

Book Reading Promotional Devices

MY READING DESIGN: GRADES 1–12. North Manchester, Ind.: Reading Circle, Inc., Box 55, 1962. Packet of Materials.

Teaching Literature through Guided Group Activities

CHAPTER THREE

PERSPECTIVE

In the preceding chapter attention was called to the need for a definite time being reserved in the school day during which the children are allowed to browse, read, or engage in other literature activities according to individual interests, and stress was placed upon the need for student freedom and student involvement.

However valuable a free personal reading program might be, it alone will not guarantee to a child a complete and enduring acquaintance with his literary heritage. This can come about only through a carefully thought out, teacher-prepared program of guided group reading and activities wherein the child acquires the skills necessary to interpret and enjoy the literature he reads.

The discussion in this chapter is centered around ways of developing interpretation skills through group activities, with particular attention being given to the unit approach to literature. The chapter first presents a systematic and planned program in literature. The literature interpretation skills to be developed are pointed out. A significant amount of space in the chapter is devoted to specific examples of how children are guided in group reading through literary units centered around (a) a single story for the primary grades, (b) a classic for the intermediate grades, (c) stories in basal readers, (d) activities in other curriculum areas, and (e) commercial literature programs.

PRINCIPLES OF GUIDED GROUP READING

The principles to be followed in guiding group activities in all phases of the curriculum are known generally to most experienced teachers, and many of those principles may be applied to the teaching of literature as well. However, a few observations specifically relative to the literature program need to be brought to the fore.

1. It is imperative that the children be involved in a literary area of real interest and genuine concern to them. Without such involvement, the program may produce little growth in literature appreciations, understandings, techniques, and skills. The selection of topics for study will not occur by happenstance. The experienced teacher triggers the identification of worthwhile topics and activities by careful preplanning and by proper motivation. In short, the area of study is carefully planned for in advance, with flexibility and accommodation for children's ideas being built into the teacher's plan.

2. Sufficient numbers of books and a plentiful array of supplies and other teaching resources must be available, and there must be an attractive environment in which the study of literature is to go forward. If unit activities are undertaken, particular emphasis must be placed on the creative arts, both in the preparation of exhibits and bulletin boards, and in a culminating activity at the conclusion of the unit.

3. The teacher must constantly rethink and revamp her expectations with regard to the children and the content of the program. Teachers must be responsible for continued additions, deletions, and improvisations, since learnings do occur among the children, weaknesses calling for immediate remediation do become apparent, and re-enforcement of certain skills does become essential. Further, schools do have expectations as to the content to be taught—as it is reflected in the districts' curriculum guides and courses of study—and these expectations must be respected and honored by teachers.

4. Materials to be studied should be drawn from many areas of literature, both fiction and nonfiction. Children should be taught to read, understand, and appreciate factual materials as well as the content of narrative works. Indeed, the quality and quantity of nonfiction has increased so dramatically in the past 15 years and it is so widely read by children today, it would be denying them part of their literary heritage if some such materials were not included in a program of guided group activities.

5. The teacher must continually look for evidence that desired learnings are taking place in the guided group program. If the teacher has provided a wealth of interesting activities, the goals of the literature

program may become obscured as enthusiastic children busy themselves around the myriad activities. Teachers need to be sensitive to the specific goals of the program and to recognize when these goals are not being met.

In most situations, facts and figures per se about literature are not major goals. Rather, evaluation is directed toward the general goal of building new attitudes and understandings about literature. The children's growth in this respect cannot be marked with a comment and a number, as "Bobby gained 12.6 per cent in literature understanding during this grading period." Teachers must recognize that growth in attitudes and understandings occurs along a continuum, and evaluation is concerned with assessing each child's progress along that line, rather than upon completion of some fixed task by each youngster.

LITERATURE INTERPRETATION SKILLS

A child's literary appreciation develops in relation to his maturity and experiences with literature, beginning with the first story or poem he hears. What he thinks about the dish who ran away with the spoon, what "mood" pictures he sees in Laura Richard's poem "Eletelephony," and how he enjoys the action of Rudyard Kipling's *The Jungle Book* represent appreciation of literature from his point of view.

To very young children, who have an almost natural love of stories, the teacher is the most frequent and satisfying contact with literature. The teacher presents stories by reading them aloud or by telling them. While the children show interest in the story for its own sake, the teacher sees this interest as the beginning of literary appreciation.

The simple enjoyment of plot development on the part of the youngsters—"what happens next?"—is an indication that children are "seeing," feeling, and appreciating literature in most subtle ways. And, of course, the teacher spurs the children on by asking them why they liked a particular character, what they disliked about a certain episode in a story, and their reasons for wanting to hear a favorite story again and again. In so doing, however, the teacher does not extract every whit of information about a book, nor does she desire a detailed analysis of the material or a complete summary of the children's reactions.

Older youngsters are interested in longer stories. In their literature they can accommodate frustration of the hero, and their understanding of human behavior and motivations is growing. Therefore, older children can recognize and understand the cause and effect of relationships that obtain in the literature they read.

The teacher of intermediate-grade youngsters employs a number of teacher- and/or pupil-led activities: group work, oral discussions, oral reading, silent reading, storytelling, and the like. When these experiences with literature provoke stimulating discussions of plots, themes, and characters, the boy and girl readers grow in their knowledge of literature as well as in their understanding of people and life around them.

Whether the children are in the primary or intermediate grades, they must be taught the literature interpretation skills that will help them accurately assess what is being read, and they must learn how to derive inferences based upon that reading. The following is a list of worthwhile literature skills to be learned at the primary and intermediate levels.

Primary Grades

Follow plot—follow a sequence of events; predict outcomes (how the story will end); recreate a scene.

Interpret character—"see" characters; identify self (by substitution) with characters in a story.

React emotionally—recognize and respond to the emotional tone and mood of the story.

React to words—learn their meanings; learn their picture-making qualities; recognize the sound values of nonsense syllables and alliterative phrases.

Recognize literary forms—recognize the difference in form of drama, poetry, prose; know real and make-believe story lines.

Intermediate Grades

Follow plot—follow a larger number of characters and events; make deductions; predict outcomes; recognize inferences from various clues.

Interpret character—read between the lines; analyze through actions and words; identify characters with self and others.

React emotionally—feel with (be) the characters; derive an emotional satisfaction from a reading experience; judge validity and interest.

React to words—know how they build suspense, help in establishing setting, and set the pace; learn their more precise and varied meanings in relation to context; recognize writing style.

Recognize literary forms—distinguish between fiction and nonfiction; discriminate among fables, fairy and folk tales; know essay form and biography; recognize types of poetry.

In order to build the above-listed literature skills and give children systematic guidance in judging literature and in drawing conclusions from what they read, the teacher of literature will want to have in mind a series of questions with which she can help the children to interpret the literature they read. Some categories of questions that help children draw valid conclusions are presented below. Although fiction and nonfiction are listed separately, it is readily seen that the fiction questions can often be used with nonfiction materials, and vice versa.

Questions That Help Children Draw Conclusions from Fiction

1. To predict outcomes

   A. Read the chapter titles. What action is suggested by these titles?

   B. Read each paragraph (or book section). What will happen next and why? What is the next problem that will arise? What will each character do with the problem and why?

2. To detect mood

   A. What was the saddest (funniest) incident and why?

   B. It was sad (funny) when.... etc. Why?

3. To interpret character

   A. Choose the character you like (dislike) the most. Describe the character and tell why you approve or disapprove of her/him.

   B. Locate and read sentences in the book that tell why each character behaved as he did.

   C. Describe changes in characters as they evolved throughout the course of the story.

4. To draw conclusions

   A. What is the situation (in a chapter, paragraph, or incident) that is described?

   B. How can this book (situation) help you in your daily life? Help you to know others better?

Questions That Help Children Draw Conclusions from Nonfiction

1. To establish validity

   A. Is this story fact or fiction? How do you know?

   B. What are the credentials of the author? Is he qualified to write on this subject? How do you know?

   C. Does the author draw valid conclusions? Leave out facts? Change facts? Is he correct in all of his facts? Explain.

   D. In what ways has this book caused you to change your mind about the subject? Explain.

2. To recognize literary style

   A. What do you like (dislike) about the author's way of writing?

   B. Locate some figurative words and phrases. What do they mean?

   C. Does the author use simple words in unusual ways? Do any words perform unusual jobs (e.g., adjectives and verbs act as nouns, or vice versa)?

D. Does the author use long sentences (compound and complex)? Does he use short sentences? Are the short sentences used to suggest abruptness?

3. To assess author's purpose

A. How do you know the author was interested in the subject?

B. Did the author succeed in getting you interested in the subject? Explain.

4. To consider relevance

A. Read section (chapter). . . . Find and list as many details as you can about. . . .

B. Use the table of contents (index) to find answers to these questions. . . .

C. How can you best use the knowledge in this book?

TEACHING A SINGLE STORY AT THE PRIMARY-GRADE LEVEL

Generally speaking, there is no one best method of teaching literature to small children. One teacher may enjoy success using stories suggested by basal readers while another may employ trade books from the library, and so on. Nor must the unit necessarily cover a large amount of material or span any given period of time. It is important that the activity be interesting and that the planning involve the children.

One approach to teaching literature is to take a well-known children's story and build around it a series of brief, interesting unit activities. The program outlined below may not cover more than 30 to 45 minutes a day for a period of two to three days, depending upon the time available and the inclinations of the pupils and the teacher.

The approach to be used in guiding the reading of the primary-level story "Goldilocks and the Three Bears," and the development of the follow-up activities, require that the teacher do three things with the children in the classroom:

1. Develop and clarify the purposes for reading the story.
2. Involve the children in a fruitful skill-building discussion of the story.
3. Help the children make use of the ideas gained from the story through a few planned literature activities.

In developing with children a set or readiness for reading and enjoying the story, the teacher will want to establish and clarify the purposes for reading in three ways: by building an experience background for the story, by introducing the new words, and by establishing a specific purpose for reading the story.

(a) To generate interest in the story and to build the concepts that the children need in order to understand the story, the teacher may initiate a pre-story discussion:

... asking the children to tell *facts* they know or experiences they or others have had with bears.

... discussing a previously read or told story about bears.

... discussing a current local happening that centered upon bears.

... showing a flat or still picture, movie or other visual aid dealing with bears.

(b) To teach unknown words meaningfully, the teacher should introduce the new words in context. To insure proper learning, a combination of techniques should be used: pronunciation of the word by the teacher, context clues, structural analysis, phonetic analysis, and the use of the dictionary, if possible. The actual words selected would depend upon which version of "Goldilocks and the Three Bears" is employed, but one such list might include: porridge, errand, latch, hospitable, impudent, bedchamber, gruff, wee, bolster, and truant. The list should not be so extensive, nor the time spent on its introduction so long, that the anticipated pleasure of hearing the story is diminished.

(c) Definite and worthwhile purposes must be established for reading the story. The purposes may be listed on the chalkboard. In one instance there may be only a single purpose: sheer enjoyment of a story. In other instances, the reasons may be many and varied, as the following:

(1) To ascertain whether the story has a basis in fact. (Could a real, live little girl visit the home of three bears?)

(2) To answer specific questions. (What facts about bears, if any, will be contained in this story?)

(3) To verify statements. (The story will suggest that Goldilocks is a foolish little girl. Who will be able to tell us why?)

(4) To follow a sequence of events. (In what order does Goldilocks encounter the bed, the chair, and the porridge? In what order do the bears speak when they first see their porridge?)

(5) To identify character traits. (Who will be the nicest bear of all? Be prepared to tell why.)

(6) To interpret figurative language. (Find out about a "middle-sized" voice.)

(7) To discover what is meant by the "climax" of a story. (Do the three bears find Goldilocks? How does the story end?)

After the purposes for reading the story are established, silent reading of individual, mimeographed, or book copies of the story takes place, or the story is told or read by the teacher. The entire selection should be read through, or told in its entirety, before any group discussion ensues.

The second major goal of the unit is to develop literature skills and appreciations. This is done in part through an informal discussion of the story, during which each reader is encouraged to react to the story and to express ideas he has gleaned from it. In particular, the discussion should center upon the purpose(s) for which the reading was done. The teacher should have in mind a series of questions that will keep the discussion lively and that will help clear up vague understandings that individual readers might harbor. Here the teacher might use the previously listed questions for helping children draw conclusions from their reading. Specifically, some questions about the story of "Goldilocks and the Three Bears" might take the following form:

... How many bears were there? What were their names? How did they get such names? What sizes were they?

... Where did the bears live? What furniture did the bears keep in their house? How many rooms did they have in their house?

... What was the name of the girl who came to the three bears' house? What did she look like? Which girl in this classroom has hair like Goldilocks?

... Goldilocks was on an errand for her mother. What do you think that errand might have been? Do you think Goldilocks ever passed through that part of the woods again? Why or why not? Of what material would the bears build their house?

Rereading or retelling a selection is often worthwhile if an educationally sound reason is available. In this instance, if the story is read again, the second reading may be oral or silent. The purpose or purposes for the second reading should be different from the first, but the suggested purposes may be drawn from those outlined previously.

The third and final goal of this brief literature unit is to help the children make use of the knowledge and enjoyment gained from the story. Further interpretation should result through group participation in literature activities. In this way understandings of the story are further clarified and story details are remembered.

A few suggestions for making use of the story "Goldilocks and the Three Bears" are given below. Additional information on various techniques and media is given in greater detail elsewhere in this volume. However a few simple approaches appropriate for the primary-grade level include:

... reading or dramatizing the story for another class group.

... making and/or bringing from home a doll dressed like Goldilocks.

... doing an iconographic telling of the story, using stuffed toys.

... writing an experience story, detailing how the class would build the house of the three bears.

... building and decorating the three bears' house, using a pasteboard carton.

... finding, displaying, and reading related poems and books.

... drawing a picture illustrating a part of the story.

... making a pictorial montage or map of the woods, and of the house of the three bears.

... writing invitations and inviting parents to an open house centered about the story.

TEACHING A CLASSIC AT THE INTERMEDIATE-GRADE LEVEL

The importance of developing in children an appreciation of literature through many experiences with the best written stories and books has already been stressed. Such pieces of literature are often identified as classics.

The term "classic" connotes different things to different people. To some, a *standard* classic refers to a book or story of the highest excellence, one that has survived a generation or more (such as *Robinson Crusoe* by Daniel Defoe). Others speak of a *modern* classic as a story with a compelling plot or theme that is particularly appropriate for today's children (such as *Charlotte's Web* by E. B. White). "Classic" is also often used to refer to a simplified or rewritten classic, a book or story that has been edited because it is too long or too complex for the average or below-average reader.

There is a place for each of the three types of classics in the literature program for children. Better readers should be encouraged to read the unexpurgated standard classics. Yet, these young people should not be denied access to the modern classics if they want to read them. Indeed, children read more for enjoyment than for an education, and if a standard classic does not meet this requirement, the child will turn away from it.

Indeed, teachers will often find it profitable to use the modern-day classics. Today's children live in a fast-paced world of machines and space. It should not be surprising to find the child more charmed by *The Incredible Journey* by Sheila Burnford or by that delightfully humorous fantasy, *Mr. Popper's Penguins* by Florence and Richard Atwater, than by *The Faerie Queene* or *The Hoosier Schoolmaster.*

How the books are presented by the teacher and *when* they are presented is often as important as *what* is presented. If the teacher takes care to apprise children of the genuine excitement, adventure, and fun in *Robinson Crusoe, The Jungle Book, Tom Sawyer,* and *Treasure Island,* the youngsters will be more than willing to use the books as study vehicles. By the same token, if children are not too young when exposed to *Alice in Wonderland, Wind in the Willows,* and *Winnie the Pooh,* they may find these books to be very enjoyable masterpieces for class study and for pleasure reading.

Rewritten or simplified classics are not to be universally denounced. If the rewritten version is faithful to the original characters, plot, theme, and style of writing, it may prove to be the worthwhile focus of a unit of study. Some of the original classics are too difficult in vocabulary and concept for the average-to-poor readers. But a class or an individual may profit from reading a simplified classic which would otherwise be missed.

For purposes of illustrating how a classic may be the core of a unit, the book-length story *The King of the Golden River* is used here. This book is a brief, yet marvelous fairy tale, which is just as popular today as it was when it was written.

THE KING OF THE GOLDEN RIVER
by John Ruskin

A STUDY OF A CLASSIC FOR GRADES 5-8

1. Gaining a Background.

    A. The teacher should read the entire book (story) so that she may locate all the concepts to be developed and to plan for the activities. With this story, a program of about five to seven days' duration is envisioned.

    B. The teacher might want to read a biographical work about Ruskin, noting particularly other books and stories that he wrote. Minimal preparation would call for reading an encyclopedia résumé of his life.

C. A list of the most difficult words should be assembled during the teacher's first reading. This vocabulary list will be expanded as the children read the story and add words to the list. The words will depend upon the edition of the story to be used, but it might include the following:

adverse	gentian	precipice
avarice	glacier	prismatic
bolster	hedgehog	repose
castellated	hob	saunter
cataract	inundate	savory
chasm	knave	tendril
crucible	magistrate	tithe
doublet	metallic	torrent
drought	mutton	traverse
fatigue	myriad	vagabond
fertile	patrimony	zenith

2. *General Outlines to be Followed in Teaching the Story.*

A. Assignments should be on a chapter-by-chapter (or section-by-section) basis; a minimum of four reading and discussion sessions is anticipated, with one or two days to be devoted to follow-up activities.

B. If discussion questions are presented in written form, questions should be distributed to students prior to the reading so they may read *for* the answers.

C. In the main, discussion questions should be handled orally. Discussion groups will vary in size from the total class to groups of four to six. Encourage spontaneous responses and informality.

D. Methods of introducing new words should vary from session to session. The new vocabulary may be presented before the children read a section of the story. Or, the pupils might read the chapter before the new vocabulary is discussed. In the former situation the teacher puts the new words on the chalkboard and holds individuals or pairs of pupils responsible for reporting to the class on the meanings of specific words as used in the chapter. *Under no circumstance should any child be asked to keep a long list of words and/or look up the definitions of all unknown words.*

The names of the characters (Hans; Gluck; Schwartz; South-West Wind, Esquire; King of the Golden River) should be presented and pronounced before the first reading of the story is undertaken.

E. In considering the interpretation skills to be built within the framework of the story, the teacher should keep uppermost in her mind the importance of (1) proper motivation for the daily reading, (2) frequent discussions of the different characters and the role they play in plot development, (3) encouraging children to make notes on questions that come to mind as they read, and (4) calling children's attention to the illustrations as aids to interpreting the story.

F. Related activities should be used to help the readers further understand and appreciate the story. These activities may take many forms; some that may be used as a preview to the study of *The King of the Golden River* are:

   (1) Write the names of the main characters on the board and make reference to the Black Stones.

   (2) If some of the students have lived in Germany, they may be able to tell about the supposed locale of this story and the presence of the two Black Stones in the Rhine River. Or the teacher might recite the legend herself.

   (3) Locate on a wall map the locale mentioned in the story.

   (4) Select a committee of children to begin planning for a bulletin board which will contain a map of the locale of the story as the children see it, pictures of the characters, words of interest from the story, and a list of related readings.

3. *Chapter I, Lesson 1: We Meet the Black Brothers and South-West Wind, Esquire (pp. 1-19).*

A. Introducing the story and Lesson 1.

   (1) Read aloud the introduction, particularly the section on how this story came to be.

   (2) Discuss some of the fine pictures in the book. If mimeographed copies of the story are utilized, show some of the pictures from the book by using an opaque projector.

   (3) Ask such questions as: What would you do if such a stranger as South-West Wind, Esquire, came to visit you? Would you be jealous of two wealthy and greedy brothers? Would you expect a reward for doing a good deed?

B. Vocabulary introduction.

bolster	hedgehog	tithe
cataract	hob	torrent
doublet	inundate	vagabond
drought	mutton	
fertile	savory	

C. Silent reading of the chapter, then oral reading of it.

D. Discussion questions. (This is a representative list rather than an exhaustive one.)

    (1) Where does this story take place?

    (2) Why were the two older brothers so mean?

    (3) How did the neighbors feel about the Black Brothers?

    (4) Why was Gluck afraid to admit South-West Wind, Esquire, to the house?

    (5) Describe South-West Wind, Esquire, using the descriptions of his personage and the pictures on pages 10 and 13 in the book.

    (6) Do you think the name South-West Wind, Esquire, fits the little man? Why or why not?

    (7) List the wealth of the Black Brothers.

    (8) How does Gluck differ in character from his two brothers?

E. Related activities.

    (1) Write another ending to the chapter based upon the possibility that Hans was as kind as Gluck.

    (2) Write a short poem about the plight of Gluck, the greed of Hans and Schwartz, or the character of South-West Wind, Esquire.

    (3) Write a brief article for the society page of a newspaper. Entitle it "The Black Brothers Have a House Guest."

    (4) Have the children use the vocabulary words in oral sentences. Have them write synonyms for the words.

4. *Chapter II, Lesson 2: The Brothers Lose Their Land, and Gluck Is Visited by the King of the Golden River (pp. 20-31).*

A. Introducing Lesson 2.

    (1) What is avarice? How do you think it will catch up with Hans and Schwartz?

    (2) What is gratitude? Does the King of the Golden River show gratitude toward Gluck when he is freed from the crucible? Do you believe he showed gratitude only because he had to?

B. Vocabulary introduction.

adverse	knave	precipice
avarice	metallic	prismatic
crucible	patrimony	saunter

C. Silent reading of the chapter.

D. Discussion questions.

    (1) How did the South-West Wind, Esquire, destroy the Treasure Valley?

    (2) What did the Black Brothers do to make a living after the valley was destroyed?

    (3) How do we know Hans and Schwartz continued their evil ways?

    (4) Describe Gluck's drinking mug.

    (5) Who spoke to Gluck in "a clear, metallic voice"? What does that phrase mean?

    (6) What command did the voice in the mug give to Gluck?

    (7) Describe the King of the Golden River. Use the picture on page 28 to help you.

    (8) What did the King of the Golden River promise to Gluck?

E. Related activities.

    (1) Draw a picture of the King of the Golden River.

    (2) Write a letter to a friend, telling him that you have just met the King of the Golden River. Describe the King to your friend.

    (3) Pretend that you are Gluck. Write a minute-by-minute diary describing your encounter with the crucible and the King of the Golden River.

    (4) Discuss this chapter as it might happen on the moon. Who are the characters? What are their names? What do they wear? How do they act? Give a playlet based upon this new setting and story.

5. *Chapters III and IV, Lesson 3: Hans and Schwartz, Separately, Seek the Golden River (pp. 32-47).*

A. Introducing Lesson 3.

    (1) How would you feel if you came upon a river of gold? Could such a river really exist? Or is the phrase "river of gold" a figure of speech?

    (2) As you read, locate examples of violence and contempt for others.

B. Vocabulary introduction.

castellated	repose
chasm	traverse
magistrate	zenith
myriad	

C. Silent reading of the chapter.

D. Discussion questions.

(1) How did Hans and Schwartz react to the melting of the drinking mug?

(2) Why did Hans and Schwartz fight?

(3) How did Hans get the holy water?

(4) Describe the mountains as Hans first saw them.

(5) What creatures did Hans encounter as he ascended the mountain?

(6) Why did Gluck have Schwartz released from prison?

(7) How did Schwartz come by his holy water?

(8) Describe the fate of Hans and Schwartz.

E. Related activities.

(1) Write a descriptive paragraph of the Golden River, or of Hans or Schwartz.

(2) If you were going to rewrite these two chapters, what character would you add? How would you change certain scenes to accommodate your new character?

(3) Locate and read in these two chapters the best example of:

(a) violence	(c) curiosity
(b) arrogance	(d) beautiful writing

(4) Make a picture dictionary of locations, characters and properties (for example, crucible, hob, bolster) discussed in the story.

6. Chapter 5, Lesson 4: Gluck Sets Out to Find the Golden River (pp. 48-56).

A. Introducing Lesson 4.

. . . Do you like to read about "magical" dwarfs and elves? Why? What temptations in real life do these "magical" people represent in this story?

. . . Gluck is about to give away his key to the Golden River. What do you suppose that key is?

B. Vocabulary introduction.

      fatigue   gentian   glacier   tendril

C. Silent reading of the chapter, then oral reading of it if there is time.

D. Discussion questions.

(1) How did Gluck earn money to seek after the Golden River?

(2) What was the first trial that Gluck faced as he went up the mountain? How did he react?

(3) What was the second trial of Gluck? Describe the path after Gluck gave the child water to drink.

(4) Who was the dog?

       (5) How had the King of the Golden River treated Hans and Schwartz? Was he right in so doing? Why? Why not?

       (6) Describe the robe of the dwarf.

       (7) What happened to the Golden River?

       (8) Where are the Two Black Stones today?

  E. Related activities.

       (1) Were the places on the way to the Golden River real or imaginary? How do you know?

       (2) List the events in the chapter in chronological order.

       (3) Read aloud your favorite passage in this chapter and tell why you liked it.

       (4) Have various groups present a pantomime of Gluck:

          (a) ascending the mountain.

          (b) meeting the old man.

          (c) encountering the child.

          (d) giving a drink to the dog.

7. *Culminating Activities.*

  A. Make a crossword puzzle from words in the story.

  B. Put together a class newspaper, a "special edition" about *The King of the Golden River*. Include advertisements, editorials, feature articles, cartoons, and news features.

  C. Produce a class play to be presented to another class and/or to your parents. Rewrite the story in script form. Form a publicity committee to advertise the play.

  D. Write an article on cruelty, using references from this story.

  E. Each child is to construct three items for a quiz: a multiple-choice question, a true-false item, and a completion problem. (Samples are given below.) The teacher will select a few items from among those submitted and the class will answer the questions with their books open.

Multiple choice:

    The main character in the story is:

    a. Gluck   b. South-West Wind, Esquire

    c. Schwartz

True-False:

    Gluck was a lazy, mean boy.

Completion:

    _____ _____ wrote *The King of the Golden River*.

UNITS FROM STORIES IN BASAL READERS

Many basal readers offer collections of good children's stories and excerpts from books centered around unit themes or topics. They are filled with many activities designed not only to build reading skills, but to increase literature appreciations and understandings as well. (It is hoped that the child-reader's enthusiasm for a particular excerpt from a book will lead him to read the entire book.) Other reading textbooks used in the course of daily lessons may also prove to be take-off points for literature units.

Basal readers are primarily skill-development tools. Therefore, to be most effective they must be used in a logical and sequential manner. About 90 per cent of all classrooms in America employ a basal reading program in this fashion. There are a great number of classrooms that also have access to supplementary basal readers. It is to these readers that the teacher often profitably turns in order to find sets of stories around which she can develop a unit activity program. There are a variety of approaches one can follow in utilizing basal and supplementary readers. Four such approaches are described below.

approach a: (One-day unit) A group of kindergarten children were read a series of Mother Goose rhymes which served to enrich their learnings about life around them. They met such community helpers as the butcher and the baker in "Rub-a-Dub-Dub." They learned of the problems of life in "Old Mother Hubbard" and "Jack Sprat." They were introduced to the garden variety of animals in "My Black Hen," "Six Little Mice," and "I Love Little Pussy."

approach b: (Two-day unit) A group of sixth-grade advanced readers had completed their week's reading in the regular basal reader. Their discussion of the story "The Pied Piper of Hamelin" had caused them to seek out other legends in a set of supplementary books. These readings further stimulated each member of the group to construct a shoe box diorama or peep show. Each person illustrated a scene from the story he liked best.

approach c: (Three-day unit) The children in a second-grade class were grouped upon the basis of their expressed preferences for particular stories in a unit in a basal reader. One group of children chose to prepare and read aloud to the rest of the class the basal reader's version of the story of "Chanticleer." A second group decided to offer their classmates the poem "Indian," using choral speaking as their mode of presentation. A third group offered for class study a large outline chart from a scene in *Winnie-the-Pooh*, while a fourth group of children erected a bulletin board based upon the book *In My Mother's House* by Ann Nolan Clark.

approach d: (Three-week unit) One fourth-grade class developed a rather elaborate unit. It began with the teacher introducing a collection of basal reader stories about domestic and wild animals. Before the opening of the unit the teacher had gathered from the school library a bundle of supplementary books suggested by the basal reader's manual and centered upon the animal theme. She also had prepared mimeographed copies of the reading lists given for each story in the series.

The day the unit began, the teacher set up the chalkboard display of supplementary books. As she led the children through an introduction to each story in the basal reader unit, they expressed much interest in what they would learn about the animals and which animals were their favorites, and they were encouraged to tell about previous experiences they had had with such animals.

After completing the story-by-story introduction, the teacher distributed to each child a copy of the mimeographed booklist and invited the members of the class to add other titles to the list. She also held up, one at a time, the chalk tray array of library books and "baited" the children by reading preselected passages, by showing attractive illustrations, and by discussing briefly the contents of the books.

Enthusiasm for the unit ran high. The initial discussion was vibrant, with each youngster eager to relate some experience or bit of knowledge he possessed about an animal to be encountered in the unit. The boys and girls descended upon the display of books and took them back to their seats, where they began poring over the pages and illustrations. There were many who pleaded for permission to gallop off to the library and obtain more books described on the supplementary list. And the children tore right into the first poem, "The Dog I Met," in the basal reader unit.

Soon the children were reading the recommended books from the teacher's list and developing literature activities based upon these related readings. The program of independent reading and the literature activities that evolved from each story or poem in this basal reader unit is charted on page 75.

The culmination of the unit was an exciting time. On a Wednesday the class made a trip to the local zoo to see the animals they had read about during the unit. (If your community does not have a zoo, do not overlook the possibility of visiting a nearby farm, going on a nature hike, bussing to a junior museum, or inviting the traveling "live-animal" museum to stop by). While at the zoo the children interviewed the superintendent and asked him questions, which they had prepared in advance, about their favorite animals.

BASAL READER STORY	SUPPLEMENTARY BOOKS THAT WERE READ	UNIT ACTIVITIES
A. "The Dog I Met" (poem)—about a boy and the playful dog he encounters one sunny day.	A.1. *The Right Dog For Joe* (by Irmengarde Eberle). A.2. *Dogs, Dogs, Dogs* (by Phyllis Fenner). A.3. *Skippy's Family* (by Stephen Meader).	A.1. Oral reports were given on the work done by different kinds of dogs: setters, St. Bernards, etc. A.2. The total class worked out and presented to another class a choral reading of the poem. A.3. The names of famous dogs were discovered and listed on a chart.
B. "A Bear Cub's Day" (story)— about a tiring day experienced by a bear cub who strays from his mother's side.	B.1. *Bear Cub* (by Ann Nolan Clark). B.2. *A Bear Called Paddington* (by Michael Bond). B.3. *The Biggest Bear* (by Lynd Ward).	B.1. Posters were drawn and illustrated in water colors, depicting woodland scenes and bears' dens. B.2. A small group rewrote "A Bear Cub's Day" from the point of view of the bear cub. B.3. A book of facts about bears was collected, and a cover for the fact book was made and decorated.
C. "The Masked Bandit" (story)— about the habits and adventures of a raccoon.	C.1. *Little Rascal* (by Sterling North). C.2. *Ringtail* (by Alice Gall and Fleming Crew). C.3. *Pepper* (by Barbara Reynolds).	C.1. Further adventures of raccoons were written up and shared with the class. C.2. The class held a discussion about what they had learned about raccoons. C.3. A group of five children read the story of *Pepper*. They rewrote the story and dramatized it.
D. "Trini's Dog" (story)—about a boy who runs away and the dog who sets out to find him and bring him home.	D.1. *The Trail of The Hunter's Horn* (by Billy Clark). D.2. *Lassie Come Home* (by Eric Knight). D.3. *Pantaloni* (by Bettina Ehrlich).	D.1. Flannelboard stories were told, with one child telling the story while the second manipulated the figures. D.2. A collage was made of the countryside, showing the reunion of the boy and his dog. D.3. A panel discussion was conducted on the right of the boy to leave home.

BASAL READER STORY	SUPPLEMENTARY BOOKS THAT WERE READ	UNIT ACTIVITIES
E. "Fly Home Soon, Loon" (story)— about a loon who thinks herself an important bird and leaves home to seek her fame.	E.1. *Honker, The Story of A Wild Goose* (by Robert McClung). E.2. *What's Inside* (by May Garelick). E.3. *Shawneen and the Gander* (by Richard Bennett).	E.1. The film, "The Loon's Neck-lace," was shown. E.2. Three girls made shoe box dioramas based upon scenes from the story. E.3. New endings to the story were devised.
F. "The Seal's Pillow" (poem)— about a baby seal's nighttime bed.	F.1. *The Sea Pup* (by Archie Binns). F.2. *Sammy the Seal* (by Syd Hoff). F.3. *Plop, Plop, Ploppie* (by Elizabeth Olds).	F.1. Pupils wrote a group poem, extending the ideas in the poem. F.2. A small group collected and mounted pictures of large sea animals: whales, seals, walruses, etc. F.3. Children were encouraged to bring from home and read to the class other poems about sea animals and the sea. Two children read exciting excerpts from *The Sea Pup.*
G. "Cage in the Woods" (story) —about a wild-animal farm and the creatures who lived there.	G.1. *My Friend Mac* (by Mary McNeer). G.2. *Dash and Dart* (by Mary and Conrad Buff). G.3. *Animal Tails* (by George Mason).	G.1. The class discussed the characteristics of wild animals which might prove that animals think. G.2. Children designed new book covers and wrote a synopsis of the story to serve as book advertisements for the three supplemental books. G.3. Original stories were written in which the animals exchanged a few characteristics and then attempted to do the things they were accustomed to doing.

BASAL READER STORY	SUPPLEMENTARY BOOKS THAT WERE READ	UNIT ACTIVITIES
H. *Harry, the Ape* (story) — about the training of an ape.	H.1. *Curious George* (by H. A. Rey). H.2. *Third Monkey* (by Ann Nolan Clark). H.3. *The First Jungle Book* (by Rudyard Kipling).	H.1. A group of children constructed a box movie depicting the development of the ape's attitude toward his keepers. H.2. The children told stories of what would have happened if the ape had escaped from the camp. H.3. What if the ape could talk? The children made up stories the ape told.
I. "Rennie" (poem) —about a fox and her pups and their warm winter den in a cave.	I.1. *Animal Homes* (by George Mason). I.2. *The Little Red Fox* (poem) (by Marion Edey and Dorothy Grider.) I.3. *Roger and the Fox* (by Lavinia Davis).	I.1. Other stories were made up and told about Rennie. I.2. Class did a choral reading, with some children playing the role of the foxes. I.3. Two boys dramatized the story of *Roger and the Fox*, using puppets and background scenery they had painted.
J. "Linda the Lion" (story)—about a pride of lions which escapes from a hunter.	J.1. *The Big Cats* (by Herbert Zim). J.2. *The Happy Lion* (by Louise Fatio). J.3. *Andy and the Lion* (by James Daugherty).	J.1. The teacher read excerpts from the book *Born Free* by Joy Adamson. J.2. Children wrote sentences using selected words and phrases from the story. J.3. After reading *Andy and the Lion*, members of the class made up and told tall stories about hunting lions.

Much of Thursday was spent preparing for Friday's book program. The children had decided to present a pageant based upon the unit. To this end, exhibit stations were decided upon, bulletin board displays were freshened, and the animal pageant rehearsed. Each child planned to display something he had made, or to participate in a skit based upon a story or book read.

On Friday morning the program was presented to various other classes in the building. The principal and a few curriculum supervisors were also present. In the afternoon, parents attended the second show. First, some of the "wild animals" appeared before the audiences. They were framed in the door of a cage and presented one-minute book reviews, read excerpts from favorite stories, told a story, or participated in a puppet play. The "domesticated animals" appeared next against a painted backdrop of a farm yard, and performed in puppet plays, showed posters, and the like.

All in all, the unit proved to be a glorious experience for the children. Both the boys and girls who were members of the class putting on the culminating activity and those who came to see it had profited. But most important of all for the children conducting the unit, they had read attentively, eagerly, and joyfully, and they had participated in a lively group activity under the guidance of a knowing and able teacher.

LINKING LITERATURE TO OTHER CURRICULUM AREAS

Literature can be correlated easily and in diverse ways with almost all the areas of the curriculum. Units can be developed around many types of books found in the library. These literature units may progress from the most simple to those calling for rather elaborate plans. It is not our intention to detail all such possible programs. Rather, we shall note a few possibilities in the area of social studies and list some selected series of books which will aid a teacher in establishing literature units in these subject-matter areas. A short unit will demonstrate how a selected series of books may serve to build an interest in literature.

Wide use of literature in the social studies invariably brings to children new and deeper understanding as well as factual knowledge in the area of study. For example, the books *Getting to Know Japan* (a nonfiction book in series, published by Coward-McCann) and *The Story About Ping* (a fiction book published by Viking Press) lend a great deal of pleasure and knowledge to a study of the Far East.

The flavor of foreign lands and little-known peoples can be sampled through a study of their folklore. The writings of Charles Perrault of

France, the German folk tales of the Brothers Grimm, the popular Norwegian tales by Asbjornsen and Moe, and the works compiled by Jacobs in England reveal a great deal of useful background information about the customs of the people of these countries. While reading of *Hansi* in the Tyrol country, of *Mei Li* in China, or of *Nkwala*, the Indian boy, we are given accurate insights into the lives of the boys and girls of these regions.

Equally rich in literature are American history and geography. Henry Steele Commager's survey book entitled *The First Book Of American History*, and such specialized volumes as Roger Duvoisin's *And There Was America* and Holling C. Holling's *Tree In The Trail* make the study of American history a vibrant, lively experience. Genevieve Foster's *George Washington's World*, James Daugherty's *Daniel Boone*, and the d'Aulaires *Abraham Lincoln* are types of biographies that help children understand the people and the times that spanned two turbulent periods in American history. A student's mind takes on new dimensions when he explores the historical fiction of Alice Dalgliesh in *The Courage of Sarah Noble*, Laura Ingalls Wilder's "Little House" books, and Carol Ryrie Brink's *Caddie Woodlawn*.

A brief, informal reading program built around biographies of American heroes and heroines might be undertaken in conjunction with a social studies unit of certain periods in American history. A skeletal outline of the unit might be as follows:

1. The teacher brings together appropriate books in a number of biographical series. The following series are of generally superior quality and usually found in abundance in many school district curriculum-library centers.

Series Name	Publisher	Reading-Level Grade	Interest-Level Grade
American Adventure	Wheeler	2–6	2–12
American Heritage	American Book Company	5–6	5–12
Childhood of Famous Americans	Bobbs-Merrill	4–5	7–9
Discovery	Garrard Press	3–4	2–5
Landmark	Random House	5–6	4–9
Lives to Remember	G. P. Putnam's Sons	5–6	5–9
Piper	Houghton Mifflin	4–5	4–8
Signature	Grossett & Dunlap	4–5	4–8

2. A list is made of famous Americans whose names will arise in conjunction with the social studies unit.

3. The teacher introduces the class to certain of the famous Americans listed whose lives are developed in the biographies she has borrowed from the library.

4. Interested children volunteer to read certain books and report on the well-known characters when their names arise during the discussion periods.

5. Opportunity is given for children who are not happy with their first choices to make another selection of a book.

6. Time is given for the boys and girls to prepare their reports.

7. Reports are given to the class; knowledge about famous Americans has been increased and, hopefully, lasting interest in biography has been established.

Another oral approach to literature was undertaken by a third-grade teacher in a school with extremely limited library facilities. She began by locating one complete set of trade books entitled the Read It Myself Books, published by Holt, Rinehart & Winston, Inc. There are 12 illustrated books in this easy-to-read, controlled-vocabulary series of folk and fairy tales. The books are categorized as follows:

First-Grade Stories:	The Wolf and the Seven Little Kids
	Goldilocks and the Three Bears
	Little Red Riding Hood
Second-Grade Stories:	Jack and the Beanstalk
	Peter and the Wolf
	The Frog Prince
	The Ugly Duckling
	The Elves and the Shoemaker
Third-Grade Stories:	Hansel and Gretel
	Snow White and the Seven Dwarfs
	The Golden Goose
	Rumpelstiltskin

The teacher aroused interest in the proposed unit by arranging a bulletin board display based upon the story "Snow White and the Seven Dwarfs." This colorful display was unveiled the same day that the teacher read aloud the story and shared with the children a sound filmstrip of the same title. At the conclusion of these exercises, a number of children suggested that the class develop a story unit.

The teacher capitalized on this enthusiasm and followed up by asking the children what other folk and fairy tales they knew. Volunteered titles were listed on the chalkboard. The teacher reminded the children that the resources of the local library were very limited, and she invited the children to bring the next day any copies of those stories in book form that they could locate at home. The teacher also revealed to the class her store of the Read It Myself Books and some other tales which she had located in the basal readers and in an anthology. She pointed out to the class how these materials might be used in the proposed literature unit.

The second day of the unit began with the teacher reading aloud to the children *The Ugly Duckling.* Then she asked if any child had been able to locate and bring from home additional books to share with the class. A half-dozen eager hands went up and brought forth their prized volumes.

At this point a plan was outlined as to how the unit might proceed. The children suggested that:

1. The teacher would read aloud some more stories from the readers and anthologies.
2. The Read It Myself Books should be made available for general circulation and silent reading in the classroom only. No one was to be allowed to take home a book.
3. Folk and fairy tales from the basal readers might be prepared for telling to other classes.
4. Certain tales could be dramatized.
5. Crayon and water color pictures could be drawn.
6. Other films and filmstrips might be located and viewed.

Due to a shortage of reading materials for all, the unit was basically an oral one. It was possible to stay close to the usual formal steps used in developing the unit.

1. The introduction of new words took place with the use of the chalkboard. The task was simplified because a word list appears on the last page of each book in the Read It Myself series. In this way new concepts were identified and the vocabulary made meaningful.

2. The teacher read aloud the story.

3. Guided questions were asked during and after the reading of each book. These questions were of the types described in this chapter under the section, "Questions that Help Children Draw Conclusions from Fiction." On one occasion a film based upon Hansel and Gretel (Baily Films) was located and used. (All of the stories in the 12-book Read It Myself Series are available from various sources in either film or filmstrip form.) After the showing of the film, a lively discussion of the story ensued.

As the unit progressed, the following activities evolved:

1. *Jack and the Beanstalk* was dramatized by one group of four children (Jack, his mother, the giant, and a narrator). The play was informally presented, with the dialogue being spontaneously given and no scenery being employed.

2. A second group dance-pantomimed the story *Peter and the Wolf* using appropriate background music.

3. Another small group of children prepared and delivered *The Golden Goose* in storyteller's form to another primary class.

4. The class decided to illustrate on a poster every story they had heard. Individual children volunteered to do particular stories. The quality of these varied, of course, but the children were anxious to see some picture of each story, and in this way every child's illustration did end up on the bulletin board.

5. Two children were motivated to write short fairy tales of their own. These tales were so well done that they were typewritten and placed on the bulletin board with the posters and other art work.

The teacher had asked the children how they might end their study. They decided to take a poll among themselves to discover their favorite tale and have it read one last time.

COMMERCIAL LITERATURE PROGRAMS

There are four basic sources from which readers can obtain prepared programs for teaching children's literature through a guided group approach. These sources are the (1) comprehensive, commercially packaged literature programs; (2) encyclopedias; (3) thematic literature sets and the firms that sell them; and (4) the anthologies. In order to help the teacher visualize the potential of these four types of materials, a few words will be said about each, after which available materials will be listed.

There are a number of complete and comprehensive literature programs for sale on the market today. They take different guises, but all

of them are basically the same: the readings in the series have been selected almost solely from the best prose and poetry for children; there is
a sequential and fairly well-defined program, with specific directions as
to how the books and material are to be used; and the focus is usually—
but not always—upon the enjoyment of literature rather than upon instruction in the basic reading skills. In the list that follows we have described only those programs considered supplementary to a basal reading
program. Only materials printed since 1960 have been included in the
listing.

Although encyclopedias do not offer developed programs to be used
in teaching literature to children, the study guide sections of these books
often give outlines of study which can be put to good use. Occasionally,
encyclopedias develop units, as on folklore and biography, which they
distribute free of charge or at a minimal cost. For example, the *World
Book Encyclopedia* (Merchandise Mart Plaza, Chicago, Ill. 60654 pro-
duces a number of teaching materials such as *Folklore* (SA–2409), *Understanding Poetry* (SA–2415), and *Literature for Children* (SA–1430), the
latter costing 25 cents a copy. A teacher should remain alert as to the
availability of these materials.

Thematic sets (for example, *The Children's Hour*) and the various
anthologies of children's stories (such as *The Illustrated Treasury of
Children's Literature*) do not offer literature programs complete with a
teacher's guidebook, but they are logically organized and usually of such
fine quality that the resourceful teacher can convert the materials to a
program in literature. Many teachers have seen the unit potential in
these sources and have used them to great profit.

It is not our intention to list all possible sources of prepared literature
programs and other related materials. The following is a representative
listing.

Commercial Programs

Best of Children's Literature. (hardbound) 1960.
A well-illustrated, six-book program for grades 1–6. Offers literature tests
and a teacher's manual. Edited by Nila B. Smith et al. Available from
Bobbs-Merrill Company, Inc., 4300 W. 62nd Street, Indianapolis, Ind.
46206.

Classic Fairy Tales. (hardbound) 1966.
Nine stories, including "Hansel and Gretel" and "Tom Thumb." For
second- and third-grade readers. Reading level indicated as 2.8. Adapted
by Audrey Claus and Evalyn Kinkead. Available from Webster Division,
McGraw-Hill Book Company, Manchester Road, Manchester, Mo. 63062.

Classroom Library Packet. (paper) n.d.
A 25-volume boxed set of well-known children's stories for use in primary

classrooms. Accompanied by teacher's guide. Available from The Economy Company, 1901 N. Walnut, P.O. Box 25308, Oklahoma City, Okla. 73125.

First Books Portable Classroom Library in Social Studies. (hardbound) 1966.
A 50-volume resource library to be used with social studies units on the United States at intermediate-grade levels. Includes book rack, wall chart, and teacher's manual. Available from Franklin Watts, Inc., 575 Lexington Avenue, New York, N.Y. 10022.

Invitations to Story Time and to Personal Reading. (hardbound) 1966.
A group of 16 pre-first-grade titles and 25 entertaining and informational books per set for grades 1–6. Accompanied by a teacher's resource book, individual reading record booklets, six posters and a mobile. Edited by Charlotte Huck et al. Available from Scott, Foresman & Company, 433 E. Erie Street, Chicago, Ill. 60611.

I Want to Be Books: Correlation with Primary Social Studies Program. (hardbound) 1966.
A 36-book program based upon these well-known books. For use in grades K-3. Package includes a 64-page handbook. Available from Children's Press, Inc., 1224 West Van Buren Street, Chicago, Ill. 60607.

Literature Sampler, Junior Edition. (paper) Also offered in secondary school edition. 1966.
A series of 120 book-preview cards, 120 reading aids, and 120 discussion cards designed to motivate free reading in grades 4–9. Program offers a teacher's guide. Available from Xerox Education Division, 880 Third Avenue, New York, N.Y. 10022.

Macmillan Reading Spectrum. (paper) 1964.
A set of materials designed to build reading skills in intermediate and upper grades. Materials are comprised of 30 different children's books, teacher's guide, pupil record book, and booklets to help teach word analysis, vocabulary, and comprehension. Developed by Marcella C. Johnson. Available from the Macmillan Company, 60 Fifth Avenue, New York, N.Y. 10018.

Owl Books. (hardbound) 1965.
Presents four sets of children's books: 20 Kin/Der Owl Books for preschool through grade 1; 40 Little Owl books for grades 1–2; 40 Young Owl books for grades 2–4; and 20 Wise Owl books for grades 4–6. The four subject areas are literature, arithemtic, science, and social studies, with all selections drawn from children's literature. Teacher's manual. Edited by Bill Martin, Jr. Available from Holt, Rinehart & Winston, Inc., 383 Madison Avenue, New York, N.Y. 10017.

Prose and Poetry Series. (hardbound) 1960.
Old and new tales and poetry organized into a nine-book program extending from the primer level through grade 8. Has a manual for each book. Developed by Marjorie Pratt et al. Available from L.W. Singer Co., Syracuse, N.Y. 13200.

Reading Caravan. (hardbound) 1964.
This seven-book series extends from grade 1 through grade 6 and emphasizes materials of literary quality. Attractively illustrated. Manual accom-

panies series. Developed by Paul A. Witty et al. Available from D.C. Heath & Company, 285 Columbus Avenue, Boston, Mass. 02116.

Reading for Pleasure. (hardbound) 1966.
This program for teenagers utilizes adaptations of well-known books, stories, articles, and plays. Three books, attractively illustrated. Manuals built into the books. Developed by Frances T. Humphreville and Frances S. Fitzgerald. Available from Scott, Foresman & Company, 433 E. Erie Street, Chicago, Ill. 60611.

Scholastic Literature Units. (paper) 1962.
Extensive units for grades 7–10, built around such themes as animals, courage, family, and personal code. One package includes 110 paperback books, teacher's guide, book-review forms, bulletin boards, and a bookcase. Available from Scholastic Book Services, 50 W. 44th Street, New York, N.Y. 10036.

Scope. (hardbound) 1965.
A two-book program, with guides, for culturally disadvantaged and reluctant readers. Uses excerpts from literature. Titles of books are *People and Places* and *Your World and Others*. Useful in upper elementary, junior high, and senior high. Developed by John C. Bushman et al. Available from Harper & Row, Publishers, 49 E. 33rd Street, New York, N.Y. 10016.

Sounds of Language Readers. (hardbound) 1966.
Based upon excerpts from children's literature sources, these five well-illustrated books present an oral approach to teaching language through the third grade. Each set of books is accompanied by an annotated teacher's edition. Developed by Bill Martin, Jr. Available from Holt, Rinehart & Winston, Inc., 383 Madison Avenue, New York, N.Y. 10017.

Told-Again-Tales from Many Lands. (hardbound) 1964.
A total of 57 old tales collected in three separate books, entitled *First Fairy Tales, Giants and Fairies,* and *Magic Tales.* Useful in upper elementary grades and junior high school. Developed by Grace E. Potler et al. Available from Charles E. Merrill Books, Inc., 1300 Alum Creek Drive, Columbus, Ohio 43216.

Treasure Chest. (hardbound and paper) 1966.
Thirty-six illustrated children's books for use at the early primary level. Readiness skills developed in four areas using books, picture cards, and holiday posters. Teacher's guidebook is included. Developed by Beth G. Hoffman et al. Available from Harper & Row, Publishers, 49 East 33rd Street, New York, N.Y. 10016.

Treasury of Literature: Read-text Series. (hardbound) 1966.
Selected stories and poems from literature, bound up in seven attractive books to be used in grades 1–6. Teacher's guide accompanies material. Developed by Eleanor M. Johnson and Leland B. Jacobs. Available from Charles E. Merrill Books, Inc., 1300 Alum Creek Drive, Columbus, Ohio 43216.

Wide Horizons Series. (hardbound) 1966.
Stories, poems, and excerpts of longer books, to be used in grades 2–9. Study guides and book lists included. Developed by Helen M. Robinson

et al. Available from Scott, Foresman & Company, 433 E. Erie Street, Chicago, Ill. 60611.

Thematic Sets and Encyclopedias

BRITANNICA JUNIOR ENCYCLOPEDIAS. 15 volumes. 1966.
Encyclopaedia Britannica Press, 425 N. Michigan Avenue, Chicago, Ill. 60611.

CHILDCRAFT. 15 Volumes. 1966. (Use Volumes 1 and 2.)
Field Enterprises Educational Corporation, 510 Merchandise Mart Plaza, Chicago, Ill. 60654.

CHILDREN'S HOUR. 16 volumes. 1953.
Spencer Press (Sears, Roebuck and Co.), 153 N. Michigan Avenue, Chicago, Ill. 60611.

COMPTON'S BEGINNER'S BOOKSHELF. 8 volumes. 1966.
Designed to develop literary appreciation in young children. Six volumes are poems, stories, and songs for children; two volumes contain games and activities. Available from F.E. Compton Co., Educational Division, 1000 N. Dearborn Street, Chicago, Ill. 60610.

COMPTON'S PICTURED ENCYCLOPEDIA. 15 volumes. 1966.
Encyclopaedia Britannica Press, 425 N. Michigan Avenue, Chicago, Ill. 60611.

FOLK LITERATURE AROUND THE WORLD. 4 volumes. 1967.
Collection of myths, fables, and legends from various cultural areas of the world for children ages 8 to 12. Available from Silver Burdett, Morristown, N.J. 07960.

MY BOOK HOUSE. 12 volumes. 1960.
The Book House for Children, Lake Bluff, Ill. 60044.

WORLD BOOK ENCYCLOPEDIA. 20 volumes. 1966.
Field Enterprises Educational Corporation, 510 Merchandise Mart Plaza, Chicago, Ill. 60654.

Anthologies

Arbuthnot, May Hill, THE ARBUTHNOT ANTHOLOGY OF CHILDREN'S LITERATURE, rev. Chicago: Scott, Foresman & Company, 1961. 1,158 pages.

Hollowell, Lillian, A BOOK OF CHILDREN'S LITERATURE, 3rd ed. New York: Holt, Rinehart & Winston, Inc., 1966. 580 pages.

Huber, Miriam Blanton, STORY AND VERSE FOR CHILDREN, 3rd ed. New York: The Macmillan Company, 1965. 878 pages.

Johnson, Edna, Evelyn R. Sickels, and Frances C. Sayers, ANTHOLOGY OF CHILDREN'S LITERATURE, 3rd ed. Boston: Houghton Mifflin Company, 1959. 1,239 pages.

Martignoni, Margaret E., THE ILLUSTRATED TREASURY OF CHILDREN'S LITERATURE. New York: Grosset & Dunlap, Inc., 1955. 512 pages.

**Selected List of Materials and
Resources for the Teacher**

Bromberg, Murray, MAKING LITERATURE LESSONS LIVE: A PRACTICAL GUIDE
TO SUCCESS IN THE TEACHING OF LITERATURE. Englewood Cliffs, N.J.:
Teacher's Practical Press (Prentice-Hall, Inc.), 1961. Booklet.

A CURRICULUM FOR ENGLISH, GRADES 1–6. Lincoln, Neb.: University of
Nebraska Press, 1966.

An eight-book collection of literature units, teaching aids, and a teacher's
manual; one guide for each grade, 1 through 6, plus one guide on poetry
and one on linguistics.

The Oral Interpretation of Literature: The Teacher Leads

CHAPTER FOUR

PERSPECTIVE

Good oral interpretation of literature is not separate and far removed from the everyday lives of children; it is part and parcel of many of their waking hours and a contributor to their genuine enjoyment and appreciation of the whole body of fine literature. For boys and girls in the elementary school a good book needs more than just a sound plot and interesting characters. It requires a teacher's voice—vital, warm, expressive—to transport the child-listener into the book, story, or poem itself, stir his emotions, stimulate his mind, and make the characters and scenes as real as the people and places he knows in real life.

Included in this chapter are ideas which the teacher may use in interpreting prose during the read-aloud periods, in telling stories to children and having children tell stories in turn, and in teaching poetry and various choral speaking selections to children. Procedures, suggestions, and materials are given for challenging the bright and the average youngsters at the primary and intermediate levels.

PRINCIPLES OF ORAL INTERPRETATION

A teacher will do a good job of reading a book, reciting a poem, or telling a story if she keeps in mind a few principles of good oral interpretation as they relate to elementary school children.

1. A genuine love for literature and a high regard for the speech arts process, a forgetfulness of self, and a lively reaction and responsiveness to the child-audience will make the teacher a successful oral interpreter of literature.

2. The teacher must have command of the requisite skills of the speech arts: clear enunciation; an agreeable, flexible voice; poise; and a mood-interpreting plasticity of face.

3. Whether the role of the teacher be that of read-aloud agent, story-teller, or definer of poetry, the activity should be in accord with the needs and interests of the children present. Realistic experiences and situations that capture the audience and involve them actively in the process are to be sought after and utilized.

4. The four vehicles of interpretation discussed in this chapter—reading aloud, storytelling, poetry interpretation, and choral speaking—are basically, but not exclusively, oral in nature. Each of the four processes has something unique to offer the child.

> *Reading aloud* adds a charm and meaning to stories which silent reading cannot.
>
> *Storytelling* brings the storyteller and the listener together in a union of unrestricted rest and refreshment, without the interjection of a book.
>
> *Reciting a poem* contributes an appreciation of rhythm not found in other forms of literature.
>
> *Choral speaking* gives boys and girls the joy of a shared group experience which is far more important than the finished product.

The teacher who understands and appreciates the unique contribution and character of each of the four means of oral expression will find ample opportunities to include all of them in the curriculum, knowing that each will add immeasurably to the richness of the child's life.

READING ALOUD

Many people feel that good literature must be heard to be appreciated fully, and children will concur with them. One of the great delights enjoyed by children of all ages, as they will tell you, is the experience of listening to a book or story read aloud in a pleasant voice.

The daily read-aloud period in the classroom is probably the single best time in which to introduce children to the finest materials in juvenile literature, and in which to increase their appreciation of it. And the teacher's role as an oral interpreter of that literature is an extremely important one. For how well she reads aloud—how well she shares and interprets the stories—will greatly influence children's acceptance or rejection of literature from that time forward.

Reading aloud well is an art which every teacher can master if she truly believes in the value of the activity, if she has a working knowledge of the techniques of the craft, and if she is aware of those books and stories that are most apt to meet the needs and interests of the children under her tutelage. When the teacher chooses *appropriate selections, properly interprets* them, and is conscious and considerate of her *audience's interests* and *needs*, the children will develop a lasting appreciation for literature.

Why Read Aloud to Children?

The justifications for including literature in the daily program are many, but the following are particularly germane.

1. *to discover good books.* Hearing stories read aloud by the teacher provides children with opportunities to gain contacts with literature that they would not usually be able to gain by reading for themselves. This is particularly true with respect to young children, who have not yet attained all of the independent reading skills, but who have a level of listening literacy that far outsteps their functional reading ability.

The teacher's custom of reading aloud to children should extend throughout the range of grades in elementary school. Too often the practice is discontinued at the beginning of the fourth grade on the grounds that there is no time for it with the press of other activities. This is an excuse designed to mask the teacher's lack of enthusiasm. A well-organized teacher can always find the time to do those things she wants to do.

There is a special reason why we should continue to read aloud to upper-grade children. They have a tendency to reject a book because of its bulk and size, and in so doing overlook some of the very best literature available. As the teacher reads aloud from these longer and more complex books, the listeners should become challenged by the language and the ideas in the books and thus be motivated to read the books for themselves. Indeed, it is not uncommon to see a youngster with a duplicate copy of a book that the teacher had begun to read to the class the day before. This youngster could not wait to see how the story developed.

2. *to build class spirit.* A group of children, seated together and listening to a tale read aloud, are engaged in a particualrly fine class sharing experience which builds group spirit and is self-sustaining. In this way the enjoyment of the story is buttressed for each individual. Take note that giggles and guffaws at humor are more contagious among children when they are listening as a group than when they read silently at their desks.

3. *to enrich thinking.* Every story and book read aloud, whether it be fanciful or factual in nature, enriches the thinking of the children and provides them with information related to their current studies. This should be one of the prime purposes of the read-aloud session. The many fine works of fiction, such as Scott Odell's *Island of the Blue Dolphins* and Ester Wier's *The Loner*, as well as books of biography and history, provide a tremendous amount of accurate and useful background material on people and the time in which they lived.

Poetry must not be overlooked as read-aloud material. Poems contain a mountain of ideas in their informative and narrative passages. Some teachers prefer to use poetry on a "squeeze in" basis, fitting it to the minute between reading and arithmetic, or using a poem just before the children are dismissed for lunch or at the end of the day. That procedure is all well and good, but one must not overlook the deliberate, planned period in which poetry is the focal point.

Nonfiction has its place as well, although on the whole the absence of plot, characters, and dialogue make this type of literature less stimulating as read-aloud material. Nevertheless, factual books are extremely useful to the teacher when she sets about to stimulate an interest in a subject area, or to introduce a new activity. And for perfect examples of beauty of writing and quality of content in read-aloud materials it would be difficult to find in any other form of literature compeers to such recent works of nonfiction as Anthony Ravielli's *The World Is Round*, Louis Darling's *The Gull's Way*, or *Digs and Diggers: A Book of World Archaeology* by Leonard Cottrell.

It is in this delightful way—learning through listening to literature— that the child increases his fund of useful and general information.

4. *to develop literary taste.* Oral reading permits the teacher to expose children to the qualities of good literature: solid characterization, finely wrought plot, beautiful language, and noteworthy styles of writing. Many teachers take the direct route: as they read aloud they point out to the child-listeners the literary qualities of the story, even if it is no more than a brief reference to some of the more subtle passages. Such a practice is well and good if the interruptions do not markedly interfere with the children's enjoyment of the story. Other teachers make no remarks about the material being shared, but take great care in selecting their material so as to provide sharp contrasts in plots, themes, characters, styles of writing, and types of books.

As she reads aloud, a teacher must be constantly on the alert for signs that children *are* developing a sensitivity to good literature. Evidence to this effect may appear in a number of ways: (a) in the form of new words from the read-aloud choices appearing in the oral and written work of the children; (b) a child's comment to the effect that "Mary Jane looks like Heidi must have looked"; (c) in a child's ability to see parallels and contrasts between the plots and themes of stories in basal readers and those in the read-aloud selections; and (d) in the application of facts and ideas gleaned from read-aloud books to lessons in social studies and other subject matter areas.

5. *to reward the teacher.* Although it may not be apparent that children can benefit from a reward to the teacher, it is a fact that what the teacher gains pleasure from, so will the children. Teachers should always choose material that they know well and that they genuinely like to read. If the teacher chooses an old favorite, her first thought might be that the book is inappropriate or out-of-date. Yet, if this volume is so revered by the teacher that she puts a little something extra into the reading, she will make the book an enjoyable one for the children, and she will herself have an opportunity to meet again with an old and dear book friend.

Many teachers employ the read-aloud period to help children regain composure, and to relax after physical exercise. Promising to read a story is usually a very effective way to quiet a group of restless children. It helps them to turn away from their cares and tedium of study as they focus upon the story line. As every teacher knows, this easing of tension is just as beneficial to them as it is to the children.

6. *to have fun.* There are other reasons why a teacher will want to read aloud to children: to stimulate creative writing, to provoke group discussion, to demonstrate dialect, to encourage dramatization. But above all, books should be read to children for the enjoyment they give, the fun they offer.

Special endeavor should be made to introduce into the read-aloud periods a number of examples of humorous literature. This type of material is especially good to get the reluctant dragons—more often the boys—started in individual reading. Particularly useful with children are those stories containing gentle and kindly incongruity, irony, wit, and slapstick. To be avoided are books which ostensibly are humorous, but which contain cutting satire and sarcasm, or which mimic and make fun of others.

The vast majority of today's picture books for young children are excellent examples of gentle humor: animals seen in incongruous situations (such as *Curious George* by H. A. Rey); and people and children in trying, difficult situations from which they must extricate themselves (as *The Man Who Didn't Wash His Dishes* by Phyllis Krasilovsky). For older youngsters there are numerous books with humorous story lines, incidents, and characters: *Homer Price* and *Burt Dow: Deep-Water Man* by Robert McCloskey; *Way Down Cellar* by Phil Stong; and A.A. Milne's *Winnie-the-Pooh*, which really is a book of puns for children nine and ten, and not for youngsters four or five years of age. Also on the market now is a generous supply of good humorous nonfiction for children: *Jokes and Riddles,* compiled by George Carlson; *Oh! What Nonsense!* a collection of light verses brought together by William Cole; and Lillian Morrison's *Remember Me When This You See,* an assemblage of autograph verses.

What to Read Aloud to Children

In choosing books to read aloud to the children of today, it is not paradoxical to say that the process is both more difficult and at the same time easier than it has been previously. It is true that the process of choosing is more difficult in the sense that there are greater numbers of books from which to choose than ever before. Contrarily, there have never been more reliable and varied aids available to help us in making our choices: publishers' catalogs, professional books and courses, better-stocked library collections, evaluation services, and many booklists and book-selection tools.

Still, the most knowing and reliable source in the selection process is the teacher. With her wealth of experience with books and literature, her understanding of children, her subject matter background, and her ability to utilize the various book-selection tools, the teacher is the only person who can match the right read-aloud book with the up-to-date needs and interests of the children in her charge.

As the teacher ponders over the numerous materials available, she will want to keep in mind the following selection criteria:

1. Is each book quality literature? Does it contain a meaningful message, consistent characterization, a plausible plot, and superlative style? If the book is nonfiction, is the content accurate, logical, and well-written? An intermediate or upper-grade teacher has only a dozen or so books she can share during a school year, so she must pick quality literature each time she selects a book for oral reading.

2. Does the book make a significant contribution to the child's world today? Does it offer him something for future use: an idea, a value, a nugget of knowledge? Does the book give enjoyment to the listener? Does it promote appreciation?

3. Does the book spark the imaginations of the children? Does it contain genuine emotion?

4. Does the book itself gain from being shared orally because of its humor, its thought-provoking qualities, its colorful phrases, or its truths? Is it a book that children could or would not be likely to read for themselves?

5. Is the book suitable to the ages and stages of development of the students? Are the children psychologically ready for it? Sensitivity to the classes' maturity, both in language development and listening set, along with an examination of the vocabulary and content of the book to be read, will help the teacher decide if the book is appropriate. Booklists often give the reading level and interest level of books, too.

6. What piece of literature is most suitable to the various class groups from the standpoint of length? If the book is for preschool or first-grade children, can it be completed in one reading? Does the longer book for older children have chapters of the proper length so that natural stopping-places may be readily identified? Does the book provide natural and stimulating "launching pads" for the next reading without necessitating undue review of what has gone before?

Because they are not generally quality literature, we rule out the high-interest, controlled-vocabulary books. But reading an historical novel to a primary-grade group would not be considered wise either, as the contents of the book would be over the heads of the children.

Occasionally a teacher might find it profitable to use a book that is a grade or two above their class level. (We would not want to do this with kindergarten and first-grade children, who should have continued exposure to the quality picture books, the nursery rhymes, and the Mother Goose tales.) Second-grade children will find delight now and then in hearing a "third-grade book," just as a sixth-grade class enjoys an occasional "eighth-grade book." All youngsters like to have a taste of what is ahead. Reading an "advanced" story gives the children some insight into the literature delights that are to be theirs.

Following is a list of top-flight read-aloud books that should prove pleasing to children. No finer grading of the books has been attempted than the designations "for primary grades (K–2)," "for intermediate grades (3–4)," and "for upper grades (5–7)." Even these designations will prove faulty in some instances, for children and books resist being labeled as being of one grade level or another. Generally though, the books for the primary-grade children are not books that the youngsters would be able to read easily for themselves. Rather, these books are suited in theme and action for the young child's level of maturity.

FOR PRIMARY GRADES (K–2)

1. Ardizzone, Edward, *Little Tim and the Brave Sea Captain*.
2. Bemelmans, Ludwig, *Madeline*.
3. Bishop, Claire, *Five Chinese Brothers*.
4. Brown, Margaret Wise, *Runaway Bunny*.
5. Burton, Virginia, *Little House; Mike Mulligan and His Steam Shovel*.
6. De Angeli, Marguerite, *Book of Nursery and Mother Goose Rhymes*.
7. de Brunhoff, Jean, *Story of Babar*.
8. de Regniers, Beatrice, *May I Bring a Friend?*
9. Duvoisin, Roger, *Petunia*.
10. Fatio, Louise, *Happy Lion*.
11. Flack, Marjorie, *Story About Ping; Ask Mr. Bear*.
12. Gag, Wanda, *Millions of Cats*.
13. Gramatky, Hardie, *Little Toot*.
14. Kahl, Virginia, *Duchess Bakes a Cake*.
15. Keats, Ezra Jack, *Whistle for Willie*.
16. Leaf, Munro, *Story of Ferdinand*.
17. Leodhas, Sorchi Nic, *Always Room for One More*.
18. Lipkind, Will, *Finders Keepers*.
19. McCloskey, Robert, *Make Way for Ducklings*.
20. Minarik, Else, *Little Bear*.
21. O'Neill, Mary, *Hailstones and Halibut Bones*.
22. Reed, Philip, compiler, *Mother Goose and Nursery Rhymes*.
23. Rey, H.A., *Curious George*.
24. Sendak, Maurice, *Where the Wild Things Are*.
25. Slobodkina, Esphyr, *Caps for Sale*.
26. Suess, Dr., *And to Think That I Saw It on Mulberry Street; Horton Hatches the Egg*.
27. Tudor, Tasha, *Mother Goose*.
28. Ward, Lynd, *Biggest Bear*.
29. Yashima, Taro, *Crow Boy*.
30. Zolotow, Charlotte, *Storm Book*.

FOR INTERMEDIATE GRADES (3–4)

1. Andersen, Hans Christian, *The Emperor's New Clothes; Steadfast Tin Soldier*.
2. Atwater, Florence and Richard, *Mr. Popper's Penguins*.
3. Bontemps, Arna, *Fast Sooner Hound*.
4. Brink, Carol, *Caddie Woodlawn*.
5. Caudill, Rebecca, *A Certain Small Shepherd*.
6. Chase, Richard, *Jack Tales*.
7. Cleary, Beverly, *Henry Huggins*.

8. Dalgleish, Alice, *Bears on Hemlock Mountain.*
9. Daugherty, James, *Andy and the Lion.*
10. deJong, Meindert, *Wheel on the School.*
11. Freeman, Don, *Pet of the Met.*
12. Kipling, Rudyard, *Just So Stories.*
13. Lawson, Robert, *Rabbit Hill; Ben and Me.*
14. Leaf, Munro, *Wee Gillis.*
15. Liers, Emil, *A Black Bear's Story.*
16. Milne, A. A., *Winnie-the-Pooh.*
17. Rounds, Glen, *Blind Colt.*
18. Stong, Phil, *Honk, the Moose.*
19. Suess, Dr., *500 Hats of Bartholomew Cubbins.*
20. White, E.B., *Charlotte's Web.*

FOR UPPER GRADES (5–7)

1. Benary-Isbert, Margot, *The Ark.*
2. Boston, Lucy, *A Stranger At Green Knowe.*
3. Burnford, Sheila, *Incredible Journey.*
4. Clemens, Samuel, *Adventures of Tom Sawyer.*
5. Cole, William, compiler, *Humorous Poetry for Children.*
6. De Angeli, Marguerite, *Door in the Wall.*
7. DuBois, William, *Twenty-One Balloons.*
8. Estes, Eleanor, *The Moffats.*
9. Forbes, Esther, *Johnny Tremain.*
10. Haugaard, Erik, *Hakon of Rogen's Saga.*
11. Henry, Marguerite, *Misty of Chincoteague; King of the Wind.*
12. Kipling, Rudyard, *First Jungle Book.*
13. Krumgold, Joseph, *Onion John.*
14. McCloskey, Robert, *Homer Price.*
15. Neville, Emily, *Berries Goodman; The Empty Schoolhouse.*
16. Norton, Mary, *The Borrowers Aloft.*
17. Pyle, Howard, *Merry Adventures of Robin Hood.*
18. Shotwell, Louise, *Roosevelt Grady.*
19. Stevenson, Robert, *Treasure Island.*
20. Yates, Elizabeth, *Amos Fortune, Free Man.*

Preparing to Read Aloud

In advance of the actual sharing of a story with youngsters, the teacher must do two basic things: (1) acquaint herself with the material to be read, and (2) consider how much class time is to be allocated to the reading.

Just as it is right for children to read over a story silently before they present it orally, so it is beneficial for the teacher to become acquainted in advance with a story or chapter she is to share with the children. For example, she needs to know certain words as to their pronunciation (such as "Nag" and "Nagaina" in *The Jungle Book,* or "cacchinations of delight" in *Penrod*). Prereading also gives her the opportunity to read the various passages with more real understanding and meaning.

The teacher who is prereading a picture book or a similar volume with a limited number of pages will not find it difficult to preread the entire book. This will not be the case with the teacher who is preparing to read aloud a 100- to 300-page book. This teacher might better leaf through the book and spot read in the chapter or chapters to be read that day, all the while making mental notes of the chapter headings, the illustrations, and how they can be used, and taking some measure of the difficulty of the various passages, both in ideas presented and in vocabulary.

Understandably, the busy teacher does not have a great deal of time to give to the prereading of a story. Therefore, it is recommended that books that have been particularly well received by the children be used again. A well-liked picture book may be reread within a day, or used six to a dozen times in a year. A longer book for older youngsters may be used year after year. In this fashion the teacher renews her acquaintance with the vocabulary, phraseology, and characters, and comes to sense ways in which she can improve her rendition of the story.

How much time should the teacher give regularly to reading aloud to children? When are the most opportune times to read aloud? As to the first question, the read-aloud periods should be on a *regular* basis. Children are in need of routine in their plans for the school day. Knowing that the read-aloud period has a fixed place in the curriculum gives them this much-needed feeling of security. They look forward with great eagerness to regular read-aloud periods with the teacher and a favorite book. Now and then a teacher might want to slip in an extra read-aloud session as a special treat or surprise.

A teacher should provide at least a *daily* read-aloud period, just as she provides class time five days a week for the other subject areas. In many instances teachers schedule read-aloud sessions more than once a day. For example, the kindergarten teacher has many picture books at hand to which she may turn for up to 25 or 30 minutes a day. These reading periods may come about during opening exercises, after recess, before dismissal, and at other quiet times when relaxation is called for. Teachers of other grades might distribute the read-aloud periods as follows:

In grades 1–2: 4 times daily; periods of 5 minutes each.
In grades 3–4: 3 times daily; periods of 5 minutes each.
In grades 5–7: 2 times daily; periods of 5 to 7 minutes each.

Beyond the kindergarten level, the read-aloud sessions may be divided equally between the morning and afternoon periods. Some teachers at the upper-grade levels may prefer to read only once a day and to make the period 10 or 15 minutes long. At the higher-grade levels a book may be so exciting and demanding of time that a teacher will say, "There are only two chapters left. Let's finish it." None of the listeners will demur!

One other word about the time element: The teacher should try to choose a restful period. During a period of relative quiescence, the children are more apt to concentrate on the story. Most teachers read to their children *after* recess, rather than before. This practice is called "cooling the horses after the recess run." After recess is not the best time for children from the standpoint of maximum attention to the story. But if no other time is available or suitable, so be it.

Tips on Technique

There are a number of techniques which the teacher must have at her command in order to be a successful oral reader. The following list, while not exhaustive on the subject, may prove valuable for the teacher to keep in mind as she prepares to read aloud:

1. *be prepared to define new words.* How shall the teacher define and explain to the children the new words she is about to read from the text? She may: (1) list the words on the chalkboard in advance of the reading, and then define them; (2) let the words define themselves in context; (3) answer children's questions about particular words *after* the oral reading; (4) parenthesize as she reads, as in "He is digging in the field for yams—that is, sweet potatoes." So that the flow of the story will not be interrupted, the first and last alternatives seem best.

2. *give the title and the author of the book.* When a new book is first introduced to the children, be sure to give the title of the book and the author's name. If the book immediately captures the fancy of the listeners, some children may wish to find in the library other books by the same author, or books containing similar contents. Many children will be already familiar with certain authors, and mention of a familiar name will set the youngsters to comparing the present story with ones read previously. The book jacket may present interesting information about the author and illustrator. These tidbits may be shared with the

class, and they do much to make the story more meaningful and enjoyable for the children.

3. group the children judiciously. The primary-grade teacher will want to gather the children closely around her on low chairs or seat them upon the floor in front of her. The teacher of older children may sit at her desk or stand. Because older children are large physically, they may have to crane their necks or move about in their seats to see the reader. For this reason the teacher should move from station to station periodically so that each child may have an occasional unimpeded view of her.

4. read with feeling. Enjoying the story herself is the first and foremost virtue that the oral interpreter of literature can possess. If the reader believes in what she is doing—if she reads with enthusiasm—the children will sense it.

At the same time she must work on matters of volume, pitch, and articulation. The voice should be used in a natural way, but it should be raised or lowered to differentiate characters as dialogue is read. Most of these things will come naturally if the reader feels that the oral reading is contributing something to the children's education.

5. hold the book carefully. The book is being held too high if it obscures the reader's face; it is being held too low and close if one reads down into its pages so that the voice is muffled. The book should be grasped in one or both hands, depending upon its size, and held from 12 to 15 inches from the chest, with the top of the book on a line with the chin of the reader.

6. play down gestures. Extreme hand gestures and quick movements of the body distract children in such a way that they lose the thread of the story. If gestures are used at all, slight facial gestures, small, descriptive movements of the hands, and slight dips and twists of the body will prove to be the most effective ones. The best suggestion is: When in doubt, leave gestures out!

7. summarize flowery passages. A book will often prove to be excellent read-aloud fare except for a few long descriptive passages interpersed throughout the text. An example of a book in which such passages are to be found is *The Adventures of Tom Sawyer*. As the teacher rereads this book, she will want to "blue pencil" the long repetitive descriptions of the Mississippi River. At the same time she will want to practice reading the conversations between Tom and his friends, for it is these bits of dialogue that the children wish to hear. Deleting the descriptive passages should not be viewed as censorship or watering down a story. On the contrary, it gives the story more vitality and movement *as a read-aloud tale.*

8. *maintain eye contact.* Every good teacher keeps eye contact with her youngsters while reading aloud to them. She does this for two reasons: (1) it steadies the restless children, and (2) it personalizes the reading. Both are important, but the second more so than the first with respect to the read-aloud period. As she reads, the teacher glances up at the end of a sentence to look into the eyes of different children seated in different parts of the room. This "singling out" gives each child the feeling that the interpreter is reading the sentence just for him, and it makes the story more meaningful.

9. *stop at an interesting place.* Every child knows where the best stopping places are in a good book: just as Jase Mason faces the renegade bear in Jim Kjelgaard's *Wildlife Cameraman*, or as Mark Anderson hears his father's distress call in Walt Morey's *Gentle Ben*. The teacher knows she has found the proper stopping place in a book, too, when her remark, "We will resume reading here tomorrow," is greeted with protestations and exclamations of disappointment from the children.

A wise teacher puts the stopping places to work for her. With them she sets up the children for the next read-aloud session, making them hunger for the next reading. The teacher also uses the children's reactions as measuring sticks to assess her own reading skills and the suitability of the story she is reading. If there are many genuine "uhs" and "ohs" from the children, the teacher knows her reading is basically good from the standpoint of technique and the story acceptable as to type.

10. *evaluate constantly.* Once in a while a teacher begins a story and immediately renders herself unconscious as to the quality of her presentation and the acceptability of the story. Only when the book is finished does she awaken, to select a new story and to begin the hibernation process over again. Every alert teacher who cares will continually evaluate her style of reading and the story she is reading by asking herself: Are the vast majority of the children interested in the story? (A few won't be, but this is normal.) Is this a story for me alone, or are the children enjoying it, too? Is my pacing good? That is, am I reading too fast? Too slow? What about my phrasing, tonal quality, volume? All of these things must be kept in mind as the reader proceeds with the story.

If the teacher has started a story in which the children are taking no pleasure, she should have the fortitude to abandon it for a better title. Two such types of books for which one must be constantly on the alert are the "old classic" and the "never miss" modern classic. The old classics are often inappropriate fare for reading aloud because they lack dialogue and are rife with slow-paced descriptive passages. A "never miss" modern classic frequently misfires with a particular group of children because the teacher forgets that the character of groups changes from year to year. Each year a teacher must assess the merits of her "tried and true" favorites against the needs, interests, and abilities, of the new class. Only in that way can she be assured of a successful read-aloud program.

Sharing A Picture Book

Sharing a picture book with small children (and sometimes big ones, too!) requires some additions to or alterations in the teacher's basic procedures of reading aloud. And primary teachers will not want to share a picture book without giving the books to be used careful scrutiny and considerable forethought as to how they are to be employed. It is most important that children's initial encounters with picture books be pleasant and profitable experiences, for therein lies the road to children's lifelong enjoyment of literature. Therefore, the considerate teacher will share picture books with them in these ways:

1. Sit on a comfortable chair, preferably a low one or one that permits you considerable movement from left to right so you can show the book to each child.

2. Seat the children on low chairs or on the floor *immediately in front* of you, where all can see the book without forcing those on the periphery to crane their necks unduly.

3. Choose a brief book with a good story line and a generous supply of attractive, story-supporting illustrations.

4. Select a "book helper" for special occasions (for example, when a child has a birthday, or when he has brought a book from home) to sit beside you and help show the illustrations. Note: A teacher should have in mind a definite policy about sharing books brought from home. Accepting one child's offering of a poor piece of literature may result in a flood of unacceptable books. The teacher should establish certain guidelines *with* children in regard to this matter.

5. Share the book carefully, showing the pictures *slowly* so that all may see them. When showing illustrations, be sure the book is held *down* to a point where the children can see.

6. Use books you are familiar with so that you do not have to keep your eyes on the page at all times. In this way your oral reading becomes

storytelling. Some teachers attach to the back of the book a sheet of paper on which is printed a "cue" word that reminds them of the contents of each page.

7. Substitute your pupils' names *occasionally* for the name of a character in the book. Relate story-illustrated events to occurrences in the lives of your students. In effect, *personalize* the story.

8. Accept remarks from children and conduct a discussion of the book as you read each page. Help youngsters to see significant ideas, events, and characters by pointing out details in the text and illustrations.

9. Above all: Be enthusiastic in your reading!

Following Up a Story

Views vary on the necessity of follow-up activities after the teacher has completed reading aloud. Some experts hold that the enjoyment of the story is the only important consideration, and that the teacher should not impose or interdict extraneous activities that would detract from that end. Others reason that children must be helped to appreciate the fine nuances of plot, theme, style, and characterization. It is this author's point of view that the story be read primarily for enjoyment. Activities should come after a read-aloud session *only* if they follow it naturally and are the outgrowth of significant student interest. In the final analysis, however, each teacher must decide the issue for herself.

Below are listed a few possible follow-up approaches and activities related to the read-aloud period.

1. Discussions of incidents, characters, plots, themes, and vocabulary, led by the intermediate- or upper-grade teacher, *after* the reading or *rereading* of a particular chapter or section of the book.
2. A brief summation and retelling by a child of an incident or chapter in the book.
3. Informal dramatization of an incident, utilizing only readily available properties and allowing free rendition of the dialogue.
4. Reading by a child of a particular passage with appropriate background music supplied by a recording.
5. Interpreting a scene or character through a variety of art media.
6. Taking the students to the library to find stories similar in content or ones by the same author.
7. Viewing a filmstrip, or watching and listening to a film or sound filmstrip based upon the book. There are a number of audio-visual materials available for such use, particularly with respect to the picture books enjoyed by little children. Source lists of these may be found at the end of this chapter.

TELLING STORIES

Storytelling is an art that has given joy and instruction to children since the beginning of time. In a technical sense storytelling may be defined as an account of an event or series of events, true or imaginary.

Storytelling has many values. Among the more obvious we would list the following:

1. It gives boys and girls an opportunity to become acquainted with the best of children's literature.
2. It details the lives of other people and creates in children a desire to know them and their cultures better.
3. It increases a child's knowledge and enriches his vocabulary.
4. When telling a story himself, the child learns to organize and express himself clearly, at the same time building confidence in his ability to face an audience.

Selecting Stories

The teacher will want to select those stories that are most suited to the age and experience of the children in the group. There is a plentitude of suitable story material for each stage of child development. Appropriate storytelling fare for given age groups are listed below.

Pre-school through kindergarten—For this age group the stories must be short and to the point. Stories should be of familiar things: animals, children, home, machines, people, toys. Humorous and nonsense story poems, jingles, Mother Goose rhymes, and the accumulative tales are especially apt choices. Typical stories would include those in The Three Series: "The Three Billy Goats Gruff," "The Three Little Pigs," "The Three Bears," and "The Adventure of Three Little Rabbits." Others: "Little Red Riding Hood," "Henny Penny," and "The Teeny Tiny Woman."

Ages 6 to 10—Animal tales, stories of child life in other lands, and the ancient and modern fairy tales are types of stories that appeal to this group. Among the many tales to be recommended we would include "The Elves and the Shoemaker," "Rumpelstiltskin," "Slovenly Peter," "The Steadfast Tin Soldier," "Hansel and Gretel," "The Sleeping Beauty," "The Bremen Town Musicians," and "Jack and the Beanstalk."

Ages 11 to 14—Children in this stage of development demand true stories, tales of adult life, hero tales, and stories that teach something about personal ideals. These children want stories of adventure, too. The 13- and 14-year-old youngsters seek out the myths, legends, and epics, along with those stories of a biographical and historical nature that teach patriotism and service to country. Tales for telling to this group would include "The Story of Aladdin," "How Thor Found His Hammer," tales of Robin Hood and King Arthur, "Pecos Bill," "Paul Bunyan," and various tales about sports heroes.

The well-prepared storyteller makes sure that each story she tells contains five basic elements: action, drama, emotional appeal, a strong beginning, and a satisfying conclusion. In order to supply stories with these characteristics, it is often necessary to rewrite or shorten stories to make them more suitable for a child audience.

Preparing the Story

The time and effort required to prepare a story for telling is significant, but the effort is rewarding. A typical routine in preparation of a story would run as follows:

1. Select a story that is worth the time of preparation.
2. Come to know the story well before you tell it. To do this, read the story once to yourself for its flavor, then reread it for plot.
3. Reread the story again. This time refresh your memory as to the scenes in the plot, the distinguishing features of the dialogue, the unique qualities of the characters, and the setting of the story.
4. Focus on "the four": the introduction, the body, the climax, and the conclusion.

A perfect thrust with a listener-capturing *introduction* is extremely vital to the success of the storyteller. The introduction should be short, to the point, and memorized. For a good opener try Kipling's words from the *Just So Stories:* "In the high and far-off times, O best beloved."

The *body* of the story contains the action, the string of steps leading to the climax. The storyteller must visualize each event as an important part contributing to the whole, and that must become a part of the storyteller, indelibly stamped upon his mind.

The *climax* is the heart of the story, giving meaning to the whole. Whatever impression the storyteller wishes to make, whatever lesson is to be given, must be emphasized here.

The *conclusion* ends the story. It does not provide any new ideas, but merely ties up the loose ends.

Telling the Story

Preliminary to the actual telling of a story, the teacher will want to do a little staging. The chairs should be placed in a semicircle in front of the teacher's chair. If children remain at their usual stations, seductive objects should be put away. Children should be seated facing away from the glare of natural or artificial light and from the numerous distractions found outside classroom windows.

When the children are seated before the teacher and their attention is riveted upon her, she is ready to begin. From the beginning the teacher should immerse herself in the story. The storyteller's voice should be used to ensnare the children in the story's magic web. Clear enunciation and adequate volume to reach each child are prime requisites of a good storyteller. Change of voice should be employed to denote differences in characters.

The teacher must take her time in telling the story. The novice storyteller often speeds up and in so doing loses the thread of the story or omits important events or details. If this should happen, the storyteller should not stop and go back, but should try to weave the events into the story as naturally as possible.

The climax is all-important and is to the storyteller what the punch line is to the comedian. The teacher wants to give the climax all that she has! The story should be closed rapidly, without a repetition of the moral or point of the tale. A story should not just straggle off, but come to a definite, but quiet, end.

Below are listed a few other principles relating to successful storytelling:

1. Just as in the books read aloud to them, children prefer stories with dialogue to those containing narration.

2. A story should contain no more than four characters. The teacher cannot interpret more; the children cannot follow more.

3. Never memorize a story verbatim. Do commit to memory the necessary phrases—"Once upon a time. . . ."; " 'Who's that tripping over my bridge?' roared the troll." Neophyte storytellers have been known to wreck upon the shoals of memorization, which induced in them a kind of stage fright from which they never recovered.

4. Some stories are better read than told. Examples are those that contain unique language such as *Winnie-The-Pooh* and Kipling's *Just So Stories*.

5. The storyteller may use cue sheets during rehearsals. A storyteller who is trying her wings the first time may find cue sheets supporting. Discard them as quickly as possible, for they do detract from the presentation.

6. Cutting a story to shorten the telling or to delete descriptive passages is an acceptable practice.

7. Tape recording a story will frequently help the teller to improve her pitch, range, and voice volume.

8. Use gestures sparingly. Facial gestures should be about all the gestures a storyteller will need. Gross bodily actions are distracting and they cause children to focus on the teller rather than upon the story.

9. Audiences occasionally become distracted. Individuals may be called back to the fold with a rhetorical question: "And, Mary Jane, what do you think happened next?"

The Child As Storyteller

Much of what has been said regarding the teacher as a storyteller applies to the child who is called upon to fill the same role. In most instances, what storytelling children are called upon to do should grow out of normal classroom activities that give children "something to talk about." Activities such as the study of a particular country, a field trip, or the care of classroom plants and animals may give rise to a story. The formal "everybody must tell a story" routine should be assiduously avoided.

The stories children tell may be original or acquired, real or imaginary, and shared because the child wants to do so. No one child or group of children should be allowed to dominate these sessions. Special days or events—Halloween, Thanksgiving, Hanukkuh, safety drives—give rise to creative oral expression.

Prior to their participation in storytelling activities, the teacher should discuss *briefly* with children the following general principles about story-telling.

1. The story must be well-prepared. This means that the teacher must give preparation time as well as assistance in planning a sequential outline of the story.

2. A story that is completely new to the class has a greater chance of being successful. Therefore, have each child try to find a fresh, sprightly tale to tell.

3. A successful story will be brief. Preparation time will be cut down, the sequence of events is more easily retained for telling, and the actual telling is better attended to by the audience. A three- or four-minute presentation is ideal, with definite cut-off signals being agreed upon by the class and the teacher.

4. Those children telling stories for the first time might find security in using visual aids such as large pictures, flannelboards, and scroll movies. These help the storyteller concentrate on the sequence of events, and take the mind of the listener off the teller.

5. The teacher should have advance knowledge of the tale to be told so she may screen it for acceptability. Further, she should remain in close proximity to the storyteller while he delivers his story. In this way she is in a position to help the storyteller with cues if he should stumble in his delivery.

6. The teacher and the storytellers should formulate a definite set of standards for storytelling. These guides should be simply stated and relatively few in number. For example:

Speak clearly.
Speak so all can hear.
Do not string sentences together with "and-uhs" or "so's."
Stand still.
Look at your audience.
Use colorful words.
Have a good beginning and ending.
Talk naturally.
Be interested in your story!

Storytelling Follow-Up

When the storyteller has completed his presentation—whether he be a teacher or a child—he may not feel that follow-up questions concerning the story are necessary. Most stories are just for the taking, and questions will ruin the inner joy of the children if the story is plumbed further. After a story has been concluded, the audience may wish to become involved in some creative interpretation of it. Following are examples of activities that may spin off the basic storytelling event.

... *Play-back time.* A dramatic repetition of the story increases the enjoyment of the story and enriches the vocabulary of younger children. For example, several groups of children may re-interpret "The Princess and the Pea" using clean handkerchiefs in place of mattresses and a pebble for the pea.

... *Tell-back time.* The story may be retold in a few sentences by a single child or by several children assuming different roles.

... *Picture-story telling.* A child may choose to tell a story as he refers to a mounted picture. The covers of *The Saturday Evening Post* and *Life Magazine's* "Miscellany" page are excellent sources.

... *Go on with the story.* The teacher begins an imaginative story in which she introduces one or two characters and an action plot. At a given point she stops and asks: "Who can go on with the story?" The story can proceed as an individual or group oral activity, or as an experience chart story.

  ... Participation story.   On the second and in subsequent tellings of a tale, the narrator pantomimes and makes sounds which the children immediately repeat after her. For example: "The chieftain walked along (slap thighs three times) until he came to the covered bridge. He crossed the bridge (slap cheeks three times with open hand) and slipped through the meadow beyond (rub palms of hands together)."

  ... Twisted tale.   One student begins a story by telling two lines. The next player adds two lines, and so on. A twisted tale will result.

  ... Storyteller's apron.   At story time the teacher wears a smock with pockets from which a child selects a story title printed on a card. The teacher tells the story selected.

  ... Shoe box story (oral or written).   Each member of the class prints the name of two unusual objects on separate sheets of paper. Ten slips are drawn from a shoe box by each of five storytellers-elect, who must weave the words into an oral or written story.

  ... Character sounds.   The storyteller assigns a sound to each character in the story he is to tell. Example: cat (purr), dog (bark), hero ("mmm"). A group of listeners must give the sound (say "bark") when the animal (say a dog) is mentioned by the storyteller.

  ... Spun-yarn.   A large ball of yarn is unwound and knotted at various intervals along its length. The story teller begins her tale and keeps the story going until she rewinds the yarn to the first knot at which time she passes it to the next child and so on.

  ... Storytelling club.   Older children form the club. Its primary purpose is to learn the techniques of good storytelling. Club members may share their stories on occasion with primary-grade children.

  ... Listen to records.   Some records may be recordings of stories told by the children. Commercial story records are also available from many sources. See the list at the end of this chapter.

  ... Storyteller's art.   Children's creative art in various media may be posted in a variety of ways, or it may be assembled in a box movie to demonstrate children's appreciation of a story.

POETRY

Poetry has a marked appeal to children. Very early in their lives they sense its beauty and its rhythm. No sooner do children begin to talk than from them flows spontaneous rhythmic expressions of the purest poetry.

The melody and movement of poetry that children sense in the simple nursery rhymes soon set their bodies to swaying and their feet to moving in tempo. It is the teacher's responsibility to see that children's interest in poetry is used to good advantage. If children are continually exposed to the best poetry appropriate to their levels, they will continue to accept poetry as a natural and vital part of their lives.

The teacher who wishes to encourage the natural poetic creativity of children wants to create a classroom atmosphere in which children can express their thoughts freely and in which their ideas are valued. The teacher who appreciates poetry and children will see to it that youngsters develop the ability to see life freshly, fully, and poetically in a classroom where there are opportunities to (1) listen to poetry, (2) study its characteristics, (3) write it, and (4) participate in special activities related to it. Above all, the teacher of poetry must enjoy sharing poetry and have a sensitivity to the beauty of poetic expression.

The Content of Children's Poetry

For the primary grades the poems chosen should be simple, vivid, and to the point. To be avoided at all levels are poems that are vague or moralizing, or poems that talk down to children. The list below reveals the basic types and examples of poetry that will prove most successful at the grades in the primary school:

Kindergarten–First Grade.
  Animals ("Piping Robin" by Annette Wynne)
  Common experiences ("City Rain" by Rachael Field)
  Famous poetry ("Animal Crackers" by Christopher Morley)
  Pets ("My Dog" by Marchette Chute)
  Repetitive jingles ("A Swing Song" by William Allingham)
  Self ("My Inside-Self" by Rachael Field)

Second–Third Grade. Continue the above and add:
  Alliterative ("Tired Tim" by Walter de la Mare)
  Appreciation of rhyme ("This Happy Day" by Harry Behn)
  Appreciation of rhythm ("B for Bus" by Phyllis McGinley)
  Fairy ("The Fairies" by Rose Fyleman)
  Humor ("Eletelephony" by Laura Richards)
  Imaginative ("Hiding" by Dorothy Aldis)

The choice of poems for the intermediate grades is especially important. Inappropriate fare more quickly and permanently spoils children's love and appreciation for poetry than does poor delivery. For the intermediate-grade children the teacher should continue using most types of poems listed for children in the primary grades. To be avoided as types, however, are the introspective or lyrical poems. It is best to rely upon poems about common experiences. Boys who are beginning to mutter that they don't like "sissy poetry" will return to the fold upon hearing some of the ballads and narrative story-poems. Specifically, the following types of poems are best suited for older children:

Fourth–Fifth–Sixth Grade.
    Adventure ("Silver Ships" by Cornelia Meigs)
    Animal ("Brown Bear" by Mary Austin)
    Everyday occurrences ("Swimming" by Clinton Scollard)
    Historical ballads ("Erie Canal" ballads by John A. and Alan Lomax)
    Humor ("Laughing Time" by William Jay Smith)
    Narrative ("Highwayman" by Alfred Noyes)
    Science ("High Flight" by John Magee)

Stimulating Interest in Poetry

In stimulating and maintaining children's interests in poetry, the teacher will want to keep in mind the following essentials of good poetry teaching.

1. The primary aims of the teacher are to build children's tastes for good poetry and to increase their enjoyment of it.

2. The teacher should memorize some poems so that she can utilize them during the "teachable moments."

3. Poetry must be heard to be fully enjoyed and appreciated.

4. The teacher must be a good oral reader who enjoys sharing poetry with children.

5. The teacher must know poetry *and* children in order to select poetry suited to the temperament, times, maturity, and experience of the pupils.

6. Poems need not be analyzed to be enjoyed. Poetry should be primarily for fun. Present the poems simply, with a short word of explanation and the establishment of the background.

7. Intensive study kills children's interests in poetry.

8. Select only the *best* poetry for sharing and study.

9. Memorization must be voluntary on the part of children, not assigned.

10. Don't overexplain poems.

11. Let the children choose some of the poetry to be read, studied, and discussed in class.

12. Teach the mechanics of poetry inductively. That is, reaching generalizations about poetry should come *after* exposure to many examples, not before.

13. Poetry is a personal thing. Therefore, do not insist that children enjoy and appreciate what you think is beautiful poetry.

14. Read and read and read again!

Although space limitations here do not permit a full exploration of all the aspects of poetry, every teacher needs to keep in mind a few objectives of teaching poetry. Generally, children should learn to enjoy poetry as they read it aloud or as they listen to it. They should strike up an acquaintance with individual poets and their works. Children need to increase their knowledge of the tools of the poet, types of poetry, and the vocabulary of poetry. Young people should have an opportunity to express themselves poetically, through original writing and through choral reading.

1. interpreting poetry. There are a number of standards which the teacher must help the child check himself against as he prepares to interpret a poem or verse for his classmates. He must keep in mind:

A. *The author's meaning.* He must find out what the author intended to say—by looking up meanings and pronunciations of new words, by interpreting punctuation marks correctly, and by ascertaining the emotions behind the author's words. He must also have knowledge of inverted word order so common in poetry.

B. *Rate of delivery.* Oral reading is slower than silent reading. The child should expect to take his time as he reads aloud. Thoughts should not be given so fast that the listeners cannot absorb them, but there should not be pauses between words unless a thought has been completed or subordination is called for.

C. *Pitch.* Ideas gain importance through a change of pitch, that is, going up or down on the vocal scale; inflection, the glide of the voice from one pitch to another, helps the voice show changes in emphasis and meaning.

D. *Volume.* The loudness or softness of a voice helps give emphasis to the poem being interpreted orally.

2. the poets and their works. The poet is an artist who creates with words, arranging these in patterns of lines and stanzas. He chooses words carefully to give us clear and exact images, and also uses some of the following tools:

A. *Rhythm* is expressed according to the mood and feeling of the poet. *Regular* rhythm has a definite beat, created through the use of *meter.* Rhythm is the rise and fall of sound within a poem, while meter is the precise number of syllables to a line. *Irregular* rhythm has a rhythmic flow or cadence.

B. *Rhyme* is the regular recurrence of corresponding sounds, usually with the same vowel sounds. Rhyme patterns come in many arrangements.

C. *Word pictures* are used to paint a fresh, vivid picture of the subject of the poem.

3. *types of poetry*. There are many different forms into which a poet may cast his poem. The subject matter of the poem usually dictates which of the forms to use.

A. A *ballad* has a singing quality, with a sudden beginning and ending, repetition and refrain. Ballads deal with heroism, tragedy, romance, fairies, and drama.

B. A *narrative* is a story told objectively in verse form. It is similar to a ballad, but greater in length.

C. The *limerick* has a nonsense or humorous theme. It is usually written in a five-line pattern and is characterized by unusual spelling, a surprise, or an odd twist in its ending.

D. *Lyric* poems are subjective and personal in nature, and are highly rhythmic and melodious.

E. *Free verse* employs an irregular rhythm, it never rhymes, and it does not resemble poetry in its usual form.

F. A *sonnet* has a rigid rhyme scheme—almost always fourteen lines in length—and themes that are serious and meditative.

4. *vocabulary*. It is inevitable that children will need to know the meaning of a number of terms related to a study of poetry. Teachers must resist the temptation to assign children to "look up and record" definitions of these words. Rather, emphasis should be on understanding the words. In addition to many of the words mentioned above, children must be able to pronounce and understand such terms as *alliteration, line, minstrel, quatrain, refrain,* and *stanza.*

The Study of Poetry

A variety of approaches may be used to acquaint children with a poem's visual images, its rhyme and rhythm, and its story element. The following experiences are illustrative of those which a teacher of poetry might use. They are not, of course, the *only* types of experiences that a class might have. With adaptations, the procedures might be used at any grade level.

A. To help children see that poems create mental pictures:
1. Teacher: "Poems help us see pictures and hear sounds. Poems thrill us or make us happy or sad or quiet. Close your eyes, listen to this poem, and feel the quietness as the moon creeps over the earth."
2. Teacher reads "Silver" by Walter de la Mare.
3. Teacher asks:
   (a) What feeling did the poem give you?
   (b) Who did the moon "walk over" ever so silently?
4. Children's reactions to the questions are discussed.
5. Teacher: "Let's listen to the poem again. This time listen for:
   (a) Interesting words (examples will be *shoon, casements, thatch*);
   (b) Pictures you see: (e.g., *moveless fish, silver reeds, paws of silver*);
   (c) Sound words you hear: (e.g., *peep, scampering*)."
6. The teacher records these words on the chalkboard as the children mention them, and the words are discussed.
7. The teacher distributes to each child a copy of the poem.
8. Teacher: "Let us say the poem together softly."
9. The children read the poem in unison, then reread it and tap their fingers to the rhythm.
10. Teacher: "How would you paint a picture to illustrate the poem, or part of the poem? What colors would you choose?"
11. The pupils draw pictures, which are then mounted on a bulletin board.

B. To point out the rhyming quality of poetry:
1. Kindergarten or first-grade children recite their favorite nursery rhymes.
2. A teacher-led discussion shows that rhyming words at the ends of the lines sound alike.
3. The children (or the teacher) repeat the nursery verses demonstrating the rhyming words by emphasis.
4. Now the children identify the rhyming words, and the teacher lists them on the chalkboard.
5. The children provide rhymes for words that the teacher says orally.

C. To illustrate the story element in a poem:
1. The teacher selects a poem with a simple expository idea.
2. Cut-out flannelboard figures are manufactured to represent the character(s) in the poem.
3. The teacher recites the poem using the flannelboard figures.

      4. At the second telling, one child tells the story while others manipulate the characters on the flannelboard.

D. To demonstrate that poems are beautiful thoughts in rhythm:
1. The teacher displays a picture of a group of animals.
2. The children give one-word or phrase responses to the picture. The teacher makes a list of these on the chalkboard.
3. Overnight the teacher constructs a poem using the words and phrases.
4. The following day the children read the poem and tap to the rhythm.
5. Another animal picture is displayed and each class member writes a poem about it.
6. The children complete their poems and share them with each other.
7. The poems are neatly copied and mounted in a poetry scrapbook.

E. To report on a well-liked poem:

1. Title of the poem: ....
2. Author of the poem: ....
3. Book found in: Title ....
                   Author ....
                   Page ....
4. What words in the poem did you like best?
   a. .... b. .... c. .... d. ....
5. Why did you like the poem? ....
....
....
6. What other poems do you know by the same author?
   a. .... b. ....

Writing Poetry As An Adjunct to Oral Interpretation

The process of writing poetry is not an easy one for children to master, for it calls for an understanding of what poetry is, a knowledge of its various forms and types, and an ability to share thoughts with an economy of words. The youthful writer of a poem must be considerate of those who will read his poem and, thus, he must provide them with a good composition that meets the standards of proper punctuation and good grammar.

The wise teacher always undertakes to provide poetry-writing experiences for her children. Her task is formidable, too, for she must provide not only direction and instruction, but variety in instruction in order to further appreciation of poetry as a whole. Below are listed a few considerations which the teacher must bear in mind as she proceeds to develop children's interests and skills in writing poetry.

... Deep appreciations and understandings must develop gradually. Start with children where they are, not where you want them to be.

... "Light" poetry is the key to the door of interest as far as boys are concerned. Initial writing experiences might well be attempted utilizing the humorous verse approach.

... Group efforts frequently help reluctant poets get underway. First attempts might find two boys paired together as authors of a single poem. Limericks and cinquains lend themselves to this type of effort.

... Don't *force* children to read aloud their poems. A classroom environment in which children feel free to express their ideas, knowing that those ideas will be respected, will usually counteract any reluctance. A teacher who is prepared to write and read aloud some of her own original verse will go a long way in overcoming the sharing obstacle.

... "Starters"—a word, a first line, an idea—given away "free" by the teacher will help many a child who says, "I can't think of anything to write about." Have at hand a prepared list, for every class has its slow starters.

... Allow children to write about the things that interest them and are related to their own experiences—pets, sports, toads, juke boxes, hot rods, tenement houses, cockroaches, rats. Don't insist that each child write a poem on the same subject, your subject—spring, daffodils, robins.

... First drafts of written poems should be for putting down ideas. Only with rewrites should the child be concerned with mechanics and spelling.

... Teach children to write brief poems. The watchword should be: "Put down your idea, then stop!"

... Don't grade children's poetry. Writing helpful comments on their papers is preferable. And don't rewrite children's poems. Teacher alteration of papers to improve a poem is a mockery, and children are the first to recognize that the poem is no longer theirs. You may help them with a word or an idea, but stop there.

.. Not every written poem need preach a lesson nor establish a moral.

... Don't overpraise a child's written poetry. Be honest in your reactions, fair in your judgments. Not every child is a Robert Frost, and the children are the first to recognize this.

Suggested Experiences in Writing Poetry

1. Writing *couplets*. These are easy-to-write verses composed of two rhymed lines with like rhythm. Each child may write one or more.

> A bear cub is a black-nosed clown
> Who tumbles up and tumbles down.

Variations:

(a) The teacher writes a first line on the chalkboard. Each child copies this and adds a second line.
(b) Students A and B write first lines, then exchange papers and try to complete their partner's couplet.
(c) Each member of the class contributes a couplet to a longer "poetry story" about a famous person, event, or holiday.

2. Writing *quatrains*. Writing a poem of two rhyming couplets, or a verse of four lines, is a natural continuation of the couplet experience. Possible construction schemes include rhyming lines as follows:

(a) 1, 2, 3, 4
  . . . more
  . . . floor
  . . . score
  . . . door

(b) 2 and 4
  . . . flow
  . . . gate
  . . . run
  . . . late

(c) 1 and 3
  . . . bat
  . . . say
  . . . cat
  . . . gone

(d) 1 and 4, 2 and 3
  . . . roam
  . . . grass
  . . . lass
  . . . home

Variation: A shaped quatrain may take the form of a square. In this instance, the child writes a poem to "Read Around the Corner."

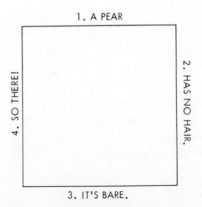

1. A PEAR
2. HAS NO HAIR.
3. IT'S BARE.
4. SO THERE!

3. Writing *triplets*. These three-line poems are relatively simple to execute:

> From across the street
> The wheat
> Smelled sweet.

Variation: A shaped triplet may look like this:

3. IF STUCK IN TAR!

4. Writing *haiku*. The singular advantage of this Japanese form of poetry is in its emphasis upon developing a thought or idea without the burden of constricting rhyme. The conventional haiku (hokku) form is a three-line, unrhymed poem of seventeen syllables, with the lines and syllables distributed as follows:

First line: five syllables	*Example: About Misty* Flowers are fragile
Second line: seven syllables	And like the soft, soft velvet
Third line: five syllables	Of a horse's nose.
	—Author unknown

Variations on writing "idea" poems:
(a) Tanka: 5 unrhymed lines, 31 syllables distributed so:

Line 1: five syllables	*Example: Snow Drop* The sparkling snow is
Line 2: seven syllables	Like a bed of diamonds
Line 3: five syllables	On the brown, dry earth,
Line 4: seven syllables	Lacing the world in a dress
Line 5: seven syllables	Of serenity and youth.
	—Author unknown

(b) **Cinquain:** 5 unrhymed lines, 22 syllables distributed thus:

Line 1: two syllables, or one word giving the title
Line 2: four syllables, or two words of description
Line 3: six syllables, or three words expressing an action
Line 4: eight syllables, or four words expressing a feeling
Line 5: two syllables, or another word for the title

Example: Coral

Line 1: Coral,
Line 2: The stone flower
Line 3: Of the sea, is the most
Line 4: Fascinating feature of the
Line 5: Sea world.
                    —Author unknown

5. Writing *limericks*. These five-line poems are always fun to write, especially after one has captured the form and rhythm. Print a few samples on the chalkboard, pointing out the rhyme scheme. A permanent wall chart like this one may be helpful:

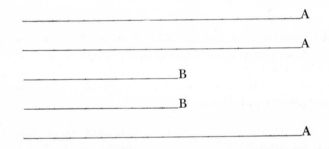

The teacher may begin a group limerick by providing the first line. Have the children build a list of rhyming words for the word at the end of line one. Continue to develop the limerick with them. It won't be long until they can construct their own.

6. Writing more poetry.
... Write in prose new conclusions to published poems.
... Write poems to background music (for example, a patriotic poem to accompany "God Bless America").
... Assign each child the portion of the world that he can see through a section of a school window pane. Ask him to write a poem about what he sees.
... Write poems which are to be mounted in a class scrapbook.

... Write individual ballads and illustrate them in any of several art media.

... Have the class contribute to a chart revealing different forms of meter.

... Draft and chart a list of standards for poetry writing.

... Select a well-known object, bring it to class, and have the boys and girls describe it in many poetic ways. Make a list of these.

... Supply a set of four rhyming words (such as you, too, few, moo). Ask: "How many verses can you make with them?"

... Add original stanzas to already written poems.

... Rewrite a fable or science article as a poem.

... Write a poem to describe a favorite book character such as Templeton in *Charlotte's Web* or Ping in *The Story About Ping*.

... Write a verse using as many words as possible that begin with the same letter. For example:

> Querulous Queenie, quiet and quick,
> Quivered and quaked as she tossed the brick.

... Appoint a class poet who is to be responsible for composing a poem of the month, or to celebrate birthdays and holidays. Rotate the class poet's position every month.

A BANG-UP idea for writing poetry. The teacher draws the pattern of a poem on the chalkboard. The children write a poem to match the pattern. For example:

_____	_____
_____	_____
	_____
_____	_____
or	
_____	_____
_____	_____

A BANG-UP idea for writing poetry. Open a dictionary page at random. Write a meaningful poem using the words found on one page. You may add extra words to help with the rhymes.

A BANG-UP idea for writing poetry. Have children write and submit entries for a "terse verse" contest. A "terse verse" definition of a "humorous rabbit" is a "funny bunny"; for a "heavy feline" it is a "fat cat." (Notice that an adjective precedes the noun.) Other contests might call for original limericks or jingles advertising a school book fair or other literature event.

Other Poetry Activities and Experiences

1. Have the class construct a "Poet Tree" (Poetry), which contains examples of different forms of poetry, favorite poems of individual class members, and pictures of poets. Construct the tree from an actual tree branch mounted in a flower pot. Cutouts of leaves, flowers, and fruit may have the poems and pictures mounted upon them.

2. Compare poetry written by different authors on the same subject (for example, contrast "The Policeman" by Marjorie Watts and "My Policeman" by Rose Fyleman).

3. Let individual children record on tape parts of poems that they enjoy.

4. Invite poets to class to share some of their poems.

5. Have poetry-sharing periods during which children read their favorites. No child should read a poem unless he has been well-prepared.

6. Each child constructs a poet's handbook containing notes on poetry discussions, his own original poems, pictures and poems of favorite poets, and so on.

7. Have children respond to roll call with a jingle, verse, Mother Goose rhyme, or poem. These may be read or recited.

8. Listen to recordings of outstanding artists reading their interpretations of famous poems.

9. Make a shadow box based upon "Catkin" or a poster of "Spring Rain" by Harry Behn.

10. Plan a bulletin board based upon poetry: "Poems We Like," "Famous Women Poets," "Beautiful Words from Poetry." The bulletin board might feature a "poet of the month," with a picture of the poet and a short biographical sketch.

11. Display an object (as a pair of overshoes) on a table. Nearby a related poem ("Galoshes" by Rhoda Bacmeister) is printed on a poster.

12. Set up a display of poetry books.

13. Have children take turns pantomiming the toad in James Whitcomb Riley's "The Tree Toad."

14. With the cooperation of the music teacher have a few boys and girls set their poems to music.

15. Using an opaque projector, flash good poems and ask: "Which words and ideas make this poem a good one? What is the pattern or form of the poem?"

A BANG-UP idea for poetry class. The class is divided into two teams. The leader of Team A gives the first line of a poem. The children on the opposing team are to supply the next line, the name of the poem, and the name of the poet. For example: Leader of Team A: "The gingham dog and the calico cat." Player 1: "Side by side on the table sat." Player 2: "The Duel." Player 3: Eugene Field (Each answer is worth two points.)

A BANG-UP idea for promoting interest in poetry. Conduct a poetry parade wherein individual children are costumed to represent their favorite personages who live in poems.

A BANG-UP idea for stimulating enthusiasm for poetry. Let a group of children write character sketches of the parts in a poem, after which they give a dramatic presentation of the poem. For example, dramatization of "The Shooting of Dan McGrew" should prove to be hilarious fun.

CHORAL SPEAKING

Technically speaking, choral speaking is the interpretation of poetry by two or more voices speaking as one. And for over twenty-five hundred years, choral speaking has been one of the most effective ways of interpreting literature orally. While it is true that the materials for choral speaking are most often poetry, selections of rhythmic prose from the Bible and certain "participation" stories in prose are considered to be choric in nature also.

Values of Choral Reading

Some of the benefits that children derive from the choral-speaking experience are direct; others are only tangentially related to the process. Among the more important values are the following:

Speech becomes more accurate and enunciation more clear.

Appreciation of poetry is heightened.

The group becomes a more cohesive social unit from having worked together.

Children are engaged in an active endeavor rather than a passive one.

An element of entertainment is introduced into the class proceedings.

The shy child learns to contribute to a shared undertaking; the bold child learns to submerge himself for the good of the group.

Literary skills are developed, including the ability to sense mood, understand rhythm, and appreciate the significance of voice tone, quality, and volume.

Types of Choral Speaking

Choral speaking is known by many names—choral reading, group speaking (in the primary grades), choric speech (combined with music) —and is distinguished by four major methods of arrangement. These methods are presented below in order of difficulty (the easiest approach appearing first), along with some observations on the character and the use of each technique with children.

1. *Refrain (chorus).* A soloist reads the body of the poem while the rest of the group or one of the voice groups joins in the chorus or refrain.

Observations:

(a) In the primary grades the soloist is invariably the "best" reader, that is, the teacher or a very able girl reader.

(b) Refrain poems, such as "Clocks" (author unknown), "Hickory, Dickory, Dock," and "The Mysterious Cat" (Vachel Lindsey), are fine for instructing the group in basic rhythm and the various moods that poems may have. The nursery rhymes and Mother Goose rhymes provide an endless array of refrain material for the primary-grade teacher.

(c) Arrangements other than the basic one may be tried after experience has been gained. A duet can replace the soloist, or the group may read the body of the poem while one or two children chime in on the refrain.

2. *Line-a-child (line-a-group, line-a-choir, sequential).* A single child (or a group of two or three children) speaks a line or couplet. Then another individual or group picks up and continues, one after another.

Observations:

(a) Poems that have relatively short lines or couplets ending with punctuation are best. Examples include "The Barnyard" (Maude Burham) and "Jump or Jiggle" (Evelyn Beyer).

(b) The director must see to it that children come in on cue; otherwise, continuity may fail and the poem may become dismembered and meaningless.

(c) Early efforts with line-a-child should find the children standing in the order in which they present their lines.

3. *Antiphonal (dialogue, two-part).* Two contrasting voice groups recite alternate lines or verses of a poem. The balanced-voice groups may be "light" voices against "heavy," boys versus girls, or the poems used may be of the question and answer variety.

Observations:

(a) Antiphonal is the most common type of choral speaking, ranging from its simplest form of opposing boy and girl choirs to rather complex combinations in which voices are grouped to obtain three or four pitch-levels.

(b) Because of the precision demanded, antiphonal choral work is primarily for middle- and upper-grade children. Poems selected should be of high quality so that interest in them will not wane as practice proceeds. "Puppy and I" (A.A. Milne) and "Laughter" (author unknown) are examples of antiphonal poetry that serve well.

(c) Dialog poems and poems of contrast make fine antiphonal pieces. In these poems boys will take the portions dominated by long vowel sounds and deep emotions, while the "lighter" parts are assigned to the girls.

4. *Unison.* The entire chorus recites together as one voice.

Observations:

(a) Unison is the most difficult choral speaking to direct because of the problems of coordinating timing and inflection. Therefore, small children should not be given a heavy dose of unison experience. In all instances, brief poems should be utilized.

(b) Blending the volume, rhythms and tones, and the various voices is the key to successful unison work. Particularly apt poems include "A Kitten" (Eleanor Farjeon), "The Bells" (Edgar Allan Poe), and many of the Mother Goose rhymes which contain scanty dialogue and little change in mood.

(c) Unison poems may be acted out and pantomimed. Nursery rhymes lend themselves to such interpretation. The anthologies and volumes by individual poets are filled with action poems which may be interpreted by one or two children as the others recite the verse in concert.

Selecting the Voice Groups

Since primary-grade children of both sexes have uniformly high voices, teachers of these grades will have little need to concern themselves with a wide range of pitch and voice quality when selecting children for parts. Further, since antiphonal and unison choral speaking are not highly recommended for use at the lower grade levels, there will be little need to be concerned with voice groups at all.

Teachers of the upper grades who wish to organize voice groups, say into high, medium, and low voices, will need to devise some scheme whereby they can group children according to pitch and voice quality. Most teachers already have some awareness of the voice qualities of the boys and girls in their classes. From this they will be able initially to form a "high" group and a "low" group of voices, with two to three individuals in each group. The remaining youngsters are asked to read or recite a short verse, and the teacher's "ear" will help her decide into which group each child should go. Many voices are relatively easy to categorize, and soon there will be ten to twelve youngsters each in the high and low groups. The children who are difficult to classify should be placed in the "medium" voice chorus. Even so, there will be much changing back and forth until the proper meshing of perfectly tuned voices takes place. For two-part choric expression, the medium group should be "halved," with the high-medium voices forming the high voices, and the low-medium voices aiding the low or dark voices.

A special note about the child with the crowlike voice. Keep the child in the group at all costs, enjoining him to speak softly. Sometimes this child can serve as an announcer or stage manager when it comes time for the performance. In whatever way, the child should be included, in the interests of his own self-esteem and respect.

Working with the Choral Group

A brief review of the procedure to be employed in the presentation of a choral selection to a group of children, and the group before an audience, may be of use to the reader. The suggestions that follow are not the only ones possible.

1. Choose a poem that will be of interest to the children. It might be advisable to start with a humorous poem, or one that has a surprise in it. Children delight in being surprised and in springing surprises upon an audience.

2. Read the poem aloud to the class. Be sure you are the only one with a copy, or read the poem from the chalkboard. Know the poem well enough to be able to enthuse the group at the first reading. Your initial rendition reflects your command of the skills of oral interpretation. Make it a good one!

3. Talk over the poem with the children, clarifying the images in the poem, defining the words, and answering questions about pronunciation. However, don't overanalyze the poem.

4. Read the poem aloud a second time, asking the group to reflect on the rhythm. Active interpretation may be brought about by having one or two children "skip" or "walk" the poem. Begin to form some thoughts as to which pupils might perform solo parts. Note: Don't choose your best pupils for all such parts. Choose some children who will grow into the parts.

5. Read the poem aloud a third time, having the children follow along with fingertip tapping, or light handclapping.

6. Distribute copies of the poem to the children. Invite the class to participate in the next reading. Direct as you do in music: one hand controlling the rate, the other hand minding the volume. Don't overdo the directing. A group must have a leader, but she should be as inconspicuous as possible.

7. Clear up any tendencies toward awkward phrasing and intonation, heavy voices and sing-song patterns.

8. Assign solo parts. After a number of choral-speaking experiences, boys and girls will be able to nominate classmates for solo parts. If memorization is required, it may begin now.

9. Total group recital of the poem begins, the teacher-leader fading more and more into the background with each rendition until she discontinues speaking with the group.

10. Choral speaking is basically an educational activity and not a showpiece to be offered to various school groups. However, occasional public performances might be considered. At those times the choir should form in a semicircle, in stairstep fashion, with the voice groups arranged from left to right in order of high, medium, and low voices. Solo speakers may be a step forward or to one side.

11. There are no bounds as to the number and types of poems appropriate for choral work. The only cautions the teacher need take is that the material not be too advanced in content nor too involved in meter and rhythm. Some specific sources of material dealing with choral materials are given at the close of this chapter, although most any book of poetry may be an excellent source.

SELECTED LIST OF MATERIALS AND RESOURCES FOR THE TEACHER

reading aloud: professional books

American Library Association, LET'S READ TOGETHER: BOOKS FOR FAMILY ENJOYMENT. Chicago: The Association, 1960.

Armstrong, Chloe, and Paul Brandes, THE ORAL INTERPRETATION OF LITERATURE. New York: McGraw-Hill Book Company, 1963.

Bamman, Henry, et al., ORAL INTERPRETATION OF CHILDREN'S LITERATURE, pp. 1–17. Dubuque, Iowa: William C. Brown Co., 1964.

Geeting, Baxter, INTERPRETATION FOR OUR TIME. Dubuque, Iowa: William C. Brown, Co., 1966.

Henneke, Ben, READING ALOUD EFFECTIVELY. New York: Holt, Rinehart & Winston, Inc., 1961.

Parrish, Wayland, READING ALOUD. New York: The Ronald Press Company, 1966.

Wagner, Joseph, and Robert Smith, TEACHER'S GUIDE TO STORYTELLING, pp. 67–85. Dubuque, Iowa: William C. Brown Co., 1958.

Willcox, Isobel, READING ALOUD WITH ELEMENTARY SCHOOL CHILDREN. Englewood Cliffs, N.J.: Teachers Practical Press, Inc. (Prentice-Hall, Inc.), 1963.

storytelling: professional books

Callwell, Eileen, A SECOND STORYTELLER'S CHOICE. New York: Henry Z. Walck, Inc., 1965.

Cathon, Laura, et al., eds., STORIES TO TELL TO CHILDREN. Pittsburgh: Carnegie Library, 1960.

Cundiff, Ruby, and Barbara Webb-Larkin, STORY-TELLING FOR YOU. Antioch, Ohio: Antioch Press, 1957.

Emerson, Laura, STORY-TELLING. Grand Rapids, Mich.: Zondervan Publishing House, 1959.

Greene, Ellin, compiler, STORIES: A LIST OF STORIES TO TELL AND TO READ ALOUD. New York: New York Public Library, 1965. Booklet.

Hardendorff, Jeanne, STORIES TO TELL. Baltimore, Md.: Enoch Pratt Free Library, 1965. Booklet.

Moore, Vardine, PRE-SCHOOL STORY HOUR. New York: Scarecrow Press, Inc., 1966.

New York Library Association Committee, ONCE UPON A TIME. New York: The Committee, 1964. Booklet.

Royal, Claudia, STORYTELLING. Nashville, Tenn.: Broadman Press, 1955.

Sawyer, Ruth, THE WAY OF THE STORYTELLER. New York: The Viking Press, Inc., 1962.

Shedlock, Marie, THE ART OF THE STORYTELLER. New York: Dover Publications, Inc., 1951.

Tooze, Ruth, STORYTELLING. Englewood Cliffs, N.J.: Prentice-Hall, Inc., 1959.

Wagner, J.A., and R.W. Smith, TEACHER'S GUIDE TO STORYTELLING, Dubuque, Iowa: William C. Brown Co., 1958.

storytelling: films

Coronet Films, Chicago.
STORY-TELLING: CAN YOU TELL IT IN ORDER. (MP). 11 min. For grades 2–6.

University of Michigan, Ann Arbor, Mich.
TELLING STORIES TO CHILDREN. (MP). 27 min. For grades 4–8.

storytelling: recordings

Weston Woods, Weston, Conn.
RUTH SAWYER, STORYTELLER. A two-record album of storytelling and commentary by Ruth Sawyer.

storytelling: related materials

Judy Company, Minneapolis.
"See-Quees" (in a series of five). Each series composed of 12 removable illustrations on a 13" x 14" board. For grades K–1.
"Story Sets": Gingerbread Boy, Three Bears, Three Pigs, Chicken Little, Goats Gruff. For manipulation as children tell the story. For grades K–1.

poetry: professional books

Applegate, Mauree, WHEN THE TEACHER SAYS, "WRITE A POEM." New York: Harper & Row, Publishers, 1965.

Arnstein, Flora, ADVENTURE INTO POETRY. Stanford, Calif.: Stanford University Press, 1951.

———, POETRY IN THE ELEMENTARY CLASSROOM. New York: Appleton-Century-Crofts, 1962.

Bamman, Henry, et al., ORAL INTERPRETATION OF CHILDREN'S LITERATURE, pp. 18–42. Dubuque, Iowa: William C. Brown Co., 1964.

Behn, Harry, CRICKET SONGS: JAPANESE HAIKU. New York: Harcourt, Brace & World, Inc., 1964.

Bernhardt, William, editor, GRANGER'S INDEX TO POETRY, 5th ed. New York: Columbia University Press, 1962.

Brewton, John, and Sara Brewton, compilers, INDEX TO CHILDREN'S POETRY, second supplement. New York: The H.W. Wilson Company, 1965.

Bruncken, Herbert, SUBJECT INDEX TO POETRY. Chicago: American Library Association, 1940.

Burrows, Alvina, et al., THEY ALL WANT TO WRITE: WRITTEN ENGLISH IN THE ELEMENTARY SCHOOL, 3rd ed., pp. 117–40. New York: Holt, Rinehart & Winston, Inc., 1964.

Dunning, Stephen, TEACHING LITERATURE TO ADOLESCENTS: POETRY. Chicago: Scott, Foresman & Company, 1966.

Hastings, Henry, SPOKEN POETRY ON RECORDS AND TAPES. Chicago: American Library Association, 1957.

Henderson, Harold, An Introduction to Haiku. New York: Doubleday & Company, Inc., 1958.

Hughes, Rosalind, Let's Enjoy Poetry. Boston: Houghton Mifflin Company, 1959.

Mearns, Hughes, Creative Youth. New York: Doubleday & Company, Inc., 1929.

Parker, Elinor, compiler, The Singing and the Gold: Poems Translated from World Literature. New York: Thomas Y. Crowell Company, 1962.

Sell, Violet, et al., compilers, Subject Index to Poetry for Children and Young People. Chicago: American Library Association, 1957.

Walter, Nina, Let Them Write Poetry. New York: Holt, Rinehart & Winston, Inc., 1962.

poetry: films and filmstrips

Coronet Films, Chicago.

Literature Appreciation: How to Read Poetry. (MP). 11 min. For grades 7–12.
Mary Had A Little Lamb: Background for Reading and Expression. (MP). 11 min. For grades K–3.
Mother Goose Rhymes: Background for Reading and Expression. (MP). 11 min. For grades K–3.
Poems Are Fun. (MP). 11 min. For grades 4–7.
Poetry For Beginners (MP). 11 min. For grades 3–5.

Grover-Jennings, P.O. Box 303, Monterey, Calif.

Poetry For Me. (MP). 14 min. For grades 1–6.
Poetry to Grow On. (MP). 18 min. For grades 5–7.

Sterling Educational Films, New York.

Hailstones and Halibut Bones. (MP). 6 min. For grades 3–6.

Sterling Films, New York.

The House That Jack Built. (MP). 6 min. For grades K–1.

Weston Woods, Weston, Conn.

The Owl and the Pussy-Cat. (FS and Sound FS).
A Picture Has a Special Look. (FS)
Sparkle and Spin. (FS)
The Tale of Custard the Dragon. (MP). 6 min. For grades 2–4.

poetry: recordings and tapes

Bill Grauer Productions, Inc. New York.

"Mother Goose Songs," Artist: Alec Templeton. For grades K–1. Bowmar Records, Los Angeles.

"Nursery and Mother Goose Rhymes." For grades K–1.

"Poems for the Very Young." Artists: Marni Nixon and Donald Murphy. For grades K–3.

"Poems of My Country." Artist: Jose Ferrer. For grades 4–8.

Caedmon Records, New York.

"American Poems of Patriotism." Artists: Ed Begley, Julie Harris, Frederick O'Neal. For grades 4–6.

"Carl Sandburg's Poems for Children." Artist: Carl Sandburg. For grades 4–6.

"A Child's Garden of Verses." Artist: Judith Anderson. For grades 2–5.

"Miracles." Artists: Julie Harris and Roddy McDowell. Original poetry of children ages 5–13. For grades K–8.

"Mother Goose." Artists: Cyril Ritchard, Celeste Holm, Boris Karloff. For grades K–1.

"Nonsense Verse of Carroll and Lear." Artists: Beatrice Lillie, Cyril Ritchard, Stanley Holloway. For grades 4–8.

Educational Audio Visual, Inc., Pleasantville, N.Y.

"I Met A Man." Artist: John Ciardi. For grades 4–7.

"A Golden Treasury of Poetry." Artist: Louis Untermeyer. For grades 4–7.

Enrichment Teaching Materials, New York. All for grades 7–8.

"Adventures." Artist: E.G. Marshall.

"Appreciation." Artist: Bennett Cerf.

"Enjoyment." Artist: Dane Clark.

"Journeys." Artist: Edward Mulhare.

"Of America." Artist: Arnold Moss

"Of England." Artist: Clifton Fadiman.

Folkways Records, New York.

"An Anthology of Negro Poetry for Young People." Artist: Arna Bontemps. For grades 3–8.

"The Song of Hiawatha." Artist: Harry Fleetwood. For grades 6–8.

Imperial Productions, Inc., Kankakee, Ill.

"Golden Anthology of Children's Verse." 8 tapes, 70 poems. For grades K–3.

Leo The Lion Records, MGM Records, New York.

"Meet Merry Mother Goose." Artists: Betty Martin and Donald Dawe. For grades K–2.

Office of Children's Services, New York Public Library.

RECORDINGS FOR CHILDREN, 2nd ed., 1964. An annotated listing of recordings arranged by subject and grade level.

Spoken Arts, Inc., New Rochelle, N.Y.

"A Child's Garden of Verses," Volumes I and II. Artists: Nancy Wickwire and Basil Langton. For grades K–3.

"Golden Treasury of American Verse." Artists: Nancy Wickwire and Alexander Scourby. For grades 7–8.

"Treasury of Nursery Rhymes," Volumes I and II. Artist: Christopher Casson. For grades K–3.

"You Know Who, Fiddler Dan and John Q. Plenty and Other Poems." Artist: John Ciardi. For grades 4–6.

"You Read to Me, I'll Read to You." Artist: John Ciardi. For grades 4–6.

Victor Records, RCA, Educational Services, Camden, N.J.

"Poet's Gold." Artists: Helen Hayes, Raymond Massey, Thomas Mitchell. For grades 4–8.

poetry: display charts

"A Child's World of Poetry." Talking Picture-Story Study Prints: Eight (8) color prints and two (2) long play records. For grades K–1. Society for Visual Education, 1345 Diversey Pkwy., Chicago, Illinois 60614.

Karb, Ruth, "Mother Goose Rhymes for Kindergarten and Primary Grades." Dansville, N.Y.: F.A. Owen Publishing Co., n.d. Set of 10 charts, 20 sides. For grades K–1.

choral speaking: professional books

Abney, Louise, CHORAL SPEAKING ARRANGEMENTS FOR THE JUNIOR HIGH SCHOOL, rev. ed. Magnolia, Mass.: Expression Company, 1959.

———, CHORAL SPEAKING ARRANGEMENTS FOR THE LOWER GRADES. Magnolia, Mass.: Expression Company, 1953.

———CHORAL SPEAKING ARRANGEMENTS FOR THE UPPER GRADES, rev. ed. Magnolia, Mass.: Expression Company, 1952.

Arbuthnot, May Hill, CHILDREN AND BOOKS, 3rd ed., pp. 220–49. Chicago: Scott, Foresman & Company, 1964.

Bamman, Henry, et al., ORAL INTERPRETATION OF CHILDREN'S LITERATURE, pp. 43–71. Dubuque, Iowa: William C. Brown Co., 1964.

Barton, Clifford, VERSE CHOIR IN THE ELEMENTARY SCHOOL. Darien, Conn.: Educational Publishing Corp., 1958.

Brown, Helen, and Harry Heltman, eds., CHORAL READINGS FOR FUN AND RECREATION. Philadelphia: Westminster Press, 1956.

Dawson, Mildred, and Mary Choate, HOW TO HELP A CHILD APPRECIATE POETRY: 100 POEMS TO EXPRESS WITH VOICE AND ACTION. San Francisco: Fearon Publishers, 1960. Booklet.

Evans, Helen, TOGETHER WE SPEAK: A COLLECTION OF CHORAL READINGS. Dansville, N.Y.: F.A. Owen Publishing Co., 1959.

Gullen, Marjorie, CHORAL SPEAKING. London: Methuen & Co., Ltd. 1957.

Hemphill, Irene, CHORAL SPEAKING AND SPEECH IMPROVEMENT. Darien, Conn.: Teachers Publishing Corporation, 1960.

Rasmussen, Carrie, LET'S SAY POETRY TOGETHER AND HAVE FUN: FOR INTERMEDIATE GRADES. Minneapolis: Burgess Publishing Co., 1963.

————, LET'S SAY POETRY TOGETHER AND HAVE FUN: FOR PRIMARY GRADES. Minneapolis: Burgess Publishing Co., 1962.

Raubicheck, Letitia, CHORAL SPEAKING IS FUN. New York: Noble ,1955.

choral speaking: films

Young America Films, McGraw-Hill Book Company, New York.
LET'S TRY CHORAL READING. (MP). 12 min. For grades 4–8.

Experiencing
Literature

CHAPTER FIVE
Orally

and Through Writing

PERSPECTIVE

The time allotted to children for talking about literature and for writing book reports and creative stories is rather short compared to the time given to other activities in the elementary school. This is unfortunate, for the values that accrue to children through these two approaches are many. Frequent experiences with speaking and writing literature develop in children a respect and appreciation for both prose and poetry. A child derives much personal satisfaction from participating in the creative act. At the same time he is giving other children pleasure or information about the literature he has read, sparking the listeners to read and enjoy the same material.

With the above observations in mind, this chapter has been designed to help teachers encourage children to participate in the processes of speaking and writing. It is hoped that this chapter will help the teacher gain a better perspective of her role in guiding children's learning in these two aspects of the literature program, while increasing her understanding of what to expect of children in each of the two areas.

For each of the two approaches discussed in this chapter—the oral and the written—there is a brief enumeration of some specific principles and values of that form of literature activity. Following that is a series of suggested classroom procedures a teacher may want to employ; the emphasis here has been placed upon compiling a *variety* of *stimulating* and *creative* approaches to sharing and viewing literature.

ORAL APPROACHES TO LITERATURE

There are many points, both practical and philosophical, that could be made about the oral reporting of literature. Listed below are a few of the basic principles and values of oral sharing, along with practical tips on techniques and a wide range of recommended classroom procedures. Included in this portion of the chapter are sections on how to construct and use flannelboards and how to develop finger plays.

Principles of Oral Discussion About Books

An often witnessed blunder in the teaching of literature is the teacher's requiring a *detailed* analysis and oral presentation of the life of an author and/or the works which he produced. No one would disagree that some such information is necessary and useful to children, but the extent and frequency of such assignments are absurd. This emphasis on facts certainly stifles the child's imagination and his interest in literature, often to a point where he turns away from literature in disgust.

Children's oral reactions to books and stories should reflect their honest statements as to what they have and have not liked in their reading. Their presentation should reflect variety, a friendly, informal style, and a purposeful period of preparation wherein they have given some thought to making the report instructive and pleasurable for the listeners.

Through all of this the teacher has in mind that the oral sharing and reporting of literature will redound to the lasting profit of the children in a number of ways, including:

1. Helping children grow in self-confidence and social adjustment as they share their interest and knowledge of literature with others.
2. Developing an ability to speak with increased ease and effectiveness before a group.
3. Learning to assemble material and organize a topic in which the child and the class are interested, including learning to limit oneself in time.
4. Coming to know that learning good speech habits also implies that you learn good listening habits.

Procedures and Approaches to Oral Reporting

The following topics illustrate effective oral approaches to literature that may be instituted to interest children in literature, whether the child be delivering a report or listening to it.

Audience reading of literature by individual children has as its purpose the enjoyment of the humor, colorful language, or information contained in the passage read. If it is well done, audience reading is a splendid device for stimulating other children to read the shared book or story. Audience reading may also be done by a group of children, who "read" a playlet or story with dialogue to their own classmates or to a kindergarten or other early primary-grade class.

The children might take turns reading a favorite passage from a fable or a fairy tale, reciting a poem, or giving a biographical sketch of a well-known children's author, after which the presentation is discussed by the listeners.

Broadcasting radio reviews, either real or simulated, is enjoyed by the children. If the school has an intercommunication system, one or two brief, well-prepared book reviews might be broadcast over it once a week. These reviews could be "live" or taped. Mock broadcasts, in which a tin cup mounted on a broomstick substitutes for a microphone, might be conducted in individual classrooms. Needed are an announcer, persons who deliver the commercials, a person who dubs in background music, a sound effects man, and three or four individuals to present their book reviews. The reading of nursery rhymes, poetry, or verses set to music might also be included. Another variation is found in the *news report*, wherein the contents of books, either fiction or nonfiction, along with sketches of famous book characters, are reported upon in a news broadcast style.

A *chalk talk* can be a highly effective routine for getting across a book. Children are usually more ready to give a chalk talk than are teachers, as the boys and girls do not find it necessary to come up with finished art work. Sketches put on the chalkboard need only be simple and of good size. Stick figures of Curious George and Little Bo Peep will later grow into more dressed-up and refined book personalities.

Character talks begin when each child or the teacher writes the name of a famous story character (Humpty Dumpty, Homer Price, Caddie Woodlawn) on a slip of paper. All the papers go into a box. Each child closes his eyes, takes a paper from the box, reads the name from the paper, and then recites two sentences about the character named. In a variation of this activity, the child takes two slips of paper and then tells how the book personalities are different in character.

Debating is a popular book reviewing approach. The aim of the debate is to stimulate thinking. First, select an issue—"Resolved, that the class should read most of its literature from books in the library rather than from basal readers." Second, select the debators, no more than two or three to a side, and restrict them to three-minute speeches. The debate, including a classroom vote on the winning team, should not run over a half hour.

Illustrated lectures, whether based upon books of nonfiction or fiction, use photographs, pictures clipped from magazines and other publications, postcards, and filmstrip slides to support the social studies program while at the same time promoting good intercultural relationships among children.

Informal and spontaneous classroom discussions in which all of the children participate are most successful when children are encouraged to give their candid opinions of books. What a child has to say about a book rightly influences the opinions of other children in the class. General participation should be encouraged so that the discussion is not dominated by just a few. The teacher should endeavor to join in the discussion as a member of the group and not as an authoritarian leader.

A man-on-the-street interview finds a classroom newspaper reporter talking with a book character from one of the critical periods in American history. Such a book character might be Ben Budge in *A Spy in Williamsburg,* a story set at the time of the American Revolution. Or the interview might be with another historical book figure (such as Rip Van Winkle) or a famous author.

My-candidate-for-election reviews come about when children make nominating speeches for favorite book candidates to be elected to offices. Offices and typical book character types to be elected might include:

For President: a famous dog (e.g., Bodger, Grey Friar's Bobby, Lassie)
For Vice-President: a famous horse (Roxana, Misty, the Black Stallion)
For Secretary: a "Newbery" character (Miss Hickory, Amos Fortune, Ginger Pye)
For Treasurer: a tall-tale character (Mike Fink, Paul Bunyan)

Other offices and categories of candidates can be devised. Three or four nominating speeches should be given for each category. Using election techniques, children then vote on their favorite character for each office.

A *monologue* delivered by a student will enable him to impersonate a book character who describes himself and his relationship to other characters in the book. Excerpts from the book can reveal his age, interests, feelings, ideas, occupation, and the setting of the story. Look to those portions of the book that are heavy in dialogue for monologue material.

Oral book reports given by individual children who stand in front of the class and "tell something about their book" is a much overworked technique. There is not as much fault in the basic approach itself as in the way it has been employed by teachers. Good oral reports should draw children to books, not drive them away as has so often happened. Therefore, the book reviews should be short, variable, and stimulating, rather than the long, tedious reports under which children chaff and rebel.

Usual Course	*Recourse*
1. *Every child* must make an oral book report periodically.	1. A child should make an oral report only if he is so stimulated by a book that he wants to give an oral précis. This may be once a year, twice a semester, or never.
2. *If* oral book reviews are mandated by the school district, require them. "Get a book from the library, boys and girls. All of us must be ready to make an oral book review."	2. Help children select books of interest by accompanying them to the library. Don't assign every child a specific book to report upon or the total class one book such as *The Yearling*.
3. "Be ready to give your oral report in about two weeks."	3. Be specific. Tell each child exactly when he will give his oral review, then remind him of this periodically. Distribute the reviews over a 6-to-8 week period, having no more than three or four reviews on any given day, and preferably not late on Friday afternoon.
4. "Read the book at home because we have no time for this at school."	4. Although portions of the book may be read at home, free minutes and an occasional planned period should be set aside during which children read toward the completion of this assignment.
5. Children are not helped to plan their oral reviews.	5. The teacher should show the children how to prepare an oral report, including giving one herself. Children's oral reviews should be confined to three-minute presentations. An egg timer is an excellent device with which to limit each report. This takes careful planning and school time must be given to planning sessions.
6. On the day of the oral reports say, "Is everyone ready to listen to Kathleen's report?"	6. Establish good standards of listening with children. Get them to listen *for something* (interesting words, correct speech patterns, etc.) rather than *to something* (Robert, and what he will do poorly).

Usual Course	*Recourse*
7. While a review is in progress, the teacher grades papers, checks the milk money, etc.	7. The teacher should sit close to the youngster presenting the review in order to encourage him or help him along with cue questions if he falters in his delivery.
8. Upon completion of the review, the class turns immediately to the arithmetic assignment.	8. A brief discussion of the story and an evaluation of the oral presentation should be undertaken.

Listed below are a number of general suggestions for children who are planning to make a stand-up oral book review before a class. Not all of these suggestions can be incorporated into one book review by a single individual, but they will lend variety to the total number of class reviews. Still other reviews might be dramatized, interpreted through an art medium, or expressed in any of the myriad ways discussed elsewhere in this book.

1. Show the book.
2. Give the title of the book and the name of the author. Write these on the chalkboard if you like. Give the date of publication if the book is of an informational type.
3. If the book is fiction, biography, or the like:

4. If the book is nonfiction, give one or two interesting facts; tell something about the book that will make others want to read it; and compare the book with others on the same topic, or with other books by the same author.

5. Read aloud the most beautifully descriptive passage or the most lifelike portion of dialogue.

6. Have a good closing sentence in which you recommend the book: "If you are looking for adventure, you will certainly find it in *Winter Danger* by William Steele.

7. Don't give away the ending of the story!

In a *panel discussion* up to five children sit before the class and share what they know and feel about the plot, characters, and illustrations of a particular book (as *Stock Car Racer* by Caary Jackson), an author (Lois Lenski), the themes of a given kind of book (the "Misty" books by Marguerite Henry, or books about horses in general), or a series of books (the "Allabout" books from Random House). The chairman introduces each panelist, who, in turn, presents his point of view. When all of the panelists have given their talks, the chairman opens the meeting to a general discussion by the class.

The *round-table discussion*, in which each member of the group is allowed to say what he thinks and feels about the subject under discussion, began during the time of King Arthur. Today, it would be highly appropriate for a group of six to twelve children to sit about a round table in a classroom and discuss Howard Pyle's book, *The Story of King Arthur and His Knights* (any edition). The group must choose a leader who is responsible for keeping the discussants on the topic and seeing to it that all members of the group participate fully and in a friendly, informal manner. The rules: be polite, speak briefly, don't interrupt another speaker, and don't make fun of another's opinions.

Sales talks may be given on the most popular books read by the children. The oral presentations should be patterned after those employed by salesmen, including the use of high pressure tactics, coaxing, promises, and guarantees. Following these talks the "critics" (the class) might vote for the salesmen who created a best-seller. A similar version of the sales talk is the *book auction*, where a boy or girl displays a favorite book, extols its virtues, then takes bids (each youngster in the class has been allocated "bid points") and sells the book to the highest bidder, who pays for the privilege of reading the book next. Cleverly designed *television commercials* may be prepared by the children, who have one minute to sell their books using visual aids and a talk based upon familiar television commercials.

A *sampler period* begins when the teacher hands two team members a new book. The teamed pair is given 15 to 20 minutes to examine the book and prepare an interesting review of its illustrations, format, and high points (this may be done by skip reading and by an examination of chapter headings). The team members are then allocated one minute in which to show the book and read selected passages to their classmates. Sampler periods are best followed by reading periods during which these "baited books" may be borrowed by interested children.

Sharing time, during which kindergarten and primary level children "show and tell" about a favorite book brought from home, is common in schools today. The teacher will want to scrutinize carefully all books brought from home. Though many books arrive and are used at the pleasure of the individual child, the teacher may choose a new person every day to bring in a much-loved book for use during sharing time. Sharing time can also give rise to spontaneous original storytelling which, with proper controls, often proves to be a rewarding experience for children.

A *symposium* on literature may be held occasionally; a group of four or five children may prepare speeches on types of books, authors, or problems encountered by book characters. For example, individuals within the symposium group might read *Up a Road Slowly, Berries Goodman, Dorp Dead, Onion John,* and *It's Like This, Cat* and then discuss the problems that the characters in these books faced in growing up. In a symposium, individuals are introduced by a chairman, after which they give their speeches. The chairman later conducts a question-and-answer period.

Talking pictures involves a class in reading a picture book together. The teacher or the child reviewer shows illustrations in a big picture book and asks volunteers to tell about each picture. Typical questions include: (1) What is happening?; (2) What would happen if the picture were alive?; (3) What will happen next?

A *"This-Is-Your-Life" program* can be conducted by two children, during which the reviewers bring out the hobbies, education, and out-standing events in the life story of a famous author, illustrator, or book character.

Other ideas for children who want to share books orally with their classmates would include the following:

...Share a book with a small group of four or five children in a "buzz group" fashion.

...When a child is ready to share a book, have him place his name tag in a bulletin board pocket entitled "Books We Wish to Tell About."

...Arrange a book report as a quiz show. A panel of experts, or a whole class, can ask the reviewer questions in order to discover the book he is to report upon. This may take the form of the game "Twenty Questions."

... Become an "expert" by reading a number of books by a given writer and/or books on particular subjects. Information gleaned from this reading would be given in an oral presentation to a class.

... Each child in class reads an animal book, after which he makes a clay model of his animal and gives a "book report" speech about the animal. Ribbons are awarded for best speech and best clay model.

... Conduct a mock trial and explore fully the situation concerning Philip Nolan in *The Man Without a Country*. Other literature figures might be brought to trial, including Johnny Tremain (if he had been caught), Huck Finn (for helping Jim to escape from his slave master), and so on.

... Review a book to musical accompaniment, with the music coming from a record player or being rendered by members of the school orchestra or band.

... Deliver a review as if the book were science fiction, a mystery, nonfiction (if fiction) and vice versa, or as one of another dozen different types of books.

... Review a book familiar to all members of the class, and add a new incident or ending to the book. See how many classmates discover the alteration.

... Contrast and criticize a book of science fiction as compared with a volume of science on the same subject. For example, review critically *The Red Planet* by Robert Heinlein after reading *Exploring Mars* by Roy Gallant.

A BANG-UP idea for an oral review requires the speaker to deliver his book review, such as a biography, as he assumes three different ages in the course of the oral presentation:

1. As a child: wears a cap and speaks in a high-pitched voice.
2. As a young man or lady: speaks in a normal voice while wearing either a man's hat or a fashionable lady's hat.
3. As an old man or woman: speaks in a weak, unsure voice, while holding a cane in his hand.

Flannelboard

The flannelboard (feltboard, flannelgraph) is one of the most versatile and inexpensive devices available to help children visualize and verbalize about a character or situation in literature. And there is no grade level at which it cannot be used successfully. Through the medium of the flannelboard the following specific needs of children are satisfied:

1. All children—but particularly the shy ones—experience the pleasure of telling stories as they manipulate the pictured characters and objects which are the center of interest. In so doing, each individual gives vent to his own impression of the story he performs.
2. Children learn to evaluate literature, noting such things as figurative language, interesting characters, dramatic plots, and the varying moods of the story.
3. Children become more critical of the speech patterns of themselves and others, leading to correction of their own faults.
4. Coordination is improved as the children manipulate the story materials.

Another obvious value of children working with a flannelboard lies in the flannelgraph's recreational nature, which provides a change of pace to the classroom routine. The teacher recognizes this, but more than that she sees in the flannelboard a medium whereby children grow in literature skills and appreciations.

A flannelboard may be used to instruct in any area of the curriculum, but the best-known use to which it is put is as a showcase for stories. The flannelboard story may be used in one of three basic ways: (1) the teacher as sole manipulator and storyteller, (2) the teacher as the storyteller, with a child or children serving as manipulators, and (3) individual children working at individual flannelboards. There is a time and a place for the flannelboard to be used in all three ways. But the teacher should remember that, by its very nature, the flannelboard invites children to participate.

materials for making a flannelboard

1. *Materials for making backing*: bristol board, a board, Celotex, fiberboard, heavy cardboard, Masonite, plywood, wallboard. Cardboard is least acceptable, although a re-enforced carton, covered on each of its four main sides with a different colored material, gives a story board to four different children simultaneously.
2. *Materials for covering the board*: long-napped fabrics such as a blanket, corduroy, duvetyne, felt, flannel, flock, interlining of a coat, jersey (wool), pellon, and suede. Dark neutral colors are best: black, blue, brown, gray, green. Flannel is preferred, since it can be colored or painted, and because it has considerable nap.
3. *Methods of attaching covering to backing*:
   a. Choose a piece of backing 24 to 36 inches square.
   b. Cut the material two to three inches longer on each side than the backing.

    c. To construct a *removable covering* (so that it may be reversed or cleaned later), hem the edges of the material, insert a drawstring, place the covering over the backing, and pull the material tight.

    d. To construct a *permanent covering*, stretch the material tightly over the backing, fold the flaps over onto the back of the board, and staple the corners. Fasten the covering securely with thumb tacks, glue, rubber cement, masking tape, staples, or a cloth binding.

    e. To further refine the flannelboard, cover the back of the board with wallpaper, enclose the flannelboard in a picture frame, append a suede brush with which to renew the nap periodically, and attach a kitchen cabinet handle along one edge for ease of carrying.

4. *Making picture characters and cutouts*:

    a. Sources of pictures with which to illustrate flannelboard stories include coloring books, magazines, toy and mail order catalogs, old textbooks, and children's original art work. Commercially made flannelboards and cutout materials are also available from any of the numerous school supply houses.

    b. Silhouette cutouts can be made directly from felt (such as old felt hats). Human figures on a three-foot board should be 9 to 12 inches high, with other objects constructed accordingly. In some instances these may be pressed directly to the flannelboard without special treatment backing.

    c. Paper cutouts of most types usually need to be backed with strips of some kind of material that will give them adhesive properties. Typical backing materials are blotting paper, burlap, felt, flannel (heavy), light carpet, monk's cloth, and sandpaper (fine). Lightweight materials, such as magazine cutouts, need to be mounted on oaktag before the backing is put on with rubber cement.

    d. Additional refinements might include the drawing on of facial features or other details with felt pens, colored crayons and pencils, and chalk, all of this being fixed in place with hair spray. For detail, buttons and beads may also be added.

5. *Parts box*: A shoe box, cigar box, or large envelope should be obtained in which to store the picture cutouts. Each child in the class may glue a piece of flannel to the inside lid of a cigar box to make a small individual flannelboard. The box also doubles as a container for his cutouts.

flannelboard technique. Theoretically, any story or poem can be adapted to the flannelboard approach, even a book of nonfiction. Practically, though, some tales are better suited for flannelboard presentation than are others. For example, the story of "Goldilocks and the Three Bears" is an ideal story in a number of ways in that it contains three elements that a flannelboard story must have: (1) familiar characters or objects (bear, tree, girl); (2) orderly, repetitive episodes which are relatively easy to remember, especially if a child is the storyteller; and (3) a story of substance, one with a satisfying plot.

But a good story such as "Goldilocks and the Three Bears" is not in itself a guarantee of a successful flannelboard experience. Knowing how to stage the story is equally important. Following are some considerations that are vital to the successful employment of the flannelboard.

1. Number the cutouts in order in advance of the storytelling period.
2. Test the cutouts to see that they adhere to the flannelboard.
3. Rehearse the story, checking to see how long it takes to tell, and noting errors in the placement of the cutouts on the flannelboard.
4. Place the flannelboard *high enough* (on an adjustable easel) and *close enough* (six feet away from the nearest child, no more than fifteen feet away from the farthest child) so that all may see.

5. Arrange the numbered cutouts—faces down, numbers up—in order on a table.

6. Stand or sit at the right of the flannelboard, the left of the viewers. Talk to the class, not to the flannelboard. Watch the audience, not the cutouts in your hand or on the flannelboard.

7. Don't overload the board with pictures. Give the audience ample time to see the pictures, then remove them.

8. Cutouts should be placed on the flannelboard when the object or character is first introduced in the story or in a new sequence within the story. For example, "Once upon a time there were three bears who lived together in a house (place picture of three bears)." After the storyteller introduces the bears' various sized bowls, chairs, and beds, these objects and the bears must be taken from the board; the action has swept by the bears—they are no longer the focal point of the story—and they must be removed to make way for Goldilocks.

The stories (S) and poems (P) listed below are deemed appropriate for adaptation as first attempts at flannelboard storytelling. The stories are divided into two categories: Primary (for grades K-3) and Upper (grades 4-8).

Primary

The Queer Visitor (S)
Ask Mr. Bear (S)
Five Little Kittens (P)
Runaway Cookies (P)
Jack and the Beanstalk (S)
Three Little Pigs (S)
Three Billy Goats Gruff (S)
Tale of Peter Rabbit (S)
Cinderella (S)
Rabbit Who Wanted Red Wings (S)

Upper

Emperor's New Clothes (S)
Princess and the Pea (S)
500 Hats of Bartholomew Cubbins (S)
And to Think That I Saw It on Mulberry Street (S)
Ugly Duckling (S)
The Nightingale (S)
Alice in Wonderland—Down the Rabbit Hole (S)
Justin Morgan Had a Horse-Pulling Bee (S)

Finger Plays

Certain finger plays and flannelboard stories have common elements. Furthermore, both the finger play and flannelboard approach to interpreting literature are mutually beneficial to children in that they help build a literature and language vocabulary, they improve coordination as children move their hands to tell their stories, and they prove to be ready vehicles of self-expression and interpretation.

Finger plays are commonly employed by the primary teacher who performs them for the younger children. But limiting the performance of finger plays to the lower grades is a grave error, for they have much to offer to older youngsters. They require minimal materials and effort, including (1) simple "finger" properties, (2) a brief, quickly memorized verse from literature, and (3) an enthusiastic finger pantomimist. With the finger play, there is no need for the flannelboard story cutouts, the papier mache figures used in puppetry, nor the elaborate properties often required for a dramatic production. All one needs is two hands, ten fingers, and the door to literature fun is open.

The techniques of telling a story with finger play are almost self-revelatory. If a primary teacher is presenting a finger play to her class, or if an older boy or girl is performing for a group of peers, the following points are about all that need be kept in mind.

1. Select a rhyme, verse, or brief story appropriate to the maturity level of the audience.

2. Choose materials that contain "action" and/or dialogue. Many poems and stories will need to be adapted rather than adopted in toto. If a middle-grade youngster is preparing a finger play, the teacher should show him models and give him time and help in preparing his first play.

3. When the finger play is presented by a teacher, the younger children will perform *with* the teacher. Upper-grade boys and girls will *watch* the performance of their classmate.

4. The person giving the finger play faces his audience. A teacher's hand movements are mirrored; that is, a movement of the teacher's right hand is followed by a left hand movement of the children who perform the finger play with her.

5. While performing the finger play, a teacher will recite the verse or action story alone one or two times, after which the children will be ready to repeat the verses with the teacher.

"Finger" puppets can add a new dimension to the finger play. Younger children like to watch the finger puppets or make their own for manipulation; older youngsters like to perform with them, especially as paired performers. Finger puppets come in a number of forms, the two most common being the ring puppet and the thimble puppet or player. The ring puppet is made by cutting out or constructing small scale models of characters, animals, or objects needed to tell a particular story. The model is pasted onto a strip of paper which is made into a form, like a cigar band, that fits the forefinger. The thimble player, with its glued-on model, is a little less fragile than the ring puppet. Thimble puppets can also contribute sound—by rasping them together, as with "Ten Little Grasshoppers"—which is something that cannot be done with ring puppets.

The Mother Goose rhyme "Little Bo-Peep" is shown below, with a description of how it may be adapted for the flannelboard and as a finger play.

As a flannelboard story	*Verse*	*As a finger play*
1. Show Little Bo-Peep standing on side of a hill.	1. Little Bo-Peep has lost her sheep,	1. Hold out both hands with fingers extended.
2. Place sheep, partly hidden, behind the hill.	2. And can't tell where to find them.	2. Put hands behind back.
3. Bring sheep to Little Bo-Peep's feet.	3. Leave them alone and they'll come home,	3. Show hand and extended fingers.
4. Move Bo-Peep to left, then "flutter" walk the sheep across the board toward her.	4. Wagging their tails behind them.	4. Wiggle fingers.

WRITTEN APPROACHES TO LITERATURE

For children, the task of writing original stories or doing written book reports often proves to be a very irksome one. Too many children have had too many teachers give them the standard written book report assignment in the standard way: "Now boys and girls, we will all write our reports using the same report form we used last time. Remember, the report must cover both sides of the paper, no more, no less. And boys and girls, watch your grammar and spelling!" Naturally, children are dissatisfied with this type of assignment as it lacks creativity, recognizes no differences in their interests, and teaches youngsters to dislike literature rather than enjoy it.

If teachers are to encourage children to report on the books they have read and to write some original literature of their own—and they should —the teachers must offer children a variety of approaches. The purpose of this section is to provide some ideas for making such writing more meaningful and enjoyable. Before proceeding, though, let us indicate a few values of using the writing approach to literature and chart a few general tips on how one might go about promoting creative writing among children.

Principles of Writing Literature

Beyond the obvious values of advancing the child's interest in literature and giving him new insights into plots, characters, and themes, there are other advantages to the writing of creative stories or the writing about books and the people who populate them. Briefly, these advantages are:

1. Children derive personal satisfaction from engaging in the creative act itself.
2. Children receive recognition as their creative efforts are shared. This is especially true in an atmosphere where children need not fear comparison (through grades) or failure.
3. Creative writing frequently develops into a hobby for some children, and for others it proves to be the spark that flames into a professional writing career in later life.

The following points on general technique are noteworthy.

1. Very few written reports or original stories are to be expected of individual primary-grade children. Cooperatively developed experience stories based upon literature are, however, worth the time that it takes to develop them.
2. Not all children should be expected to produce the same number, nor quality, of writings about books. But quality is a far loftier goal than quantity.
3. Give children time for writing, allowing them ample opportunity for idea development as well as actual writing. And remember that creative thought cannot be turned on automatically at 1:00 P.M. and shut off at the snap of a finger one half hour later.
4. Maintain a quiet atmosphere for writing. The teacher moves to the children to help with difficult words or ideas not the other way around.
5. Have children share the results of their work, and do evaluate their work. But do not attach letter grades to children's original stories.
6. Don't teach spelling and grammar with first drafts of creative writing of any kind.

7. Do not demand a formal written book report for every book a child reads.

Approaches to Writing About Literature

It is hoped that the written reports or creative stories that children write in conjunction with a literature program will be forceful and stimulating reactions to books they have read, or that the works will be exciting original stories created for a particular occasion. Of course the nature of the presentation will vary with the purpose for which the writing is intended. For example, one written report will be intended to stimulate interest in a particular book, while another report on a work of nonfiction will call for an informative type of report. An original story will be designed to pique the imaginations of the listeners. But whatever the audience, each report should be fresh and stimulating, reflecting the author's true feelings about the literature involved. In short, the written material should not be a rehashing or redoing of a book or story.

The following approaches to writing literature are offered as effective classroom procedures designed to help children share their knowledge of and interest in good books.

"art" writing: There are a number of writing activities that may be combined with various approaches in art. *Package stories* develop when a "mysterious something" (such as a book) is wrapped in a light cloth and displayed before the writing class. The children complete a one-paragraph story about the mystery object, after which it is unveiled. Hilarity ensues when those who have analyzed incorrectly read aloud their descriptions of the shrouded object.

A class *book tree* is constructed from a tree branch set upright in a wastebasket and anchored with stones. Each child folds a small piece of oaktag or construction paper to form a "book." On the front cover, the child records the title and author's name of a real book he has read. On the inside pages the pupil writes a brief book review. He adds an illustration to the outside back page. The "books" are then attached to the book tree by means of a string passed through a hole punched in the corner of the book and then tied to the tree.

Children may design and illustrate full-sized *book jackets* in much the same way as described above. In addition to the written summary of the story, biographical material about the author and illustrator may be placed on the back flap of the jacket.

Still other children may design, illustrate and distribute *handbills* which advertise their favorite books.

booklists: Various types of booklists may be drawn up by individuals or by an entire class. List subjects may include books about Christmas, animals, humorous literature, those that can be purchased for $1.00 or less, and the like. A list of books currently popular with children in a class can be published to form the classes's choice to receive the Newbery prize. Lists may be posted on the bulletin board, backed by a sheet of attractive colored paper.

creative stories: After children have listened to the reading of a tall tale about Tony Beaver or John Henry, they may be in a mood to write an original story. With their enjoyment of exaggeration, children readily create their own tall tales with "stretched out" episodes and characters.

Creative writing may be touched off in other ways, too. The teacher may display a picture from a calendar or magazine, a child's drawing, or a series of two or more pictures from some other sources and then ask the children to write a story about the picture(s). The teacher may wish to discuss the picture with the class, noting the center of activity in the illustration, and listing any useful words related to the picture. The children then choose a particular "one scene-one theme" picture and write their story by (a) selecting and naming the characters they see, (b) constructing the scene, (c) defining the theme, (d) developing the dialogue, and (e) selecting an appropriate title.

Further creative writing experiences may arise from the use of sensory stimuli. After listening to the story of "The Little Engine That Could," children might contribute sentences to a paragraph about the sound a train makes. An actual doughnut-tasting session brought on by a reading of *Homer Price* might be followed by attempts to describe in writing how a doughnut feels, smells, and tastes.

Here are another baker's dozen suggestions for creative book summaries:

1. Write a *legal brief* defending or repudiating the actions of a story character.
2. Write a *character sketch* about a well-known book character. Title it: "My Most Unforgettable Book Character."
3. While listening to a recording of Toscanini, write a three-paragraph *essay* on the book, *The Art of Ancient Rome* (Shirley Glubok).
4. Make a list of ten *facts* learned from reading a particular book of nonfiction.
5. Write a *new ending* to an old favorite.
6. Devise a *literary model* by rewriting a well-known poem as a piece of prose.

7. *Rewrite* a story from literature in which a fairy tale is modernized, or rewrite an episode from a *Henry Huggins* story and place Danny Dunn in the place of Henry.

8. Write a highly *descriptive paragraph* about the leading characters in a book (Julie, Uncle Haskell, Aunt Cordelia, and Danny from *Up A Road Slowly* by Irene Hunt). Read these descriptions aloud to other pupils and let them try to guess the names of the characters described.

9. Write an interview between (a) a book character and author, or (b) two characters in a book.

10. Add another episode or short chapter to a book.

11. Compile a short biographical sketch of an author.

12. Write to an imaginary publisher and tell him you have just completed a manuscript. Describe the story and tell the publisher the type of reader who would enjoy reading the book.

13. Original poems, essays, and stories not exceeding 400 words may be submitted for possible publication to The Horn Book League, The Horn Book, Inc., 585 Boylston Street, Boston, Mass. *Highlights Magazine* also accepts original materials for possible publication if the poems or stories are sent to its Editorial Office in Honesdale, Penn. 18431.

dictation: Various dictation activities make appropriate creative writing procedures in the primary grades. A group book report could take the form of an experience chart story which children compose and dictate to the teacher after she reads to them Virginia Lee Burton's *Mike Mulligan and His Steam Shovel*. Or captions might be dictated for illustrations drawn by individual children.

glossary: Have the class assemble a glossary of unusual words, new words, and the characters' names from a particular type of story being studied (for example, myths). Form a committee to make up a *bingo game* using these words and names, making the individual cards from oaktag, or make a *picture dictionary* to help define the words.

invitations: Writing and addressing invitations to a library tea for parents, at which time a book program will be presented, is an enjoyable experience. The book and poem "title-tilted" invitations are the tickets for admission to the event. An invitation might read:

> *Listen, Rabbit!* There will be a "Tea Party" and a book program in *Miss Hickory's* room (really Miss Scott's room) at 3 P.M. on March 12. *The Duchess Bakes A Cake*, and there will be *Twenty-One Balloons* for all. *Come Hither!*
>
> *Yours Till Niagara Falls,*
> Johnny Bledsoe

journals: A creative writing *notebook, envelope*, or *file* may be maintained by individual children or by the class. A notebook may contain lists of colorful words encountered in reading, "story plot" pictures, story ideas, titles for stories to be written, and the like.

A file box of 3-by-5 cards may be maintained. On each card the children list the title of a book they have read, along with the author's name and a short annotation of each book. These reviews are signed by the individual children, then filed alphabetically and referred to by other children seeking a good book to read.

Children who are reading adventure stories may want to keep a *diary*, recording adventures or accounts of travels mentioned in the stories. A *ship's log* or *pilot's log* may be kept by boys and girls who are reading a sea story or the adventures of an astronaut or airplane pilot, respectively.

A further extension of this idea is seen in the *class storybook*, in which children collect original illustrated stories, riddles, poems, and other creative work and organize the material under such titles as Tall Tales, True Tales, Funny Tales, and the like.

letters: Letters of various types may be composed. One child may write a letter to a friend recommending a particular book, telling what he liked about the book and commenting upon the quality of the illustrations. Another child may drop a note to a book character, such as *Brighty of the Grand Canyon*, questioning Brighty about certain adventures, his master, and his work. Or a class may compose and address a letter to a community librarian requesting that certain books be purchased for the library collection. Whenever practical, letters should be mailed.

Individual children are encouraged to write letters to authors and illustrators in care of the publishers. The child might ask the author questions, tell the author what he liked about a favorite scene or character, share his ideas on a subject broached in the author's book, or send the author a creative story the child has written on the same subject. Care must be exercised to see that only one child in a classroom writes to a given author.

mottoes: Mottoes or *proverbs* to accompany a story may be composed. Girls may illustrate their mottoes by sewing samplers while boys do their mottoes as wood carvings. Or pupils may write one-sentence *morals* to sum up the theme of a chapter or a book.

newspaper: A weekly classroom literature newspaper or monthly *magazine* might be established. Included would be news articles and feature articles (Tom and Becky Are Found!). Other sections of the publication would include advertisements for new books, book review columns, articles about authors, editorials, fashions in literature, cartoons about characters, a society column (reporting on the ball which Cinderella attended), and a lost and found column (Lost: A glass slipper!). One writer might imagine himself as a war correspondent and write a lively account of John Tunis' *Silence Over Dunkerque.* In a related activity, a teacher might inquire to see if a local newspaper would be willing to print an occasional child-written book review in its Sunday supplement.

outlining: Outlining a story very often serves to reinforce in a child's mind the sequence of incidents and their relationship to one another. The procedure to be used in teaching outlining through a book of literature is to have the children: (a) read the story silently; (b) read the story orally; (c) contribute to a teacher-designed phrase outline that is written on the chalkboard; (d) copy the outline; and (e) listen while one pupil tells the story, referring to his copy of the outline, after which the other children point out where their interpretations and understandings of the story differ.

The *story ladder* is another form of story outlining. In this activity, the children are asked to provide endings for a set of sequential step-ladder sentences which, when completed, result in a story. It is not long before the children will be making and exchanging original story ladders like the following:

1. Mildred ran across the lawn toward ....
2. She saw something that was ....
3. Mildred picked up ....
(Six to eight additional line steps are added to bring the story to a satisfying conclusion.)

In another version of the story ladder, each child is asked to originate an outline by preparing a sequential arrangement of questions about the plot of a story.

story bakers: Mix n' match stories are begun when the teacher places in five different cigar boxes a series of essential ingredients for a story cake. There is one set of ingredients for each child in the class or story group. Each child pulls one "ingredient" (slip of paper) from each of the five boxes and writes a story based upon his selections. The five boxes are labeled as shown below, and each contains the requisite number of ingredients—one for each story baker:

1. Central character: a girl, age 11; a druggist; an old man; a teacher; etc.

2. Central character's trait: talkative; bashful; evil; ambitious; etc.
3. Story setting: at home; aboard ship; in a secret tunnel; at a party; etc.
4. Problem: loses jewels; finds a new job; car crashes; loves girl; etc.
5. Outcome; policeman arrives; boy is found; killer is unmasked; club-house is built; etc.

title fun: Titles of books may be the center of the writing activity. Children may prepare an eight-course *menu* of book titles. As a salad they may have *Onion John* by Joseph Krumgold; for dessert they could eat *A Apple Pie* by Kate Greenaway.

Children can make up an *alphabet* of animal names from book titles: *Alligators All Around* by Maurice Sendak, *First Book of Bears* by Robert Whitehead, *Millions of Cats* by Wanda Gag, and so forth. Book-title category activities are plentiful: girls' names (beginning with *Alice's Adventures in Wonderland* by Lewis Carroll); clothing (*Ballet Shoes* by Noel Streatfeild); colors (*Big Red* by Jim Kjelgaard): and so on.

Riddles and *Rhymes* about titles of books may be constructed, as well as conundrums about characters, authors, and book plots.

unfinished story: Completing an unfinished story is often a help-ful step along the way to creative writing for the slow starters who are devoid of ideas for launching a story. Less able writers may need no more than a one-word title to get started, while others may want a be-ginning paragraph, such as the following:

> At the first stroke of midnight, Padric woke from his restless sleep. Against the face of the grandfather clock, the moon shone bright as day. Mirrored in the clock's face was the head of a strange little man.
> "Come, Padric," said the little man. "Hurry! Time waits for no one."
> Padric jumped from his bed, ran to the grandfather clock, and ....

traditional reports: Many children are asked to make periodic written book reports on a rather standard or traditional report form. Teachers justify these reports on the grounds that they help children develop skill in analyzing literature, that they encourage other children to read the same books, that they further the writer's own reading, and that they develop in a child the ability to write creatively. To some degree, all of these statements are true. But any teacher who repeatedly employs one such form, month in and year out, will probably drive children away from accomplishing any of the goals outlined above.

Success in using a written book report form periodically lies in recog-nizing that children differ in chronological age and mental maturity—that young children cannot make adequate reports if they lack the basic writing skills, and that differing reading and writing abilities among older boys and girls warrant giving assignments of a different number and character to different children. Further, the nature of the book that has been read should have some bearing upon the form the report takes; one should not expect a child to write the same type of report on a book of fiction that he does upon a book of nonfiction, a biography, a classic, or a book of poetry. Insofar as possible, adherence to a traditional reporting form or technique should utilize as much variation and adaptation of the form and the system as is feasible.

The forms to be used for the traditional written book report may be outlined on the chalkboard, printed on permanent charts, or mimeographed in quantity and distributed. Following are some forms that have been used by teachers.

1. **Primary-grade form (fiction)**
   My name: .... Book title: ....
   Author's name: .... Main character's name: ....
   What is the story about? ....
   ....
   Part I liked best: ....
   ....
   A favorite picture (below or on the back of the paper)

2. **Primary-grade form (nonfiction)**
   My name: .... Date: ....
   Book title: .... Author's name: ....
   The book was about ....
   ....
   An important fact I learned was ....
   ....
   I would or would not (underline one) recommend this book because ....
   ....

3. **Check sheet form (for primary-grade children or less-able readers)**
   My name: .... My age: .... My grade: ....
   Title of book: .... Author's name: ....
   Number of pages: .... Illustrator's name: ....
   Kind of book (check one): Fiction .... Nonfiction: ....

This book: (check one box in each column)

☐ Is one of my favorites.	☐ Is too hard.	☐ Not much happened.
☐ Is a good book.	☐ Is just right.	☐ Was all right.
☐ Is not interesting.	☐ Is too easy.	☐ Was good.
☐ I did not like.		☐ Was great!

It was a book of: (check one or more)

☐ adventure	☐ fables	☐ information	☐ poems
☐ animals	☐ fairies	☐ mystery-detective	☐ science
☐ autobiography	☐ geography	☐ myths-legends	☐ science fiction
☐ biography	☐ history	☐ nature	☐ short stories

4. Primary-grade form (convertible to intermediate-grade use when the questions are phrased to demand longer, more explanatory answers)

My name: .... My age: ....

My grade: .... Date: ....

Name of book: ....

1. Is this story true?   Yes ☐   No ☐   (check one)

2. The book is about (check one): Animals .... Mystery .... History ....
   Adventure .... Science .... Other (name) ....

3. Which person did you like best? ....

4. Name a character you did not like. ....

5. Was the book funny?   Yes ☐   No ☐   Tell why. ....
   ....

6. What place does the book tell about? ....

7. What did the book teach you? ....

8. Would you like to read this book again?   Yes ☐   No ☐
   Why? Why not? ....

9. Could children act out this book?   Yes ☐   No ☐
   Why or why not? ....

10. Who wrote the book? ....

11. Who drew the pictures? ....

5. Intermediate-grade form (fiction)

Name: Jack Delaney

Title: Onion John

Author: Joseph Krumgold

Publishing date: 1959

Setting: When: about ten years ago

        Where: small town called Serenity, New Jersey

Plot: The author pretends this is a story that happened when he was twelve years old. He writes in the first person as if he were remembering exactly how he felt then. He is Andy Jr. and is Onion John's best friend. Andy has many interesting adventures with Onion John and these adventures help him grow up.

Characters: **Andy Jr.:** A star player in Little League, Andy helps his dad in the
(main)   hardware store. Because he is kind and helpful he discovers
                              that he is the only one who can understand Onion John.

           Onion John: This man came from a far-away country to make his home in
                              Serenity. He speaks little English; most of the time he sounds
                              as if he is speaking "a high speed language full of x's and
                              z's." He has strange ways and works as a handyman. He is
                              independent, hardworking, and lonely. He makes friends with
                              Andy and his gang.

Evaluation: Grade level 5–8 For boys_____For girls_____Both____ # ____
              Easy to read____ # ____Difficult to read_____
Type: Humorous____ # ____Serious _____Factual_____
Pictures: Some____ # ____Many_____Black and white____ # ____Color_____

6. Intermediate-grade form (fiction)

   1. Title: The 500 Hats of Bartholomew Cubbins 2. Author: Dr. Seuss

   3. Publisher: The Vanguard Press, New York 4. Publication Date: 1938

   5. What is it about? This story is about Bartholomew Cubbins and the 500 hats
      that he couldn't keep off his head. Bartholomew's life was
      saved by his beautiful 500th hat. The King bought it for 500
      gold pieces.

   6. Where and when does the story take place? The story takes place many years
      ago in the Kingdom of Didd.

   7. Describe one of the characters: Bartholomew Cubbins is a happy, soon-to-be-sad
      boy who was just as surprised as the King to see one hat
      after another appear on his head.

   8. What is your honest opinion of this book? This is a funny picture book. I really
      liked it.

   9. The book is for: boys .... girls .... both ...X.... in grades ....1-5....

   10. The book is: funny ...X... serious .... factual ....

   11. The book is: easy ...X... hard .... to read.

   12. Pictures: some .... many ...X... in b & w ...X.... color ....(red hats).....

   13. Name: Ruth Fenton

7. Intermediate-grade open-end form (fiction)
   Have you read *Mr. Popper's Penguins* by Richard and Florence Atwater? If you haven't . . . you should.

I'm Captain Cook, born and raised in Antarctica. Only gradually did I get to like living in Stillwater with the Popper family. Once they converted the refrigerator into comfortable nesting quarters, and winter arrived to change the living room into an icy toboggan-room, I felt more at home. You will want to read about how Mr. Popper became world-famous with his penguin act, too. (That's me and my family!)

Actually, I'm the main character in this book. But Mr. Popper sometimes steals the show. I was his bird— and became his problem.

This book is for boys and girls, grades 4-6.
It is *very* funny, and *easy* to read.
Mr. Popper's Penguins is a good book to read aloud; show Robert Lawson's illustrations, too!

Form developed by: Sister Mary Assisi, I.B.V.M., student, Sacramento State College, California.

8. Intermediate-grade open-end form (fiction)
   Complete the following statements by writing no less than two sentences about each statement.
   a. *This book made me decide that. . . .*
   b. *This book made me realize that. . . .*
   c. *This book made me wish that. . . .*
   d. *The author showed admiration for (name of character) when. . . .*
   e. *The author showed pity for (name of character) when. . . .*
   f. *The author enjoyed a laugh with (name of character) when. . . .*

9. Intermediate-grade form (nonfiction)
   Title of book: .... *Illustrator:* ....
   Author's name: .... *Publisher:* ....
   My name: .... *Copyright date:* ....
   Subject of the book: ....
   ....
   Most interesting information: ....
   ....
   My opinion of the book: ....
   ....

10. Intermediate-grade open-end form (nonfiction)

Our Senses and How They Work
by Herbert S. Zim
Illustrated by Herschel Wartik

This is an accurate, factual science book for fifth and sixth graders. The book is easy to read, and the illustrations make what Dr. Zim is writing about easy to see.

See

The book tells about the wonder of the human senses. How do we see a beautiful sunset?

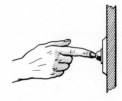

Taste

Can you tell the difference between a strawberry that is sour and one that is ripe?

Smell

How does the aroma of a delicious apple pie travel from the kitchen to your nose—and make your mouth water?

Touch

Would we be better off without a sense of touch, so that we would not feel hot and cold objects, or is it necessary for man that this sense be developed?

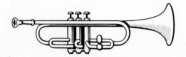

Hear

How does the brain operate the controls of all these senses?

For the questioning, curious boy and girl: *Our Senses and How They Work* has the answers.

Form developed by Sister Mary Assisi, I.B.V.M., student, Sacramento State College, California.

11. Intermediate-grade form (biography)

Title of book: .... *Author:* ....

My name: .... *Number of pages:* ....

Publisher: .... *Date of publication:* ....

The central figure of the book is ....

Where did he live? .... *When did he live?* ....

The outstanding positive characteristics of this person were ....

....

How did this characteristic make possible the subject's accomplishments? ....

....

The subject had to overcome the following problem(s): ....

....

The high point of the story was when ....

....

What proof do you have that the author (biographer) was qualified to write this story? ....

....

A BANG-UP idea for writing stories. Design a large sign with the words "Story Boxes" on it. Place the sign above a table upon which are placed two boxes. One box is labeled "Ideas-In!" From it children may select slips of paper upon which are story-starter phrases based upon children's book characters: "Henry and Beezus started . . ."; "Jack and Jill went up a . . . ."; "One day *Alphonse, That Bearded One* took . . . ." After these phrases have been developed into stories, they are deposited in a slitted box labeled "Ideas–Out!" This box is opened once a week and the stories are read aloud.

A BANG-UP idea for promoting wide reading. Literature passports are constructed from oaktag by each child. The titles of books that they have read represent each country visited. When a book has been read, a dated rubber stamp is pressed alongside its title and the title is entered into the passport book.

SELECTED LIST OF MATERIALS AND
RESOURCES FOR THE TEACHER

Oral Reports—Books

Applegate, Mauree, EASY IN ENGLISH. New York: Harper & Row, Publishers, 1960.

Children's Book Council, AUTHORS AND ARTISTS AVAILABLE FOR PROGRAMS. New York: The Council, n.d. Pamphlet listing of available speakers organized by states and by regions of the country.

Cortright, Rupert, and George Hinds, CREATIVE DISCUSSION. New York: The Macmillan Company, 1959.

Courts, Ann, TEACHING LANGUAGE ARTS CREATIVELY. Minneapolis: T.S. Denison & Co., Inc., 1965. Booklet.

Gillespie, John, and Diana Lembo, JUNIOR PLOTS: A MANUAL FOR BOOK TALKS. New York: R.R. Bowker Co., 1967. Plot Summaries of 80 books for young people 9 to 16.

Huckleberry, Alan W., and Edward S. Strother, SPEECH EDUCATION FOR THE ELEMENTARY TEACHER. Boston: Allyn and Bacon, Inc., 1966.

Pronovost, Wilbert, THE TEACHING OF SPEAKING AND LISTENING. New York: David McKay Company, Inc., 1959.

Rasmussen, Carrie, SPEECH METHODS IN THE ELEMENTARY SCHOOL. New York: The Ronald Press Company, 1949.

Sansom, Clive, SPEECH IN THE PRIMARY SCHOOL. London: A & C Black, Ltd., 1965.

Wolfe, Don M., LANGUAGE ARTS AND LIFE PATTERNS. New York: The Odyssey Press, Inc., 1961.

Oral Reports—Films and Filmstrips

Coronet Films, Chicago.
PREPARING YOUR BOOK REPORT. (MP). 11 min. For grades 4–7.
Educational Audio Visuals, Inc., Pleasantville, N.Y.
A set of 32 transparencies and guide on stimulating imaginative compositions. For grades 4–8.

Finger Plays—Books

Ellis, Mary, FINGER PLAY APPROACH TO DRAMATIZATION. Minneapolis: T.S. Denison & Co., Inc., 1961. Booklet.

———, FINGER PLAYTIME. Minneapolis; T.S. Denison & Co., Inc., 1963. Booklet.

Grayson, M., compiler, LET'S DO FINGERPLAYS. New York: R.B. Luce, c/o David McKay Company, Inc., 1962.

————, and F. Lyons, FINGER PLAYTIME. Minneapolis; T.S. Denison & Co., Inc., 1960.

Scott, Louise Binder, and J.J. Thompson, RHYMES FOR FINGERS AND FLAN-NELBOARDS. St. Louis: Webster Publishing Co., 1960.

Flannelboard—Books

Anderson, Paul S., and Irene S. Francis, STORYTELLING WITH THE FLANNEL BOARD. Minneapolis: T.S. Denison & Co., Inc., 1963.

Di Sarro, Lucy, LET'S MAKE AND USE THE FLANNEL BOARD. Minneapolis: T.S. Denison & Co., Inc., Booklet.

Koskey, Thomas, HOW TO MAKE AND USE FLANNEL BOARDS. San Francisco: Fearon Publishers, 1961.

Osborn, Merton, THE FLANNEL BOARD. Redlands, Calif.: Merton B. Osborn, Box 3, 1956. Booklet.

Scott, Louise Binder, STORIES THAT STICK ON THE FLANNELBOARD. Dansville, N.Y.: F. A. Owen Publishing Co., 1959. Booklet.

Flannelboard—Films and Filmstrips

Association Films, New York.
THE MAGIC OF THE FLANNELBOARD. (MP). 20 min. For use in grades 4–8.
Audio-Visual Consultation Bureau, Wayne State University, Detroit.
THE FELTBOARD IN TEACHING. (MP). 10 min. For use in grades 4–8.
Bailey Films, Hollywood.
FLANNELBOARDS AND HOW TO USE THEM. (MP). 15 min. For grades 6–10.
Ohio State University Audio-Visual Center, Columbus, Ohio.
HOW TO MAKE AND USE THE FELTBOARD. (FS). For use in grades 4–8.
University of Minnesota, Minneapolis.
FLANNELGRAPH. (MP). 27 min. For use in grades 6–10.

Flannelboard—Related Material

Instructo Products Co., Philadelphia. "Favorite Stories: Flannel Board Aids." Character and scenery cutouts of seven well-known stories (e.g., "Ginger Bread Boy"). For grades K–1.

Written Reports—Books

Barbe, Walter, compiler, CREATIVE WRITING ACTIVITIES. Columbus, Ohio: Highlights for Children, 1965. Individual and group writing activities in single copies or pupil packs (five booklets in all).

Carlson, Ruth K., SPARKLING WORDS: TWO HUNDRED PRACTICAL AND CRE-

ATIVE WRITING IDEAS. Champaign, Ill.: National Council of Teachers of English. 1965. Booklet.

Christensen, Fred B., and Hope M. Scrogin, RECIPES FOR CREATIVE WRITING. Santa Fe Springs, Calif.: Creative Teaching Press, Inc., n.d. Over 100 4 x 6 cards covering motivation, story-starters, plot ideas, writing techniques, and evaluation.

"Imagine and Write." Columbus, Ohio: MY WEEKLY READER. A creative writing program consisting of four, 48-page booklets and a 32-page Teacher's Guide. For grades 3–6.

Petty, Walter T., and Mary E. Bowen, SLITHERY SNAKES AND OTHER AIDS TO CHILDREN'S WRITING. New York: Appleton-Century-Crofts, 1967.

Tiedt, Sidney, and Iris Tiedt, CREATIVE WRITING IDEAS. San Jose, Calif.; Contemporary Press, P.O. Box 1524, 1964. Booklet.

Ullyette, Jean M., GUIDELINES FOR CREATIVE WRITING. Dansville, N.Y.: F. A. Owen Publishing Co., 1963. Booklet.

Written Reports—Films, Filmstrips, and Tapes

Audio-Visual Center, University of Michigan, Ann Arbor, Mich.

"Authors for All." A series of taped interviews with children's authors, illustrators, poets, and editors of children's books. (Send for catalog.)

Coronet Films, Chicago.

HOW TO WRITE EFFECTIVELY. (MP). 11 min. For grades 6–9.

CHAPTER SIX

Appreciating Literature Through the Creative Arts

The interpretation of literature through dramatization and art is often the outgrowth of children's delight in a book or story that they have encountered. It is the nature of children that when they have had their imaginations stimulated by a story, they want to do something with it: to present it as a dramatic production or to interpret it through an art medium. For in these two forms of endeavor, the children find an outlet for their creative bents and a locus for their desires to *do*.

There are many opportunities for the teacher to fuse children's interests in literature, drama, and art. Dramatization of literature and the interpretation of literature through creative construction are often directly interrelated. For example, certain forms of drama, such as informal dramatizations and pantomimes, may call for the construction of simple properties to be contributed by the children. Nor can plans for a puppet show go forward until the figures to be manipulated have been artfully made by the children.

Of course dramatization and art also may be utilized as an individual activity to support and enhance the literature program. Dramatization may take the form of rhythms, pantomimes, puppet plays, informal dramatizations, and so on. With respect to art, numerous opportunities should be presented and materials made available in order that children can demonstrate their knowledge and appreciation of book settings and characters through handwork of all kinds: in constructing dioramas, in making literature maps, in building mobiles and the like.

This chapter notes the advantages of children interpreting literature through dramatizations and artistic expression. It first presents a series of principles that reveal the common elements shared by drama and the arts as they relate to children's literature. The main body of the chapter is devoted to a description of various drama and art experiences that are suitable for use in the literature class.

PRINCIPLES OF A CREATIVE ARTS PROGRAM

The utilization of dramatization and art activities in conjunction with a literature program will add zest to the daily teaching routine while increasing children's understandings and appreciations of literature. The teacher will want to keep in mind the following points as she proceeds with the program.

1. Interpreting literature through the creative arts helps children acquire skill in the use of the various media and modes of expression. If the work is in art, the children have an opportunity to use the various tools of art and to sharpen their skills and appreciations by working in the various media. Creative dramatics provides them with the opportunity to develop good speech qualities—audibility, clarity, flexibility—while acquiring the basic dramatic movements such as body control, correct posture, and stage movement.

2. Using drama and art in conjunction with the literature program provides children with an opportunity to reflect and think creatively about their literature experiences, and then to express themselves as individuals. Every child needs an outlet for free, honest, original expression, and the avenues are available in the form of appropriate artistic and dramatic activities.

3. Art and drama will add a new dimension to books, stories, and poems. As children watch a puppet show based upon Rachel Field's *Calico Bush* or look at a friend's mobile depicting *John Billington, Friend of Squanto* by Clyde Bulla, they will see the characters, plots, settings, and themes of their favorite stories in a new light.

4. Children learn to cooperate and interact socially as they participate in the drama and art portions of the literature program. Both areas provide children with opportunities to participate in meaningful group activities, to appreciate the contributions of classmates, to share materials, and to contribute, in general, to the advancement of the group's general well-being.

5. Dramatization in particular develops in children an increased ability to evaluate dramatic literature and dramatic acting. Television, movies, and children's theatre increasingly use the best children's books as vehicles to teach and delight children, giving youngsters an opportunity to compare these productions with what they have read in the books.

In summary, literature experiences with both art and drama should assist pupils in developing their powers of observation and evaluation in order that the children may learn to apply them in present and future encounters with book characters, plots, themes, and settings.

DRAMATIC ARTS

The dramatization of literature begins in the primary grades as children react naturally to creative rhythms, engage in unstructured dramatic play, and participate in pantomimes, puppet shows, and shadow plays. These last three activities continue to be a part of the dramatic arts program in the intermediate grades. Along the way children also develop an interest in informal dramatization of stories from literature, and in an occasional production of a formal play. A discussion of each of these forms of dramatization is entered into below. A list of ten Bang-up ideas for dramatic interpretation is also included.

Creative Rhythms

Creative rhythms dominate the drama portion of a kindergarten program. The rhythms spring naturally from boys and girls as they express their thoughts and feelings through such fundamental body movements as skipping, jumping, galloping, and hopping. A teacher does not usually have to teach creative rhythms. All she does is serve as a catalyst for such creativity by giving children the run of their own imaginations and feelings. At times the teacher may want to facilitate children's rhythmic interpretations by playing some musical instrument or by providing a recording of background music as the children dance like ghosts after reading *Georgie* by Robert Bright or skip like rabbits after listening to the teacher read *The Velveteen Rabbit* by Margery Bianco.

Dramatic Play

In the primary grades, dramatic play is a natural part of the school day and a suitable companion to a program in creative rhythms, for it makes use of children's rhythmic responses and their natural bodily movements, facial expressions, and gestures. In dramatic play, children act out the daily dramas of life: delivering the milk or the mail, impersonating a tiger or a train, play-acting as a father or a fawn.

Dramatic play may be instigated by any occurrence in a classroom. It may arise spontaneously or may stem from a literature situation. For example, after the reading of the story *Little Toot* by Hardie Gramatky, one teacher asked her class: "Who can steam out of the harbor like *Little Toot?*" As it turned out, there were some 35 Little Toots in that classroom, each with a different way of "steaming" and, of course, each with a different "toot."

Dramatic play may arise during the show-and-tell period as a child recites a newly learned nursery rhyme for the class:

> Little Miss Muffet
> Sat on a tuffet (explain!),
> Eating her curds and whey (explain!);
> Along came a spider,
> Who sat down beside her
> And frightened
> Miss Muffet away.

What a wonderful experience for the children who are called upon to give their interpretation of this verse in pantomimed dramatic play as a beaming boy is asked by the teacher to "tell it again while all the other children act it out." Reciting or reading aloud the Mother Goose rhymes may frequently give rise to dramatic play in which one or more children act out, with or without dialogue, a well-known story situation.

Pantomime

Pantomime as related to literature is the interpretation of characters, book plots, and story situations without the use of dialogue. Pantomime can be employed and enjoyed by children at every grade level, with kindergarten and preschool children engaging in its simplest form— single incident interpretations—and older youngsters participating in pantomime plays, the most complex of all the pantomime productions. Between these two performance types lie other commonly used pantomime activities which can be used from primary grades through junior high school: the group, pair, and individual pantomimes.

The kindergarten teacher is not introducing anything completely new when she directs children's attention to the art of pantomime. Very small children practice it spontaneously every day as they engage in dramatic play with their peers. The Mother Goose rhymes and other simple poems that have a lively lilt to them provide a fine backdrop for the interpretation of literature through pantomime for these children. For example, the possibilities for silent interpretation are readily seen in this nursery rhyme:

> One, two, buckle my shoe;
> Three, four, knock at the door;
> Five, six, pick up the sticks. . . .

The teacher would introduce the above rhyme by demonstrating the actions that might accompany each line. Children must be taught that the mark of an effective pantomime is that it is precisely and clearly presented and that it is easy to identify. Often children get the erroneous impression that the well-performed pantomime is one in which the audience has been fooled and no one has been able to guess the pantomime. The teacher would not want to linger too long on explanations, however, as small children are activity oriented and eager to give their own interpretations of "Seven, eight, lay them straight."

If older pupils are unfamiliar with pantomiming, there will be a natural hesitancy on their part to engage in such drama. These barriers may be overcome by teacher demonstration and by the adoption of a "game" atmosphere during initial exercises. The teacher's demonstration of a situation from literature should be made up of large-movement gestures and action, and easily recognized characters and scenes: Tom Sawyer fishing, William Tell shooting the apple from his son's head, and so forth. Having the children guess the situation may be conducted under the banner of a game entitled "Who Am I?" or "Secret Scene."

Group pantomimes are the best introductory activities for self-conscious children or older children who are unfamiliar with pantomiming. In a group performance no one person is in the spotlight alone. Group scenes from literature—the seven dwarfs trying to awaken Snow White; Dr. Dolittle, Chee-Chee, Dab-Dab and the *Dr. Dolittle* characters packing to go off to Africa—provide good introductory material.

Pair pantomimes are situations performed by two youngsters: Peter Rabbit's encounter with Mr. McGregor; the frolicking of the gingham dog and the calico cat from Eugene Field's poem "The Duel," or the scene where Danny must *Ask Mr. Bear*. Pair pantomimes constitute a big step up from group pantomimes, for now there are only two performers. But even in this type of pantomime some children remain self-conscious. Any embarrassment may be ameliorated by having a fluent reader read aloud the portion of the story being enacted.

Confidence gained in doing group and pair pantomimes should lead children to individual pantomimes of literature characters and scenes.

A teacher should establish a climate in which individual pantomimes are offered voluntarily by the children. In these solo performances we may see Paul Bunyan chopping down a forest, Casey at the Bat, or Homer Price mixing doughnut batter.

A pantomime play, sometimes called a tableau, may involve the total class or a small group in a performance. The play may go forward in a fluid, continuous pantomime or it may be posed in a series of separate, still frames as in a picture. The tableau story line may be advanced by a narrator, a choral group, a ballad set to original music and sung by a group, or a combination of these. Costumes and simple properties may enhance the performance. Pantomime play scenes may arise from such literature sources as "Jack and the Beanstalk," "Hansel and Gretel," *The Story of Ferdinand, What Can You Do With a Shoe,* "The Four Musicians," *Treasure Island, Millions of Cats* (many possibilities for ingenious cats!), and *The Matchlock Gun* (for the active boys). All the children can be involved by (1) allowing groups of two or three pupils to prepare different pantomimes, or (2) having different groups work out the same situation so that comparisons can be made.

The game approach to pantomime has great appeal to children. Four pantomime games are described here.

1. In *title charades* the class is divided into two teams. Each team sends a pantomimist to look at a book title the teacher has written down on a slip of paper. At a signal the actors begin to pantomime the title for their group. The team guessing the title first scores a point. A time limit is imposed. A second pair of pantomimists then interprets a second title, and so on.

2. A *pantomime box*, which may be real or imaginary, is "carried" to the front of the room. From it a child takes out an imaginary object which he uses in a pantomime—Eeyore's tail, *The Enormous Egg, Jimmy's Own Basketball*. The children are allowed three guesses to identify the object. The one who guesses correctly then gets to select another make-believe item from the box and describe it by his motions. If no one guesses the object correctly, a new pantomimist is appointed.

3. *Short paragraphs* are read from literature. Three children are asked to pantomime the part. The child who gave the best interpretation—by class vote—gets to elect a pantomimist for the next excerpt. From Arna Bontemps' *The Fast Sooner Hound* we might have an interpretation of this scene:

> The Boomer didn't answer. He just threw his head back into the cab and began to shovel coal. He shoveled without much spirit, shaking his head sadly.

4. For *story-team pantomimes*, the class is divided into teams and given 15 minutes to prepare a story for pantomiming. Every member of the team must participate as each team presents its story to the other teams. The winning team is selected from ratings by the other teams (15 points for excellent to 5 points for adequate). Familiar stories are best: "The Three Little Pigs," "Chicken Little," or "Henny Penny."

Children find pantomime activities to be genuine fun, and literature comes alive as children give lifelike reenactments of situations and characters from books and stories. This is especially true if the teacher is willing to demonstrate techniques through her own pantomimes, and if she shows sincerity and empathy with the children in their interpretations of characters and scenes.

Puppets

The types of puppets that can be made and the stories that can be adapted to puppet drama are many and varied.

The word "puppet" describes two types of hand-manipulated, artificial figures: (1) *puppet*, a doll worked directly by hand, and (2) *marionette*, a doll operated by strings. Most grade-school children will find puppetry more enjoyable if they stay with the simple puppets and leave the marionettes to junior and senior high school students. As a matter of fact, marionettes will not be considered within the scope of this book, although admittedly they can be used by skillful children at the upper

range of the elementary grades. But no matter what type of puppet is constructed—whether it be a hand, rod, or simple string puppet—nor by what age child, too much time must not be taken in constructing the puppets. If this is done it detracts from the fun of telling and interpreting the story and manipulating the figures.

The first requisite for a puppet show is the selection of a good story to be played. For purposes of illustration, let us suppose a class chooses to produce a puppet show based upon L. Frank Baum's *The Wizard of Oz*. More specifically, let us say they have decided to interpret the chapter entitled "The Discovery of Oz, the Terrible." The book (and this scene) is a good one to convert to a puppet play because it contains the necessary ingredients for a successful puppet play: (1) considerable lively dialogue, with many brief monologues; (2) a fast-moving plot (necessary because the facial features of the puppets remain frozen during the performance and the action of the play must hold the audience's attention); (3) several playlets which can be drawn from the same book; (4) "speeches" which the children can convert to their own words; (5) no more than three to five puppeteers required on stage at one time; (6) a few simple settings; and (7) characters who are recognized by children of many different age and grade levels.

Once the book and/or its story situations have been selected, the type of puppets to be constructed must be decided upon. A series of teacher-led discussions will help determine this. At the same time decisions will need to be made about types of costumes and about how to give the puppets expressive faces. This latter point is most important. A puppet's face is focal, as the body is relatively immobile and lacks individuality unless "character" is built into the eyes, nose, mouth, facial contours, and hair. We don't expect the Cowardly Lion to look *exactly* as he is pictured in a book. Being that "real" would detract from the charm a child would bestow upon him. But he still must look like a Cowardly Lion, or at least a lion.

Dorothy, Tin Woodman, Cowardly Lion, Scarecrow, and Oz, the Terrible will take the form of hand (glove) puppets, which consist of a head and a small costume that fits over the head of the figure. These puppets can be fashioned from almost every conceivable kind of material including balls (rubber, tennis), bars of soap, corncobs, darning eggs, driftwood, fists (with features painted on), fruits (apple, banana), gourds and other seed pods, light bulbs, milk cartons, potato mashers, pine cones, soft drink bottles, spoons, tin cans, vegetables (carrot, potato, turnip), and wood scraps. Five other commonly made hand puppets based upon our chosen characters are sketched below, along with brief directions as to how to build them and a list of materials needed to construct them.

Materials:
Paper bag, paint or crayons, paper or cloth scraps, other decorative material (such as straw to make Scarecrow).

Instructions:
Color in features, making mouth opening fall on the fold of the bag. Clothe the puppet in torn paper *glued* on, or dress him in bits of fur or leather. Glue on straw for hair.

**Paper Bag Puppet
(of Scarecrow)**

Materials:
Clay, newsprint or paper toweling, wallpaper paste, Vaseline.

Instructions:
Mold the head from clay. Grease with Vaseline. Dip paper strips into wallpaper paste and lay layers over head mold. Let dry. Cut in half, remove the clay, and paper the two halves together again.

**Papier Mache Head
for Puppet
(of Oz)**

Materials:
Paper towel roll, poster paint, papier mache head, strips of colored paper, velvet, a ring.

Instructions:
Form head (from papier mache) around paper towel roll. Paint on face. Glue on paper "hair" strips. Make the dress from velvet. Convert the ring into a necklace.

**Paper Towel Tube Puppet
(of Dorothy)**

Materials:
Old sock, pieces of cotton or cloth, buttons.

Instructions:
Stuff the sock with cotton or cloth. Sew on strips of cloth for ears. Sew on buttons for features. Add strips of shredded cloth for mane.

Sock Puppet
(of Cowardly Lion)

Materials:
Wooden spoon, paint, can, paper scraps, cone. (Or make the whole figure from tin cans of various sizes, laced together with string.)

Instructions:
Paint a face on a large wooden spoon. Clothe the puppet in a "can" or cloth costume. Add the cone as a hat.

Wooden Spoon Puppet
(of Tin Woodman)

A plentiful supply of materials, inventively used, is the key to making functional hand puppets. The DO's and the DON'T's of hand puppetry materials might be: DO make puppet hair from crepe paper, scouring pads, steel wool, and yarn. DON'T use paste on anything, use glue. DO make puppet hands from wire, pipe cleaners, asbestos, sponges, and styrofoam. DON'T use expensive materials. DO have available lots of materials of various kinds: foil, screws, hooks, paper clips, sandpaper, coat hangers, paints, paper, old jewelry, tape, thread, buttons, beads, and tacks. DON'T bother with small details on puppets such as eyelashes and nail polish. DO provide children with saws, scissors, knives, hammers, files, pliers, and rulers.

Making Dorothy and her friends as rod or stick puppets would be quite easy, too. We would start with original drawings, cutouts from magazines and old books, or clothbags or paper bags stuffed with torn paper. We would then back the lighter materials with oaktag, draw on any other features we desired and then staple, tack, tie, or otherwise fasten the characters to a broomstick, cardboard roll, dowel rod, rolled newspaper, pencil, piece of plywood, stick, tongue depressor, yardstick, or any rodlike object.

Further, our "Oz" puppets could be constructed as string puppets. Any of the hand or rod puppets described above, if left dancing at the end of a string, could actually be called string puppets. But from the standpoint of materials, there are other kinds of string puppets, too. A paper cup string puppet of Dorothy could be manufactured by collecting paper cups of various sizes, letting the largest represent the body of the girl, the next largest the head, and so on. These could be threaded together loosely with string. Similar Oz character string puppets could be made from various size boxes, cans, pine cones, corks, seed pods, nut shells, paper bags, and spools.

Finally, the characters need a stage upon which to act. The stage for a puppet show will probably be right at hand in a classroom. A long table turned on its side will do, as will a chair, a card table, or even an open doorway. On the overturned piece of furniture, for example, a curtain can be stretched from leg to leg and supported by a window pole. The same curtain might be hung across the doorway. Other workable stages may be constructed from plywood, orange crates or a large appliance box. In making a refrigerator box stage, cut *back* the upper half of the front of the box so the puppets may be shown and cut *out* the lower half at the back of the box so the puppeteers can enter from the rear. Large boxes should be anchored with stones so they will not tip over.

To improve the over-all effect of the production, you can decorate the puppet stage, both inside and out, and install a string of Christmas-tree bulbs or a strong flashlight or electric lantern to serve as a source of lighting. On a puppet stage properties must be kept to a minimum. In the case of our scene from the Wizard of Oz, the inside of the Wizard's castle might be painted on. But the Tin Woodman's ax may be cut from some rigid material and set in clay on the stage or attached to the puppet's hands by a magnet-to-magnet arrangement. Sound effects, such as the Cowardly Lion's roar, may come from a puppeteer speaking into a can. And the crashing screen, behind which the Wizard had been hiding, may be effected by slapping a yardstick against a table top, and so on.

Manipulating the puppets and staging the show are all important, and the children will learn much through experience. If children adhere to the following half dozen ground rules, a successful production is likely to emerge:

1. Each puppet scene should be rehearsed at least once, since speaking lines and manipulating puppets at the same time are difficult tasks.
2. Children should devote some time to developing different "character" voices. The Tin Woodman must have a voice pitched at a different level than that of the Cowardly Lion.
3. Improvisation and free interpretation of story dialogue are to be preferred to memorization.
4. If at all possible, involve the audience in an occasional dialogue exchange.
5. While they are on stage, have the puppets engage in some "business" rather than having them remain completely motionless. When the puppets leave the stage, have them walk off the stage, rather than having them jerked out of sight.
6. Employ a good sound effects man and a capable prompter.

There is an ample supply of prose and poetry which can be adapted for puppet drama. The following selections are recommended because, generally, they meet the seven characteristics of a good puppet story advanced earlier in this section.

Primary	*Intermediate*
1. Andy and the Lion (James Daugherty)	1. Aladdin and other Arabian Nights' Tales
2. Angus and the Ducks (Marjorie Flack)	2. Charlotte's Web (E.B. White)
3. Babar stories (Jean de Brunhoff)	3. A Christmas Carol (Charles Dickens)
4. Hansel and Gretel	4. The Dark and Bloody Ground: Stories of the American Frontier (Phyllis Fenner)
5. The Little Red Hen	5. The Enormous Egg (Oliver Butterworth)
6. Mother Goose verses	6. Fairy Tales (Hans Christian Andersen)
7. The Runaway Bunny (Margaret Wise Brown)	7. Gone is Gone (Wanda Gag)
8. Snipp, Snapp, Snurr stories (Maj Lindman)	8. Johnny Tremain (Esther Forbes)
9. Story of Ferdinand (Munro Leaf)	9. Judy's Journey (Lois Lenski)
10. Any of the "Three" Stories (Bears, Pigs, Goats Gruff)	10. Just So Stories (Rudyard Kipling)

11. Tiger in the Cherry Tree
(Glen Dines)
12. Winnie-the-Pooh
(A. A. Milne)

11. The Lion, the Witch, and the
Wardrobe (C.S. Lewis)
12. The Merry Adventures of
Robin Hood (Howard Pyle)
13. Thee Hannah! (Marguerite
de Angeli)
14. Treasure Island (Robert Louis
Stevenson)
15. Wind in the Willows (Kenneth Grahame)

Shadow Play

Whether puppets or human figures are used, the shadow play or shadow pantomime is suitable at any grade level. In this drama the human figures either stand or hold puppets behind a screen, upon which a strong light throws their shadows. Stories chosen for shadow play interpretation should contain certain essentials: action, considerable dialogue, an attention-holding plot, and distinctive characters and settings. In particular, the successful shadow play must have well-defined silhouette figures and settings: Pinocchio, big-horned Thidwick, Heidi's mountain homeland.

When the teacher develops shadow plays with primary-grade children she should employ the Mother Goose rhymes or stories centered upon holidays for which plenty of literature material is available. Older children enjoy interpreting and watching the folk tales, ballads, and stories of high adventure.

The shadow play screen is made from any translucent material (a white sheet, tracing paper, a white window shade, unbleached muslin). A practical size is 8 x 12 feet. The screen should be tacked or stapled rigidly to a wooden frame or suspended from a rod so that it is wrinkle free. About six feet behind the performers arrange a light source: a 200-watt bulb and a reflector, a slide projector, or a strong bulb in a metal-lined box, mounted atop a table. Both the light and the screen should be fairly high, so that if puppet figures are to be manipulated from below, the puppeteers will not cast their own shadows.

Color may be introduced into the shadow play by placing a sheet or (alternately) sheets of translucent colored gelatin over the light source. Cellophane-covered shapes and scenery also add dimension to the shadow play, giving an effect of yellow moon, orange sunset, or pink sunrise. Any properties, puppeteers, actors, and light sources may be concealed from the audience seated out front in the darkened room by a valance around the screen and by standing portable partitions.

Scenery for the shadow play may be made from (1) cut-out silhouettes manufactured from tagboard or heavy cardboard, or (2) stencils or figures painted directly onto the screen. If the shadow play is performed "puppet style," objects (trees, tables, buses) and animals may be mounted on sticks for easy movement. Figures cut from black oaktag and manipulated *in front* of a white background provide another form of shadowgraph.

A successful shadow play requires careful preparation and practice. Oral interpretation of parts may be done by the actors behind the screen, by a single narrator, or by a tape recording, or the production may be entirely in pantomime. Musical accompaniment will also enhance the production.

Whether the shadow play is done with puppets, marionettes, or children, the figures must be close to the screen to give a sharp outline. If it is performed by puppeteers, the puppet manipulators must sit or kneel below the screen and they must remember to move their puppets only right or left, never forward or backward. Because of lack of space behind the shadow play screen, stories selected for presentation should be reduced to their simplest components: a limited number of scenes and a minimum number of characters. To give more children an opportunity to perform, a number of casts may be formed to present the play.

One story that meets the criteria above is the story of "Goldilocks and the Three Bears." Four characters are required and each has a distinctive appearance as seen through a screen: a girl, and three bears of different body sizes. The following scenes might be enacted:

1. Goldilocks arrives at the cottage of the bears.
2. Goldilocks "tries out" the bears' porridge, chairs, and beds, falling asleep upon the big bear's bed.
3. The three bears arrive home.
4. The bears repeat the routines about the porridge, the chairs, and the beds.
5. Goldilocks is awakened and sits up on the big bear's bed.
6. Goldilocks runs from the cottage of the three bears.

Informal Dramatization

Children's engagement with dramatics other than pantomime, puppets or shadow plays falls in the realm of informal dramatization. Indeed, so easily may the transition be made that the teacher working with second- or third-grade children may still get good mileage from the Mother Goose rhymes. In one instance, a teacher may challenge a class to do informal dramatizations reciting "Baa, baa, Black Sheep, have you any wool? Yes sir, yes sir, three bags full!" Then she elects a group of children to recite the rhyme as if they were sad, happy, angry, flippant, etc. At the same time she may ask other children to recite the rhyme as they assume various character roles: Aladdin, King Midas, *Alphonse, That Bearded One* (by Natalie Carlson), and so on.

Usually informal dramatization begins with the end of something: a completed story in a literature reader, a chapter that the teacher has just finished reading from a favorite book, a poem recited by the teacher. From these arise an extemporaneous dramatization of the piece of literature. The performance does not evolve from a lengthy analysis of plot and characters. Rather, the children are so inspired by the story as to want to play it out, right away.

Typical of the books that can be used in this fashion is Munro Leaf's delightfully funny *The Story of Ferdinand*. This is a simple tale, brief, full of action, and with enough characters so the whole class may participate. The cast of characters might include Ferdinand, his mother, a few "extra" bulls, five selectors, a bee, two or three Banderilleros and Picadores, a Matador, and the crowd to cheer on Ferdinand. Props (properties) called for are few: flowers (to sniff and for the ladies' hair), wooden spears, a cape, and a wooden sword.

The story may be performed impromptu; that is, it is just put on without any analysis. Everything—dialogue, action, properties—are spontaneously thought up and delivered. Some fluent reader may serve as narrator and read aloud certain portions of the story as the cast acts it out.

Or, the action and the dialogue may be worked out in part, with the actors memorizing only the sequence of happenings and then rendering freely their interpretation of the dialogue. Individual tryouts for the various character parts are possible. This should prove interesting if the *The Story of Ferdinand* were to be presented, for many children would want the role of Ferdinand, the central figure. Who is to receive the role should be decided by vote of the class after they have viewed the spontaneous interpretations and ideas that flow from each potential actor.

As we have noted in the case of *The Story of Ferdinand*, there are enough roles to occupy the whole class in the production. However, if some of these roles are dispensed with, it would be possible to form a number of different casts which, in turn, can work out their own interpretations of the story. In most instances, and particularly at the upper-grade levels, this is to be preferred because all of the children want and demand a place in the informal shows.

Through all of this the teacher serves in a supportive role, helping the children to visualize the scenes and characters, serving as a source of properties, and helping with room arrangement and staging. Once the play is in progress, the teacher melts into the background, coming forward only if the continuity of the play falters, or acting as a prompter if a bit of dialogue is momentarily displaced. When the informal dramatization is over, the teacher leads the class in an analysis of the production.

Following are some books and stories that offer potential for informal dramatization. From among these titles, a teacher can undoubtedly find several pieces of material suited to children in grades one through six. Many old folk tale favorites are to be found here, along with some of the standard book favorites. These two categories are particularly useful because children can more easily remember and follow the sequence of the story and give their interpretations of familiar characters. Also listed are some repetitive, cumulative tales for younger children, and a few fast-paced, lively, "our hero" tales for the older boys and girls.

primary level

Andy and the Lion (James Daugherty)

Ask Mr. Bear (Marjorie Flack)

Bremen Town Musicians (Brothers Grimm)

Caps for Sale (Esphyr Slobodkina)

Cinderella (Charles Perrault)*

Elves and the Shoemaker (Brothers Grimm)

Epaminondas (many versions)

Five Chinese Brothers (Claire Bishop)

Golden Goose (many versions)*

Hansel and Gretel (Brothers Grimm)

Henny Penny (Joseph Jacob's edition)

Jack and the Beanstalk (many versions)

Just So Stories (Rudyard Kipling)

Little Pear (E.F. Lattimore)

Little Toot (Hardie Gramatky)

Millions of Cats (Wanda Gag)

Mother Goose rhymes

Painted Pig (Elizabeth Morrow)

Pelle's New Suit (Ella Beskow)

Peter Rabbit (Beatrix Potter)

Poppy Seed Cakes (Margery Clark)

Red Riding Hood (Charles Perrault)*

Rumpelstiltskin (Brothers Grimm)*

Sleeping Beauty (Charles Perrault)

Snow White and the Seven Dwarfs (Brothers Grimm)

Story of Ferdinand (Munro Leaf)

Tar Baby (Joel Harris)

Three Bears (many versions)

Three Billy Goats Gruff (many versions)

Three Little Kittens (many versions)

Three Little Pigs (many versions)

Walter, the Lazy Mouse (Marjorie Flack)

Wolf and the Seven Little Kids (Brothers Grimm)

intermediate level

Adam of the Road (Elizabeth Gray)

Adventures of Pinocchio (Carlo Lorenzini)

Aladdin (many versions)*

Ali Baba and the Forty Thieves (many versions)

Augustus and the River (Eddie LeGrand)

Ben and Me (Robert Lawson)

Benjamin West and His Cat Grimalkin (Marguerite Henry)

Caddie Woodlawn (Carol Brink)

500 Hats of Bartholomew Cubbins (Dr. Suess)

Golden Touch (Nathaniel Hawthorne)

Homer Price (Robert McCloskey)

Huckleberry Finn (Mark Twain)

Johnny Appleseed (many versions)

King's Stilts (Dr. Suess)

Lentil (Robert McCloskey)

Many Moons (James Thurber)

Mary Poppins (Pamela Travers)*

Miss Pickerell Goes to Mars (Ellen MacGregor)

Moffat stories (Eleanor Estes)

Mr. Popper's Penguins (Florence Atwater)

Mrs. Piggle Wiggle stories (Betty MacDonald)

Penrod (Booth Tarkington)

Pied Piper of Hamelin (Robert Browning)

Rapunzel (many versions)*

Robin Hood (Howard Pyle)

Robinson Crusoe (Daniel Defoe)

Secret Garden (Frances Burnett)

Spice and the Devil's Cave (Agnes Hewes)

Swiss Family Robinson (Johann Wyss)

Tom Sawyer (Mark Twain)

Treasure Island (Robert Stevenson)

Wind in the Willows (Kenneth Grahame)

Winnie-the-Pooh (A.A. Milne)

Formal Dramatics

Formal production of literature plays at the elementary-school level is an involved process, which calls for costumes, properties, memorization of lines, rehearsals, and the acquisition of suitable scripts. Formal play production is often decried because of these very requirements, and some consider the process too difficult and trying in proportion to its rewards. Rather than abandoning the idea of formal production of

*This story, as well as many others, has been adapted and published as a formal play for children's theatre. Catalogs of such plays may be obtained by writing to the following companies: (1) Baker's Plays, 100 Summer Street, Boston, Mass.; (2) Children's Theatre Press Coverlot, Anchorage, Ky.; (3) Coach House Press, 53 West Jackson Blvd., Chicago, Ill.; (4) Plays, Inc., 8 Arlington Street, Boston, Mass.; (5) Samuel French, 25 West 45th Street, New York, N.Y. *The Grade Teacher Magazine* and *The Instructor Magazine* are also excellent sources of plays, particularly of the story for informal dramatization.

literature plays, teachers should attempt to adjust to the needs and capabilities of groups of children who can profit from such an experience. For some children do find a great deal of satisfaction in the production of a polished theatrical performance.

Undertaking the preparation of a literature story for formal dramatic presentation is an intricate task, necessitating a knowledge of many details and a discussion of many topics. Examination of these details and a discussion of all salient points of formal dramatics is beyond the scope of this publication. However, a number of excellent books about formal dramatics is listed at the end of the chapter.

Ten BANG-UP ideas for creative dramatization:

1. Each child acts out the title of a book or poem which has a color in it (for example, *Little Blue, Little Yellow*; "Purple Cow").

2. The teacher plays a record containing the score from the movie version of, say, *Mary Poppins*. The children act out what the music says to them.

3. A narrator and selected children read aloud the dialogue from a literature story in a basal reader while a cast acts out the story being read.

4. Hundreds of recordings of children's stories are available (such as "The Sorcerer's Apprentice" under the RCA Victor label). One of these records may be played, after which the children may interpret the story dramatically.

5. Dramatize a single line of poetry, or a complete poem, from such works as "Casey at the Bat."

6. Academy Award scenes may focus upon characters from well-known books, who act out their most famous scenes. These performances may be conducted at a banquet table where a toastmaster serves as master of ceremonies and introduces the characters and their acts.

7. Each child dresses as a character from literature and relates an incident from a book or story. For example, one child dresses as Dr. Dolittle (in baggy pants and a tall black hat, and carrying a satchel). The class can prepare musical verses to greet each character (for example, the verse "doctor, lawyer, Indian chief" can be altered and set to music).

8. Have children bring to class a *Classic Comic*. Ask them to dramatize the story, letting their friends portray other characters mentioned in the comic book story.

9. Writing original scripts is an activity common to many grade levels. Groups with little experience may want to begin by adapt-

ing and rewriting a well-known story whose characters are familiar to them. In so doing they serve more as editors who select dialogue rather than writers who create dialogue.

10. Television interviews of famous characters may be conducted, during which the book personality acts out a role for the interviewer and his "fans" who are watching.

FINE AND PRACTICAL ARTS

This section contains a variety of art and construction projects organized into fourteen categories. The teacher may use these activities to make the broad field of fine and practical arts a part of the literature program. The utilization of these creative art approaches will add zest to the daily teaching routine, at the same time increasing children's appreciation and knowledge of literature.

Books

Regular books may be composed and constructed by the children. After reading *How Baseball Began in Brooklyn* (Eddie LeGrand) to the children, one teacher cut out a replica of a large baseball to make the coverlet for the class storybook. On sheets of paper shaped to match the cover, the children each wrote an original baseball poem or story and illustrated it. These sheets were bound together and fastened to the cover with a brass paper fastener.

Students who find writing and drawing difficult can build a scrapbook about a well-known author, illustrator, book, or book character. The scrapbook may be "antiqued" by using old window shades for its linenlike pages. From newspapers, magazines, real book jackets, catalogs, and the like the students may collect pictures, articles, biographical data, and other material on the subject of the scrapbook.

Bookends

These may be made from a variety of materials. In one method, milk cartons are filled with sand and burlap is then rubber-cemented to all surfaces of the carton. Or, a carton may be filled with plaster of Paris; when dry, the carton is torn away and the burlap applied to all surfaces of the molded bookend.

A heavy wire coat hanger may be bent to form an open book-holder.

A similar device may be made by screwing two wire coat hooks into a piece of wood measuring about 8″ x 12″ x ¾″. The coat hooks should be placed about six inches apart to provide maximum support for the book.

Box Theater

Box theaters are of three basic types: the roller movie, the peep show, and the diorama. Common to each of these is that their construction usually begins with a box.

(1) The *roller theater* or box movie helps children analyze and interpret books. One teacher read aloud *Mr. Popper's Penguins* by Florence and Richard Atwater, after which the class planned and executed the story as a delightful box movie in the following manner:

    a. Twenty-nine important scenes from the book were identified.

    b. Each of the children volunteered to contribute an illustration of one of the scenes. These were numbered sequentially.

    c. Each child interpreted his scene in a 9″ x 12″ frame drawn on a 12″ x 15″ sheet of manila paper (shelf paper or wrapping paper could be used also). Pictures were drawn with crayon (paints or pasted-on colored paper cutouts can serve as well).

    d. Finished pictures were assembled sequentially and fastened together with masking tape. (If lightweight paper is used for the frames [pictures], edging them with masking tape will give them extra durability.) The first frame was put farthest to the right in the series so the pictures would unroll from left to right. Note: some box movies may operate on rollers that roll from bottom to top.

    e. The 29-unit roller movie about *Mr. Popper's Penguins* was then pressed on its back side with a hot iron.

    f. The movie box was constructed from a carton approximately 18″ x 24″ (an apple box, crate, or frame made from plywood will serve, too). A 12″ x 15″ window was cut in the carton. Holes were made in the top and bottom of the carton to the left and right of the window, into which dowel rods (or broom handles), 2″ in diameter and 26″ long, were inserted to serve as rollers. The back of the carton remained hinged to open and close.

    g. The two ends of the "movie strip" were attached to the two dowel rods by means of tacks *and* masking tape. This was done through the back of the carton with the dowels already in place in the holes. Handles with which to turn the dowel rods were made from scrap wood.

h. For the show the sequence of pictures was rolled from the left roller and onto the right dowel rod, the pictures passing through the aperture in the box as one child narrated the story.

There are a number of variations to the basic roller theater described above. Picture panels are painted upon a *window shade roller*, which is unrolled to tell a story. Individual *slit movies* are made by children who do pen and ink drawings on strips of adding machine paper, which is drawn through two slits cut in a heavy envelope. *Box bottom movies* use thin suit boxes with cardboard characters which have paper clips attached to them. A powerful magnet, attracted to the paper clips, moves the characters around the box bottom stage. A *cigar box* movie uses stick figures that move in and out through slits cut in the bottom of the box. An *individual shadow box* is an abbreviated version of the larger roller theater. A decorated shoe box is the stage, and everything else is scaled down in size. A burning electric light bulb is run into the back of the box, the box lid put on, and the shadow box movie is ready to go on. Pictures done in crayon show up best.

(2) A *peep show* is constructed in much the same manner as is the aforementioned shadow box. To make a three-dimensional peep show, a box with a removable lid—such as a shoe box or shirt box—is called for. One girl built a miniature scene of *McElligot's Pool* (by Dr. Suess). The inside of the box was painted light blue. Various materials—sand, pebbles, shells—were arranged in the box. Paper cutouts representing fishes and other water creatures were either stuck in the sand or pasted upright in the bottom of the box. Most of the box lid was cut away and replaced with a light green cellophane paper. When the lid was placed on the box and the viewer looked down, he had the feeling he was peering down into the water of *McElligot's Pool*. A small peep hole was also cut into one end of the box.

A series of numbered peep show boxes made by a class, with written clues attached to the boxes, may be converted into a game in which children try to guess the title of the book which the 3-D display represents. This is an excellent activity for a book fair.

(3) A *diorama* is a three-dimensional scenic arrangement of figurines and objects in front of a decorated background. They can be made to represent characters and scenes from books, plays, and poems. Although all dioramas are of this same general nature, they may be built from different materials. A *box diorama*, with one open side, has a painted-on inside background scene. Clay objects, paper cutouts, papier mache figures, or salt and flour figurines are then arranged in the box in front of the background. The box diorama pictured here represents a barn scene from *Charlotte's Web* by E. B. White. Other semi-enclosed dioramas

may be built into wooden frames and hat boxes. For example, one boy mounted three scenes from K.M. Peyton's *The Maplin Bird* on a lazy susan, dropped a hat box over it and cut a window in the side of the box. By means of a dowel rod attached to the scene separators and the lazy susan, the youngster was able to "dial" the different scenes.

Open dioramas may be made by placing figures in front of (1) a decorated bookend, (2) a folded piece of cardboard which provides a flat and an upright surface, and (3) a piece of cardboard, folded twice,

to provide two leaves on either side of a background. Dioramas can be built without background scenes by placing the objects and figurines in a pleasing arrangement on a table top, a sheet of plywood, a cake serving tray, or on a record player turntable if movement is desired. One inventive child obtained a battery-operated Alka-Seltzer display unit from a local drugstore and converted it into an animated scene from Louis Darling's *The Gull's Way*.

Clay Models

Nonhardening or plasticene clay may be used to model an incident or character from a book. Older youngsters are particularly adept at interpreting character: the Crooked Man; Pinocchio and his nose; Homer Price and the doughnuts (the doughnuts made of Cheerios). The models may be mounted on tables or in dioramas, with the other trappings of the scene made from a variety of materials.

Electric Board

An electric board is a proven teaching tool, not only in literature classes, but in other curricular areas as well. The electric board is built on a 15 x 12 inch board, and question bolts are matched against correct answer bolts by means of a dry cell battery and insulated wire. On a "Literature 'Lectric Board," to which children may contribute illustrations and the like, youngsters are asked to match (1) book titles to author's names, (2) book scenes to pictures of characters, and (3) questions about plots to answers about themes. Because of the complexity of constructing an electric board, the task belongs to the teacher. Simple, clearcut directions for building an electric board are given in Leslie Nelson's *Instructional Aids: How to Make and Use Them* (William C. Brown Co., Dubuque, Iowa, 1964).

Exhibits

Literature displays provide children with opportunities to express their reactions to books. Display material may be simply a single object or the display may be made up of a combination of articles mentioned here or elsewhere in this book. A display should be attractive, be placed where it may be seen and evaluated, and be a product of a child's imagination. A title card or poster should accompany the exhibit.

There are thousands of items and approaches that can be utilized in a literature exhibit. In addition to those already mentioned, we would add:

1. *Models.* A likeness of *The Cat in the Hat* (Dr. Suess) may be made by lapping papier mache over a "hair spray can" body and a "fruit juice can" head. A copy of the book is displayed with the object. Or interwoven pieces of colored yarn form a model of *Charlotte's Web*.

2. *Realia.* An old bed warmer displayed on a table shows an object important to the occupants of *The Little House in the Big Woods* (Laura Ingalls Wilder). Helmets, flags, model planes, and scale models of World War II weapons make *Silence Over Dunkerque* by John Tunis more vivid to the reader and the viewer.

3. *Sand tableaux.* Simple, homemade electric toys displayed with a copy of Ira Freeman's *All About Electricity* and John Lewellen's *The True Book of Toys at Work* make an exciting display when set in a sand table. Kindergarten children will love to model Mother Goose characters from clay, paper, or pipe cleaners and then place them in the sand table.

4. *Dolls.* Costumed dolls may be made from cardboard, paper, rags, wire, or ready-made dolls. Vegetables may be dressed to represent characters in *Down Down the Mountain* (Ellis Credle). Painted or costumed bleach and detergent bottles with burned-out light bulb heads provide striking Dr. Suess characters.

5. *Sculpture.* Book characters, animals, and objects may be carved from soap, wood, clay, plaster, and plasticene. Ships and boats carved from wood may remind the sculptor of Lois Lenski's *Little Sail Boat*, while a plaster stockade and a wooden cutlass reflect another child's appreciation of *Treasure Island* by Robert Louis Stevenson. A bar of soap can be fashioned into *The Biggest Bear* or *Little Pear*.

Jigsaw Puzzle

Made from book jackets or original drawings of story scenes glued on very heavy cardboard or plywood, the pieces of the jigsaw puzzle are cut out and placed in a large envelope. After a child has assembled the puzzle correctly, he might be encouraged to read the book or story.

Literature Maps

These may take many forms:

(1) In studying the myths, enlarge a map of the Mediterranean Sea

area using an opaque projector. Important names and places from mythology are drawn on the map.

(2) Drawings or pictures of famous authors of fairly tales (such as Hans Christian Andersen) and excerpts from their stories may be mounted around a large map of Europe.

(3) From a blank outline map of the world make a Biography Map, upon which children record the names and birthplaces of persons whose biographies they have read. Or small book replicas made of folded sheets of paper may be mounted on the map. These "books" contain book titles, author's names, and the name of the child who read the book.

(4) Draw a simple map of a book scene or a large movement map of a book or story. Animate it with symbol pictures of characters, objects, and "arrows" to show the action of the story. A map might be of (a) the floor plan of *The Borrowers'* house, (b) *Huckleberry Finn's* hometown, or (c) Tangerina and Wild Island described in *My Father's Dragon* by Ruth Gannett.

(5) A large map or individual desk maps of a locale or a state may chart children's reading of regional books by means of pictures that are drawn in.

(6) Literary maps which help children to place authors and books in time and place may be purchased. For example, *Literary America*, a 28″ x 37″ full-color map describing literary figures and their works, may be purchased for $2.00 (1966) from Civic Education Service, 1733 K. Street, N.W., Washington, D.C. 20006.

Magnetic Board

The magnetic board, like the felt board, has great possibility as a story-telling device. It accommodates properties, scenery, and objects, and even allows for a "walking" movement of the characters across the stage under certain circumstances.

A magnetic board that is to be used by a teacher in front of the class should be made from a thin, rolled sheet of iron measuring about 2 x 3 feet. Children's individual magnetic boards are ideally found in baking sheets or old metal trays (but not aluminum trays). Character cutouts and scenery made from cardboard, along with lightweight toys, can be fastened to flat or rectangular magnets with heavy glue, epoxy, or mending cement.

A strong magnet behind the board can be manipulated to move the story characters across the surface. An ideal story to demonstrate the utility of a magnetic board would be "The Old Woman and Her Pig," wherein the woman chases the pig along a road outlined in silver-sprayed wire. Another amusing story the children love to tell is *The Mouse and the Motorcycle* by Beverly Cleary.

Mobile

Character cutouts, illustrations from the book, objects portrayed in the story, miniature book replicas, and book jackets are balanced and suspended by flexible wire, light string, or thread from an umbrella frame stripped to the bare ribs, balanced dowel rods, or a real tree branch. The book *Bruno Munari's Zoo* may provide the stimulus for a class to make a series of paper, fabric-coated animals suspended inside a wire coat hanger cage. The zoo cage mobile hangs from the ceiling by a heavy cord.

Paper and Paint

Creating a series of original illustrations for a story, using paper, paint, and other art media requires good judgment in the selection of story incidents to interpret and careful thought in the choice of materials to execute them. There are several media in which children may work: charcoal, colored chalk, crayon, fabrics, India ink, paper, pencil, and paint (water and oil). There are many forms that the interpretation of the story could take: (1) book markers; (2) a collage; (3) individual pictures painted or pasted on Manila, textured, or white paper covered with

fabrics, other materials, or paints which have been applied as finger paint or splatter paint; (4) a mural; (5) paper cutouts, mosaics, torn paper figures, paper masks and silhouettes; and (6) posters.

(1) *Book markers* may be made by cutting off corners of colored envelopes and decorating them with scraps of cloth or ribbon and yarn, or painting on them pictures of book characters, titles of books, or author's names. Other book markers may be made by (a) cutting short strips from old belts and stitching on a representation of a book object, (b) wrapping tongue depressors in light paper decorated with a picture of a book character, and (c) drawing or painting a picture of a book character on one end of a heavy, but slender strip of paper which is inserted between the pages of a book.

(2) A *collage* based upon Ezra Jack Keats' book *The Snowy Day* (a book with a collage effect itself) is made by draping cutout representations of the boy and his mother with scraps of fur, burlap, or another cloth. Collage book jackets of the characters and scenes from *Wait for William* by Marjorie Flack can be constructed of heavy shelf paper coated with rug samples, sponges, wallpaper, yarn, rickrack, crepe paper, twigs, and grass. These materials should be covered with plastic wrap to prevent the pieces from falling off.

(3) Illustrating well-liked stories and poems as original *drawings or paintings* makes for a showy display and adds to the attractiveness of a room. Primary children would enjoy drawing a pictorial representation of a famous nursery rhyme. Older boys and girls might like to bind their original paintings as a booklet entitled, "Animals We Loved in Literature" after reading a series of books on this subject.

(4) A *mural* is a colorful medium for presenting characters and scenes distinctive to a story. Murals may be done on wrapping paper, oilcloth,

the chalkboard or even the school's back fence. And a variety of effects may be obtained by using chalk, paint, and so forth. After the over-all effect of the mural is planned, each child is allocated a fixed space on it. An excellent book for young children to interpret in this way would be *The City-Country ABC* by Marguerite Walters, from which the differences and likenesses between farm and town life can be portrayed.

(5) *Paper*, either cut or torn, may be shaped and fashioned into book characters and scenes. Kindergarten children might try their hands at cutting from paper the animals and objects necessary to tell the story, *The Rabbits' Wedding* by Garth Williams. The cutouts illustrating a scene from this very popular book could be mounted on a poster. Or torn paper mosaics based upon scenes from "The Story of the Little Red Hen" might prove interesting. Silhouettes of *The Black Stallion* (Walter

Farley) made from black and white paper, and paper masks of Long John Silver, *The Grinch Who Stole Christmas* (Dr. Suess), and other characters would prove more challenging to older boys and girls. The paper masks call for a supply of variously colored construction paper for the basic "face," plus quantities of paper scraps, yarn, paste, and paints to flesh it out.

(6) *Posters* are excellent devices with which to publicize a book. One class painted a series of large posters centered around mystery stories they had been reading as a group. The public library was happy to display the posters in a prominent place. Any outstanding character, idea, scene, or object from a book may be interpreted through an original

painting, drawing, paper sculpture approach, crayon, or collage placed upon a poster.

Pleat Story

Accordion boards or pleat books are made from six to ten pieces of cardboard, each 9″ x 12″. Hinge the 12-inch sides with binder linen, but leave a one-quarter-inch space between the pieces so that the strips can fold accordion-fashion. Small pictures of scenes and characters, made as paintings, montages, or collages, may be pasted to the panels to tell the story in sequence. The front panel may have a printed title. Both sides of the pleat folder may be used, accommodating one long story or two different stories. Two variations of this basic idea are a fan that is unfolded to reveal a sequence of painted-on panels, and a four-panel pop-out story made from a cardboard box and four fold out panels showing scenes from a story.

Stamp Imprints

Stamped prints of book characters and scenes may be made upon cloth, paper, a handkerchief, tablecloths, and quilts. The stamps can be made of potatoes, corks, felt, rubber, and linoleum. Book jackets and book posters may also be printed in this fashion.

Time Lines

Time charts are used to plot relationships between and among various authors, books, events, and times. Time lines are done on long, narrow sheets of paper. A particular amount of space on the line will represent a given period of time. For example, one foot may represent 100 years. Points on one chart might show a picture of a famous writer, with his birthdate or the date of publication of his best-known book. A time line can be developed into a mural, with pictures of authors or their book creations being shown along the line.

A final baker's dozen art-and-literature-based ideas may be found in the following projects:

1. Cutouts of story characters are fashioned as *lapel pins*.

2. Original paintings, drawings, or silhouette cutouts of favorite book characters are painted, pinned, or sewn onto multicolored cloth *pennants*, one fluttering from a flag holder (made from an empty plastic bottle) at each child's desk.

3. By pulling on the control cords of a *venetian blind*, a child can dial alternating scenes from *The Happy Lion* (Louise Fatio) or other book that have been painted by two children.

4. A tinker-toy or erector set converts into a revolving *ferris wheel* with gaily colored paper dolls seated astride it to represent famous literature characters.

5. A heavy cardboard disc spins around a *record player turntable*, carrying with it cutout characters from literature.

6. A series of scenes from a story are bound together and then thumbed rapidly, giving action to the *flip movie*.

7. On a *paper shadow plate*, paint or paste pictures of book characters. Hang up the shadow plates by applying a gummed picture hanger to the back.

8. *Book plates* are prepared from gummed paper upon which are drawn or pasted construction paper silhouette illustrations of book scenes and characters.

9. Several scenes from a book are drawn on a long narrow paper. Brief descriptions of the scenes are lettered in, after which the ends of the paper are glued to two dowel rods and the paper rolled up to form a *scroll*.

10. Build an *oversized book*—at least as tall as the shortest child in the class, and big enough to stand upright on the floor. Make the cover of heavy cardboard from an appliance box, and decorate.

On the heavy butcher paper or wrapping paper pages have the children paste in original stories and illustrate them.

11. Have children contribute to a four-panel *cartoon* strip showing *Angus and the Cats* by Marjorie Flack. Picture Angus showing off and write what the characters are saying by drawing in balloons over their heads.

12. Give each child a 2′ x 2′ sheet of heavy paper. Have him neatly print a favorite quotation or portion of dialogue from *The Matchlock Gun* by Walter Edmonds or any other book. The children then go over the words with yarn, after which they make a decorative border and mount their *literature sampler* in a frame.

13. After reading *Three Golden Oranges and Other Spanish Folk Tales* by Ralph Boggs and Mary Davis, one or two children might make an orange *sachet* by inserting cloves in a real orange. Place the sachet on a display table with the book.

A BANG-UP idea for a resourceful literature class. A group of capable youngsters, each of whom has read *The King's Fifth* by Scott Odell, may salute the book by each of them illustrating the book in a different art medium: watercolor poster, charcoal etching, mobile, clay model, diorama, and other expressive art and craft materials. These are displayed, along with the book, at the *One Book Show*.

SELECTED LIST OF MATERIALS AND RESOURCES FOR THE TEACHER

dramatics—books

Allstrom, Elizabeth, LET'S PLAY A STORY. New York: Friendship Press, 1957.

Burger, Isabel B., CREATIVE PLAY ACTING: LEARNING THROUGH DRAMA. 2nd ed. New York: The Ronald Press Company, 1966.

Chorpenning, Charlotte, TWENTY-ONE YEARS WITH CHILDREN'S THEATRE. Anchorage, Ky.: Children's Theatre Press, 1962.

Daniels, Elva S., CREATIVE RHYTHMS FOR YOUR CLASS. Dansville, N.Y.: F.A. Owen Publishing Co., 1965. Booklet.

Davis, Jed H., and Mary J. Watkins, CHILDREN'S THEATRE: PLAY PRODUCTION FOR THE CHILD AUDIENCE. New York: Harper & Row, Publishers, 1960.

Fitzgerald, Burdette S., LET'S ACT THE STORY. San Francisco: Fearon Publishers, 1957. Booklet.

————, WORLD TALES FOR CREATIVE DRAMATICS AND STORYTELLING. Englewood Cliffs, N.J.: Prentice-Hall, Inc., 1962.

Forkert, Otto M., CHILDREN'S THEATER. . . .THAT CAPTURES ITS AUDIENCE. Chicago: Coach House Press, 1962.

Howes, Alan, TEACHING LITERATURE TO ADOLESCENTS: PLAYS. Chicago: Scott, Foresman & Company, 1967.

Kamerman, Sylvia E., CHILDREN'S PLAYS FROM FAVORITE STORIES. Boston: Plays, Inc., 1959.

Kase, Robert, STORIES FOR CREATIVE ACTING. New York: Samuel French, 1961.

Lease, Ruth, and Geraldine B. Siks, CREATIVE DRAMATICS IN HOME, SCHOOL AND COMMUNITY. New York: Harper & Row, Publishers, 1958.

Rasmussen, Carrie, SPEECH METHODS IN THE ELEMENTARY SCHOOL, Chapters 3 and 9. New York: The Ronald Press Company, 1962.

Schattner, Regina, CREATIVE DRAMATICS FOR HANDICAPPED CHILDREN. New York: The John Day Company, Inc., 1967.

Scott, Louise Binder, FAIRY TALE PLAYS IN RHYME. Dansville, N.Y.: F.A. Owen Publishing Co., 1961. Booklet.

Siks, Geraldine B., CHILDREN'S LITERATURE FOR DRAMATIZATION: AN ANTHOLOGY. New York: Harper & Row, Publishers, 1964.

————, CREATIVE DRAMATICS; AN ART FOR CHILDREN. New York: Harper & Row, Publishers, 1958.

————, and Hazel Dunnington, eds., CHILDREN'S THEATRE AND CREATIVE DRAMATICS. Seattle: University of Washington Press, 1961.

Walker, Pamela P., CREATIVE CHILDREN'S DRAMATICS. New York: Hill and Wang, 1957.

Ward, Winifred, PLAYMAKING WITH CHILDREN, 2nd ed. New York: Appleton-Century-Crofts, 1957.

————, STORIES TO DRAMATIZE. Anchorage, Ky.: Children's Theatre Press, 1952.

dramatics—films and filmstrips

Baily Films, Hollywood.
   MAKE A MOBILE. (MP). 11 min. For grades 4–8.

Brandon Films, New York.
   STEADFAST TIN SOLDIER. (MP). 14 min. For grades K-6.

Coronet Films, Chicago.
   THE PEDDLER AND THE MONKEYS (Acting Out Stories). (MP). 11 min. For grades 2–4.
   STORY ACTING IS FUN. (MP). 11 min. For grades 4–6.

Northwestern University Film Center, Evanston, Ill.
   CREATIVE DRAMA: THE FIRST STEPS. (MP). 29 min. For Grades 1–4.

dramatics—records and tapes

Leo the Lion Records, New York.

CURTAIN GOING UP. Artists: Ruth Roberts, Richard Kiley, Julie Harris. For grades 3–6.

RCA Victor Records, New York.

DANCE-A-STORY-AT THE BEACH. For grades K-2.

pantomime—books

Bruford, Rose, TEACHING MIME. London: Metheum & Co., Ltd., 1958.

Howard, Vernon, PANTOMIMES, CHARADES AND SKITS, New York: Sterling, 1959.

Hunt, Douglas, and Kari Hunt, PANTOMIME: THE SILENT THEATER. New York: Atheneum, 1964.

Taylor, Loren E., PANTOMIME AND PANTOMIME GAMES. Minneapolis: Burgess Publishing Co., 1965.

puppetry—books

Adair, Margaret, DO IT IN A DAY: PUPPETS FOR BEGINNERS. New York: The John Day Company, Inc., 1964.

Arnott, Peter, PLAYS WITHOUT PEOPLE: PUPPETRY AND SERIOUS DRAMA. Bloomington: Indiana University Press, 1964.

Baird, Bil, THE ART OF THE PUPPET. New York: The Macmillan Company, 1965.

Batchelder, Marjorie, THE PUPPET THEATRE HANDBOOK. New York and London: Harper & Row, Publishers, 1947.

———, and Virginia L. Comer, PUPPETS AND PLAYS: A CREATIVE APPROACH. New York: Harper & Row, Publishers, 1956.

Binyon, Helen, PUPPETRY TODAY. New York: Watson-Guptill, 1966.

Creegan, George, SIR GEORGE'S BOOK OF HAND PUPPETRY. Chicago: Follett, 1966. Booklet.

Cummings, Richard, 101 HAND PUPPETS. New York: David McKay, Inc., 1962.

Curry, Louise H., and Chester M. Wetzel, TEACHING WITH PUPPETS. Philadelphia: Fortress Press, 1966.

Howard, Vernon, PUPPET AND PANTOMIME PLAYS. New York: Sterling, 1962.

Jagendorf, Moritz, PENNY PUPPETS, PENNY THEATRE AND PENNY PLAYS, rev. ed. Boston: Plays, Inc., 1966.

Lewis, Shari, and Lillian Oppenheimer, FOLDING PAPER PUPPETS. New York: Stein and Day (J.B. Lippincott Co., distributor), 1962. Booklet.

MacNamara, Desmond, PUPPETRY. New York: Horizon Press, 1966.

Scott, Louise B., et al., PUPPETS FOR ALL GRADES. Dansville, N.Y.: F.A. Owen Publishing Co., 1960.

Slade, Richard, YOU CAN MAKE A STRING PUPPET. Boston: Plays, Inc., 1966. Booklet.

puppetry—films and filmstrips

Bailey Films, Hollywood.
  ABC OF PUPPETRY—Two Parts. (MP). 10 min. For grades 4–8.
  HOW TO MAKE A PUPPET. (MP). 12 min. For grades 4–8.
Walt Disney Productions, Glendale, Calif.
  SIMPLE HAND PUPPETS. (MP). 18 min. For grades 1–6.
Encyclopedia Brittanica Films, Wilmette, Ill.
  PUPPETRY: STRINGED MARIONETTES. (MP). 11 min. For grades 4–8.
Library Films, New York.
  LET'S MAKE PUPPETS (MP). 10 min. For grades 4–8.

puppetry—related material

Instructo Products Co., Philadelphia, Puppet Playmates, Five sets of 12" x 34" story characters (e.g., "The Three Bears") in color on laminated craft board. For grades K–1.

Milton Bradley Co., Springfield, Mass., Drama and Puppet Stage. Size: 27" x 18". For grades K–3.

shadow plays—books

Blackham, Olive, SHADOW PUPPETS. New York: Harper & Row, Publishers, 1960.

art—books

Beringer, Doris, 3-D ART. Dansville, N.Y.: F. A. Owen Publishing Co., 1965. Booklet.

Currie, Dorothy H., MAKING DIORAMAS AND DISPLAYS. Dansville, N.Y.: F. A. Owen Publishing Co., 1965. Booklet.

Doan, Eleanor, MORE HANDCRAFTS AND FUN: SIMPLE HANDCRAFTS FOR BOYS AND GIRLS 4–10. Grand Rapids, Mich.: Zondervan Publishing House, 1966.

Erickson, Janet D., and Adelaide Sproul, PRINT MAKING WITHOUT A PRESS. New York: Reinhold Publishing Corp., 1966.

Honda, Isao, HOW TO MAKE ORIGAMI. New York: Ivan Obolensky, Inc., 1959.

Johnson, Lillian, PAPIER MACHE. New York: David McKay Company, Inc., 1958.

———, SCULPTURE: THE BASIC METHODS AND MATERIALS. New York: David McKay Company, Inc., 1960.

Johnson, Pauline, CREATING WITH PAPER. Seattle: University of Washington Press, 1959.

Krinsky, Norman, and Bill Berry, PAPER CONSTRUCTION FOR CHILDREN. New York: Reinhold Publishing Corp., 1966.

Kuwabara, Minora, et al., CUT AND PASTE. New York: Ivan Obolensky, Inc., 1961. Booklet.

Lynch, John, HOW TO MAKE MOBILES. New York: Thomas Y. Crowell Company, 1953.

Marantz, Kenneth, compiler, A BIBLIOGRAPHY OF CHILDREN'S ART LITERATURE. Washington, D.C.: National Education Association, 1965. Booklet.

Massoglia, Elinor, FUN-TIME PAPER FOLDING. Chicago: Children's Press, 1959.

Murray, William D., and Francis J. Rigney, PAPER FOLDING FOR BEGINNERS. New York: Dover Publications, Inc., 1960. Booklet.

Zarchy, Harry, SCULPTURE: CLAY, SOAP AND OTHER MATERIALS. New York: Alfred A. Knopf, Inc., 1952. Booklet.

art—films and filmstrips

Coronet Films, Chicago.
CUTTING AND PASTING. (MP). 11 min. For grades 1–3.
FINGER PAINTING METHODS. (MP). 10 min. For grades 1–3.
LET'S DRAW WITH CRAYONS. (MP). 11 min. For grades 4–6.
LET'S PAINT WITH WATER COLOR. (MP). 11 min. For grades 4–6.
Film Associates, Los Angeles.
WHAT SHALL WE PAINT? (MP). 11 min. For grades K–3.
International Film Bureau, Chicago.
FINGER PAINTING. (MP). 6 min. For grades 1–3.
Making a Mask (MP). 6 min. For grades 4–8.
PAPER SCULPTURE. (MP). 6 min. For grades 3–8.
McGraw-Hill Text-Films, New York.
HOW TO MAKE AND USE A DIORAMA. (MP). 20 min. For grades 4–8.
PAPER IN THE ROUND. (MP). 11 min. For grades 4–8.

art—related materials

G. W. School Supply Specialists, Fresno, Calif. Raggedy Ann and Andy Rag Dolls. For preschool and kindergarten.

CHAPTER SEVEN

PERSPECTIVE

Games and puzzles can be used to good advantage in a literature program because they have two obvious qualities: (1) games capitalize upon children's universal inclination to play, and (2) games and puzzles reinforce a child's knowledge of book plots, settings, titles, authors, and characters.

Some of the literature activities presented herein are old, tried, and true. But most of the games are bright and new, especially to children. Each of these games and puzzles has been popular with some group or individual at some time. Most importantly, the games and puzzles are educational and fun.

There is one game that is more fun than any of the others. That is the game of making a new literature game. A little ingenuity on the part of the teacher and her students will enable the class to get fun twice from a game or puzzle: the fun of making a new game and the fun of playing it. Further, many of the games and puzzles can be adapted to fit into different categories and situations, and the teacher should keep this in mind as she examines them for possible classroom use.

This compilation of literature games and puzzles is a relatively brief one. The teacher who faithfully reads the trade journals, such as *Instructor Magazine* and *Grade Teacher Magazine*, will uncover fresh games as they are developed and described by practicing teachers. Nor should the teacher forget the gamelike pastimes of playing charades or doing pantomimes as described elsewhere in this volume.

The literature games and puzzles presented herein appear under the following subject headings: Book Title Quizzes, Book Character Quizzes, Riddles and Puzzles, and Group Games. The collection closes with an assortment of game activities listed under the title, Odds to End With.

No attempt has been made to segregate activities according to school grade. It is felt that, with appropriate adjustments, most of the activities may be attempted as well at one grade level as at another.

PRINCIPLES WHEN DEALING WITH LITERATURE GAMES AND PUZZLES

The teacher who uses literature games and puzzles in the classroom should keep in mind the following guiding principles:

1. The purpose of the game is to further stimulate wide reading on the part of children, or to let them reflect joyfully on the pleasures they have gained from their past reading. Games are not to be used to force the students to amass a collection of literary facts and figures.

2. Children can derive a great deal of pleasure and knowledge if allowed to construct their own literature puzzles, games, and riddles.

3. Short puzzles and riddles are good fillers to be used during brief waiting periods between regularly scheduled activities.

4. Longer group games and activities should be included periodically as a part of the regular literature period.

Book Title Quizzes

1. Half Title
    Directions: Try to think of a word (or words) that completes each book title below. The first two are done for you.
    Example: Paddle-to-the (Sea)
    (Jack) (the) *Giant Killer*
    Justin Morgan .... *Horse*

2. Numbers Into Books
    Directions: Add these numbers correctly and then substitute letters for the numbers according to the key. You will find a well-known book title.
    Example: 22   1111
    101 212100
    123 301202
    ──────────
    246 514413
    OLD YELLER

1 = E		4 = L
2 = O		5 = Y
3 = R		6 = D

3. **Anagrams**
   Directions: Rearrange each of the following groups of letters to spell the name of a famous book.
   Example: Het Bohtib   (The Hobbit)
              Utstar Tillet   (Stuart Little)

4. **End with a Title**
   Directions: Complete each sentence with the title of a book.
   Example: Lee became involved with a leather-jacketed gang and almost got in

   ....

   (Trouble After School)

5. **Name the Book**
   Directions: On the line at the end of the sentence write the title of the book that is asked about.
   Example: What is the name of the book that:
   a. Tells about a bull and a bee? ....
      (The Story of Ferdinand)
   b. Tells about Jane and Michael having tea on the ceiling? ....
      .... (Mary Poppins)

6. **Three Titles**
   Directions: Provide three book titles that begin with the word "silver."
   Example: .... (Silver Branch, The)
              .... (Silver Button, The)
              .... (Silver Chief, Dog of the North)

7. **What Book?**
   Directions: Fill in the line with the title of a book.
   Example: .... convinced Lamp-Wick and Marionette that they should take off their caps together. (The Adventures of Pinocchio)

8. **Titles of Things (animals, hats, foods, etc.)**
   Directions: Think of all the book titles with the word "hat" in them.
   Example: .... The Cat in the Hat
              .... Caps for Sale
              .... Five Hundred Hats of Bartholomew Cubbins

9. **All About**
   Directions: What is the one thing that these book titles have in common?
   Example: Stone Soup   (They all have
              Ice Cream for Two   the name of a
              Popcorn Dragon   food in them.)

10. **Strike It Out**
    Directions: Strike out the title of the book that does not belong in this list.
    Example: Big Red   (dog story)
               The Incredible Journey (dog story)
               ~~Misty of Chincoteague~~   ~~(horse story)~~

11. **Book Title Word Game**
    Directions: How many words can you make from the letters found in the book title? You may mix up the letters.
    Examples: Lentil (lent, net, ten, till, lit, tin, nil, lilt, nit, let, it, ill, etc.)

12. **Hidden Titles**

Directions: Underline the 21 book titles that are hidden in the following story. You may use each title only once.

Example: "Come, play with me," said the little cowboy.

"No, I can't," said Homer Price. "Company's coming for dinner. If I play at the beach I will get nothing at all to eat."

So the little cowboy ran away over the meadow. He saw Charley the horse, the little lost lamb, and little bear. When he reached McElligot's pool, the little cowboy met Eloise.

"Come to the farm," Eloise called.

"No, let's take a Saturday walk," said the boy.

"All right," said Eloise. "This will be a happy day. We can take a giant step to the little island in shoes fit for a king."

"And we can make houses from the sea," said the little cowboy. "We will wait till the moon's full before we go back to Peter's sugar farm."

Check your titles against these: Play with Me, The Little Cowboy, Homer Price, Company's Coming for Dinner, I Play at the Beach, Nothing at All, Over the Meadow, Charley the Horse, Little Lost Lamb, Little Bear, McElligot's Pool, Eloise, Come to the Farm, Saturday Walk, Happy Day, Take a Giant Step, The Little Island, Shoes Fit for a King, Houses from the Sea, Wait Till the Moon's Full, Peter's Sugar Farm.

13. **Hidden Books**

Directions: Hidden in the following sentences are the names of well-known books. Can you find them?

Example: "It is beginning to rain," said the robin. "Hoods up, everyone." (Robin Hood)

It snowed throughout the long winter. (The Long Winter)

Book Character Quizzes

1. **Famous Characters**

Directions: Match each of these authors with the name of his or her famous book character by putting the number of the author on the line before the famous character.

Example:
1. Beverly Cleary   (3)   Madeline
2. Joel Harris   (4)   Little Bear
3. Ludwig Bemelmans   (2)   Brer Rabbit
4. Else Minarik   (1)   Henry Huggins

2. **What Character Is It?**

Directions: Name the famous character described in the phrase. Provide the answer on the line.

Example:
1. .... The girl who went underground. (Alice)
2. .... A pioneer tomboy. (Caddie Woodlawn)

3. **Guess Me**

    Directions: Uncover the name of the book character by working out the letter puzzle for each line. Write the answer to the puzzle on the line provided.

    Example: My first letter is in cup, but not in up: ....
                    My second is in due, and also in pup: ....
                    My third is in run, but not in sun: ....
                    My fourth is in sit and also in big: ....
                    My fifth is in cow, but not in caw: ....
                    My sixth is in bump, and also in dug: ....
                    My last is in has, but not in hat: ....
                    My first is in pig, but not in pit: ....
                    My second is in ten, but not in tin: ....
                    My third is in dog, and also in hot: ....
                    My fourth is in rat, but not in hat: ....
                    My fifth is in go, and also in dug: ....
                    My last is in eat, but not in at: ....

                                        (Answer: Curious George)

4. **Who?**

    Directions: Here are some sentences and phrases from Mother Goose rhymes. Fill in the name of the person who was left out.

    Example: .... see how they run. (Three blind mice)
                    .... lived in a shoe. (An old woman)

5. **Who Lived Where?**

    Directions: Provide the name of the character who lived in each of these places.
    Example: Who lived in an orphanage with 11 other little girls? ....
                    (Madeline)
                    Who nailed a bearskin up to dry? .... (Johnny Orchard)

6. **Who Ate What?**

    Directions: What did each of these characters eat? Write your answer on the line.
    Example: The owl and the pussycat. .... (mince and slices of quince)
                    Three little kittens. .... (pie)

202

7. **Who Did What?**
   Directions: Draw a line between the name of each book character and the thing that he did.
   Example: Tom Thumb ——————— slept for a long time.
   Sleeping Beauty ——————— lived in a bottle.

8. **Animals, Animals**
   Directions: On the line provided, identify the type animal that each of these famous characters is.
   Example: Flip .... (dog)
   Thidwick .... (moose)

9. **The Character's Pet**
   Directions: Identify each story character by drawing a line to his or her favorite pet.
   Example: Mary ——————— cat
   Bo-peep ——————— lamb
   Dick Whittington ——————— sheep

10. **Where Did They Go?**
    Directions: Draw a line from the name of the character to the place where he went.
    Example: This little pig ——————— to bed
    My son John ——————— to market

11. **Presents**
    Directions: The Crooked Man received a great number of presents for his birthday. On the line provided tell the name of the Mother Goose character who sent him these gifts.
    Example: A peck of pickled peppers. .... (Peter Piper)
    A bag of wool. .... (The Black Sheep)

12. **Characteristics of Characters**
    Directions: Fill in the blanks with the names of famous characters in fiction, and defend your choices.
    Example: You're as inventive as .... (Amos in Ben and Me)
    You're as humble as .... (Uriah Heep in David Copperfield)

13. **Pairs**
    Directions: The first of a famous pair of characters is given below. On the line write the name of the character's partner.
    Example: Jack and .... (Jill)
    Hansel and .... (Gretel)
    Penrod and .... (Sam)

14. **Find These Books**
    Directions: From the reading table select a book in which these characters will be found.
    Example: A boy who met some tigers. (Little Black Sambo)
    A rabbit who went to a farmer's garden. (The Tale of Peter Rabbit)

15. **Who, In Order?**

    Directions: Write the names of the characters on your paper in the order in which they are described below under the word "Who?"

    Example: WHO?

    fooled a rabbit   (Tar Baby)

    turned into a swan   (Ugly Duckling)

16. **Book Character Puzzle**

    Directions: Fill in the word square below from the three clues so that there will be a famous book character in the heavily outlined squares.

    Example:

(L)	I	D
	(A)	
		(D)

    1.
    2.
    3.

    1. Cover for a box
    2. Opposite of good
    3. Another name for father

17. **Know Your Characters**

    Directions: Can you make the name of a famous story character by adding the same letter to each box? Write the name on the line.

    Example:

    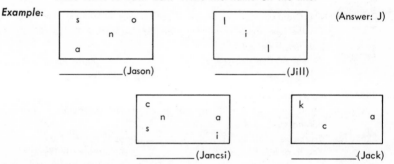

    s   o
         n
    a

    (Answer: J)

    _____(Jason)

    l
       i
        l

    _____(Jill)

    c
       n   a
    s   i

    _____(Jancsi)

    k
                a
         c

    _____(Jack)

18. **Mother Goose Game**

    Directions: Write down the titles of five Mother Goose Rhymes that have in them the names of boys (or girls, cats, dogs, etc.).

    Example: 1. Peter, Peter Pumpkin Eater

    2. Jack and Jill

    3. ....

Riddles and Puzzles

1. **Riddle Me This**

    Directions: Supply the name of the character described. Write his name on the line.

    Example: I climbed a vegetable into the sky.

    I came upon a big man in his big house.

The man was very wealthy.
I ran down the vegetable with some of the man's treasures.
I had to kill the big man.
Who Am I?

.... (Jack in "Jack and the Beanstalk")

2. **Next Line**

Directions: This game may be played in a number of ways:
(1) mimeograph the poems, leaving the last line for the children to fill in; (2) read the poem aloud and have the children write the last line; (3) read the poem aloud and have the children finish the poem vocally.

Example:
If wishes were horses
  Beggars would ride;
If turnips were watches
  (I'd wear one by my side)

Sing a song of sixpence,
  (Pocket full of rye)
Little Jack Horner
  Sat in a (corner).

3. **Who Is Who?**

Directions: On the line to the right of the verse, write the name of the character described.

Example: This little girl, at half past nine,
Left the house in rain or shine. .... (Madeline)
Who rode to give the folks a warning;
Rode through the night into the morning? ....

(Paul Revere)

4. **Book Chain**

Directions: Start each chain in the upper left-hand corner. The last letter of each word is the first letter of the next.

Example:

Chain A

1. Along came a ...., and sat down beside her.
2. The .... books were first published in 1834 by Jacob Abbott.
3. Walt Disney made a movie about the dog, ...
4. The Caldecott Medal was awarded in 1946 for the book The .... Crows.
5. .... in My Pocket is a book of riddles by Carl Withers.
6. The Norse god of thunder was ....
7. .... around a rosy.
8. .... liver went on a long journey to Lilliput.

Chain B

1. .... Alive was written by Pope.
2. John Masefield's "................. Fever" is a beautiful poem.
3. Tom Sawyer really did love his .... Polly.
4. The poem "The Coin" was written by Sara ....
5. A sign of spring is Janet Konkle's .... Kitten.
6. ....-a-dub-dub.
7. This little pig had roast ....
8. There was never a more speedy dog than the .... Sooner Hound.
9. .... Tomboy is about a girl who wants to become a ranch-woman.

Chain A

9. Terhune wrote about ...., a Dog.

10. Margaret Wise Brown wrote a story about a .... bird.

11. Hugh searches for The .... Colt of William Penn.

12. The Peterkin Papers was authored by Lucretia ....

Chain B

10. Toki comes face to face with .... of the White Mane.

11. .... am of the Road loses his dog, Nick.

12. James Daugherty wrote a book about the famous pioneer, ...
....

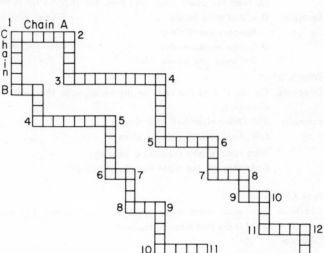

Chain A

Answers: Chain A: 1. Spider; 2. Rollo; 3. Old Yeller; 4. Rooster; 5. Rocket;
6. Thor; 7. Ring; 8. Gul; 9. Lad; 10. Dead; 11. Dutch; 12. Hale.

Chain B: 1. Snakes; 2. Sea; 3. Aunt; 4. Teasdale; 5. Easter; 6. Rub;
7. Beef; 8. Fast; 9. Texas; 10. Simba; 11. Ad; 12. Daniel Boone.

Note: *Book chains are to be preferred to the conventional crossword puzzle
as they are easier to construct.*

5. Storybook Matching Puzzle

Directions: Duplicate the page as seatwork. The sentences should be cut out and pasted under the pictures before the coloring is done.

Example:

Humpty Dumpty
Sat on a Wall.

Picture of a steam shovel, from Mike Mulligan and His Steam Shovel	Picture of a cable car, from Maybelle, the Cable Car	Picture of a mouse, from Cheerful	Picture of a fox, from Chanticleer and the Fox
Picture of an elephant, from The Story of Babar (here you will have to refer to the book)	Picture of a tugboat, from Little Toot (tug must have eyes)	Picture of an ape in a cape, from Ape in a Cape	Picture of a ladybug, from Fast Is Not a Ladybug

Picture of a pig, from The Clean Pig	Picture of a spider's web, from Charlotte's Web	Picture of a tree from A Tree Is Nice	Picture of a "boy cowboy," from The Brave Cowboy.

This is the ladybug	This is the ape in a cape	This is the mouse, Cheerful.	This is a Tree That Is Nice.
This is Maybelle, the cable car.	This is Charlotte's web.	This is the steam shovel.	This is the Clean Pig.
This is the fox.	This is Babar.	This is Little Toot, the tugboat.	This is the Brave Cowboy.

6. Literature Crossword Puzzle*

Directions: Fill in the crossword puzzle in the customary manner.

Example:

¹M	²O	³W	⁴G	⁵L	I	▓	▓	⁶P	⁷E	⁸N	⁹R ¹⁰O ¹¹D

1 M	2 O	3 W	4 G	5 L	I	▓	▓	6 P	7 E	8 N	9 R	10 O	11 D
12 E	L	I	A	S	▓	13 G	14 A	▓	15 H	E	I	D	I
16 L	I	N	G	▓	17 D	R	U	18 M	▓	19 E	U	E	N
20 I	V	E	▓	21 B	R	E	G	E	22 R	▓	23 E	S	K
24 S	E	S	▓	25 A	U	T	U	M	N	▓	26 T	S	E
27 J	R	▓	28 N	29 M	E	S	O	▓	30 H	▓	31 A	Y	
32 A	▓	33 G	Y	34 M	▓	35 L	T	▓	36 P	A	37 N	▓	S
▓	38 H	O	M	E	R	▓	39 M	I	D	A	S	▓	
40 T	▓	41 A	P	T	▓	42 H	43 P	▓	44 P	E	T	▓	45 S
46 I	47 V	▓	H	▓	48 P	E	E	49 P	▓	S	▓	50 G	A
51 N	O	52 S	▓	53 W	I	N	N	I	E	▓	54 T	R	W
55 K	I	L	56 T	▓	57 A	N	N	E	▓	58 G	R	A	Y
59 E	L	I	O	60 T	▓	61 Y	Y	▓	62 K	N	A	V	E
63 R	A	M	O	N	A	▓	▓	64 P	A	U	P	E	R

*Constructed by Lucy Ter Avest, student, Sacramento State College, California.

Note: Puzzle designs that can be related to the story are highly motivating. Examples would be a skate design for a series of questions about the setting, plot, and characters from *Hans Brinker or the Silver Skates*, or a spinning wheel from *Rumpelstiltskin*, or a dragon from *My Father's Dragon*.

Across

1. Boy in Kipling story
6. Friend of Sam
12. A Prophet
13. Abbreviation for Georgia
15. Lived with her grandfather
16. Rhymes with Ping
17. Fife and ....
19. .... Steven (share alike)
20. I have (as a contraction)
21. Cartoonist
23. Abb. for a Dog of the North
24. Sir Ernest Seton (initials of adventurer, author)
25. "................... Woods," a poem
26. Initials of the poet, T. S. Eliot
27. Abb. for Senior
29. Greek word for middle
31. Yes
32. An article in grammar
33. Setting for Go Team Go!
35. Abb. for Lieutenant
36. Peter ....
38. Boy who made doughnuts
39. King with the golden touch
41. Likely
42. Initials of author of Men of Iron
44. Mr. Popper's penguin was a strange one
46. Roman numeral four
48. Little Bo ....
50. Abb. for gallium
51. "Us" in Spanish
53. .... the Pooh
54. — , • — • , • — — (in Morse Code)
55. Scottish skirt
57. .... of Green Gables
58. Elizabeth Janet .... (author)
59. Children's poet with initials T. S. E.
61. — • — — , — • — — (in Morse Code)
62. Stole the tarts
63. Written by Helen Jackson
64. Prince and the ....

Down

1. Whit and .... in frontier story by Cannon
2. .... Twist
3. Made from fruit of the vine
4. Children's authoress who wrote Millions of Cats
5. Initials of author of "Four Little Foxes"
7. Expression of inquiry
8. Used to introduce a maiden name
9. To fasten firmly
10. City on the Black Sea
11. Small locomotives or trolley cars
13. Hansel and ....
14. The eighth month
17. Same as 17 across
18. A note to oneself
21. Bachelor of Arts
22. Registered nurse
28. Nature goddess
30. Greek name for Pluto
33. Country south of Bombay
34. The Day and the Way We ....
36. Main character in Great Expectations
37. Nickname for Nathaniel Hawthorne
40. .... Bell
42. .... Penny
43. Henny ....
45. Tom ...., Huck Finn's friend
47. French, meaning behold
48. Latin for pious
49. Made of four and twenty blackbirds
50. Home for the dead bird
52. Jack Sprat was very ....
54. The mouse saved the lion from a ....
56. Also
58. An animal
60. Abb. for thoron
62. Abb. for kathode

Further directions: Color the steamshovel blue and yellow; color the cable car tan;
color the mouse gray; color the fox silver; color the elephant gray;
color the boat red; color the ape black and the cape orange; color the
ladybug black and orange; color the pig black; color the web black;
color the tree brown and green; color the cowboy's pants brown.

7. A Book Crossword
   Directions: The clues to this crossword puzzle are from well-known nursery rhymes,
   book titles, or plots of books. One word from each line is missing. The
   missing words are the words you should write in the crossword.

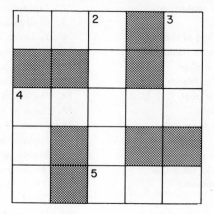

Example:

Across

1. *Rikki-Tiki-Tavi killed ....*
   (Nag)
4. *The dish ran away with the*
   .... (spoon)
5. *The .... and the*
   Dormouse. (Elf)

Down

2. *Mother .... (Goose)*
3. *Robert Lawson wrote*
   .... and me. (Ben)
4. *Five, ..., pick up sticks.*
   (six)

8. Mix and Match
   Directions: Match the questions with the answers by putting the number before
   the answer on the line after the question.

   Example: WHAT did Ferdinand smell? *(5)*   1. Mowgli.
              WHEN did I meet a man with
              seven wives? *(3)*   2. His hat would not
              WHERE did the old   come off.
              woman live? *(4)*   3. On the way to
              WHO knew Baloo? *(1)*   St. Ives.
              WHY did Bartholomew   4. In a shoe.
              Cubbins go to the castle? *(2)*   5. Flowers.

9. A Book Title Code
   Directions: Each box below represents a letter of the alphabet. Look at the secret
   code at the bottom of the page. Find the letter that uses the same

circles or crosses as each box and fill in the letters. You will have the title of a book. The first one is done for you.

Example:

| °. G | I | ° N | ° G | ° E | R ˣ | | P | ˣ Y ˣ | ˣ E ˣ | |

BOOK CODE

° A	B °	C °	° D	° E	F °	° G	° H °	I °	° J °
° K °	° L °	° M °	° N	O ˣ	P ˣ	ˣ Q	ˣ R ˣ	ˣ S ˣ	ˣ T	ˣ U ˣ	V ˣ
ˣ W ˣ	ˣ X ˣ	ˣ Y ˣ	ˣ Z ˣ

10. To Arrive at E

Directions: Start at number 1. Follow the arrows to the E by filling in the boxes according to the clues below. Each word begins with the last letter of the word before it. The first one is done for you.

Example:

1. (Peter) Rabbit.
2. A famous outlaw's first name. (Robin)
3. First name of a famous girl "book" detective. (Nancy)
4. Story of a horse. (Yearling)
5. His first name is Curious. (George)

1 P	E	T	E	2 R
6			5	
	➝ E		
4				3

11. Across to a Book

Directions: If you fill in the puzzle correctly, it will read the same down as across.

Example:

Across:

1. a letter in dig and do. (d)
2. Each of the three bears had one of these. (bed)
3. Author of Robinson Crusoe. (Defoe)
4. Lassie is a .... (dog)
5. The fifth letter of the alphabet. (E)

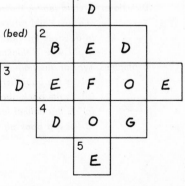

Group Games

1. **Book Bee**

   Directions: The children are divided into two teams, each with a scorekeeper. First, each team compiles a list of literature questions about authors, titles, and characters. A team captain asks each member of the opposing team to answer one of the questions. (In a variation of this game each team member asks a counterpart on an opposing team to answer a question.) Five points are given for each correct answer.

   Example: Who wrote the book, Ask Mr. Bear? (Marjorie Flack)

   In what story did two boys find a moose in a livery stable? (In Honk the Moose by Phil Stong)

2. **Story Circle**

   Directions: Seat the class in a circle. Have the players count off by fours. In each group of four, the first player gives the title of a book or story that the group has read. The second player gives the author's name. The third player gives the name of a character; the fourth tells some incident from the book.

   Example: Harvey: "The book is entitled The Good Master."

   Jean: "The author is Kate Seredy."

   Phil: "One of the main characters is named Jancsi."

   Jeanine: "I will tell what made Kate behave so badly when she first came to her uncle's ranch."

3. **Hard Clues, Easy Clues**

   Directions: Each person writes a series of progressively easier clues as to the identity of a book character. After each clue, the other members of the class guess the name of the subject. The game can be played as a radio or TV quiz show with points being awarded to the students for each correct answer. Knowing the name of the character after the first clue would be worth five points and so on down the scale.

   Example: I was a poor boy.   (5 points)

   I worked for a mean cook.   (4 points)

   I sent away my pet.   (3 points)

   The cat brought back money.   (2 points)

   I became mayor of London.   (1 point)

   (Answer: Dick Whittington)

4. **Twenty Questions**

   Directions: A child leaves the room while those remaining select the title of a book. The first child returns and is permitted to ask 20 questions in an attempt to discover the title of the book. (In a variation of this a class questions a girl who is thinking of a book or story.)

   Example: Typical questions might include:

   (a) Is the book fiction?

   (b) Is the book about animals?

   (c) Is the animal four-legged?

   (d) Is it a book about horses?

5. **Guess Again**

   Directions: The child who is "It" thinks of the title of a well-known book. The object of the game is for his classmates to guess the title by finding out what letters it contains. "It" chooses *Rabbit Hill* by Robert Lawson. He writes this title on a piece of paper and numbers the letters as follows:

   R A B B I T   H I L L
   1 2 3 4 5 6   7 8 9 10

   "It" says that his chosen title contains 10 letters. The players write 1 to 10 on their papers. Player 1 asks, "Are there any I's in the title?" "It" answers, "Yes, numbers 5 and 8." Player 2 asks, "Are there any M's?" "No," says "It." This goes on until someone guesses the title. Everytime a player asks about a letter that is not used, "It" scores one point. Everytime a player asks about a letter that is used, the players score one point.

6. **Authors**

   Directions: Each child will have a dozen slips of paper on his desk. Half of the slips will have book titles on them; the others will have the names of authors. When one child holds up the title card *Onion John,* any other child having the matching author card, Joseph Krumgold, will hold it up. For a variation, a pack of cards, consisting of three title cards and an author card for each book, can be designed. Children take turns drawing cards from the deck until they complete their hands of three title cards and an author card. A variation of this game, called the *Book Time Card Game,* can be purchased from the Children's Book Council, 175 Fifth Avenue, New York, N.Y. 10010.

7. **Book Bingo**

   Directions: Tagboard cards are made with titles, authors, characters, and descriptions of settings on them. A caller reads matching information squares and the players place markers over the proper squares. Each player must have a different card. A winner is one who covers a row diagonally, horizontally, or vertically, or one who covers his card completely.

8. **Hurry Home, Characters!**

   Directions: This table game makes use of episodes, authors, titles, and characters in a number of books. The game is played by twirling a spinner in order to move markers (paper characters) around a 40-station course. When a marker stops on certain squares, the player must draw a card which asks him about a book and/or which tells him to move ahead or go back a number of squares. The game continues until one player reaches the finish line, having answered correctly all the questions posed to him by the game board (shown on page 214).

Constructed by Arlice Tune, student, Sacramento State College, California.

9. **Book Football**

   Directions: Each team prepares a set of questions about books and stories, and scores the questions as to difficulty ("5 yard advance," "10 yard advance," etc.). A diagram of a football field is drawn on the chalkboard, with numbered lines for the yard stripes. Two teams play the game, with players being asked questions in turn. To begin the game the offensive team puts the ball in play on the fifty yard line. For a correct answer, the "ball" is advanced the designated yardage.

10. **Book Baseball**

    Directions: Four corners of the room serve as bases. A team captain "pitches" literature questions at the opposing team members in turn. A correct answer moves "the batter" to first base and on around the bases as team members answer other questions correctly. A missed question is an out. Three outs bring the other team to bat. Scoring may be based upon the usual rules of baseball or as in the game One-Eyed Cat, in which only first base and home plate are employed.

11. **Hot Potato Literature**

    Directions: The group may be seated in a row or a circle. A leader gives the name of a book and calls upon a player to respond with an author's name, a character from the book, or the like. Or the leader may mention the name of a character and call upon the player to name another book character whose name begins with the same letter as the last name of the character mentioned by the leader. In all instances, as soon as the leader calls upon someone, he tosses the player a small ball or chalkboard eraser. The player must provide his answer within ten seconds of catching the object or he becomes "It."

Odds to End With

1. **Book Alphabet**

   Directions: Using the description given, can you complete the title, author's name, book character name, or description of an event in the books mentioned, one for each letter of the alphabet.

Example: Went up the hill with Jill.   J .... ck   *(A)*

A book about Billy and his horse.   .... laze   *(B)*

2. Number for a Story in Literature
   Directions: Give the right number to complete the statement about these nursery
   rhymes and other stories.
   Example: .... blackbirds baked in a pie. *(4 and 20)*

Bartholomew Cubbins had .... hats. *(500)*

3. Storybook Addition
   Directions: Remember the correct numbers that are mentioned in each of these
   stories or books. Then add them correctly.
   Example: The number of bears that met Goldilocks: 3
   The number of Billy Goats Gruff: 3
   The number of Chinese Brothers: 5
   (from the Five Chinese Brothers)   ——
                                                                    11

4. The Color of Literature
   Directions: Tell the color of each of the following:
   Example: The fleece .... *(golden)*
   The bah bah sheep .... *(black)*

5. Famous Words in Literature
   Directions: What famous literature characters said the following words and in
   what book or story were they said?
   Example: "Somebody has been eating my porridge" (in a great, rough, gruff
   voice). .... (the Great Big Bear in Goldilocks and the Three
   Bears)
   "Pray do not send me to Singapore on a Shutter. . . ." ....
   (Godfrey Gordon Gustavus Gore from the poem by the same name
   by William Rands)

6. What Kind of Animal?
   Directions: Tell what kind of dog each of the following is and in what book you
   would find him.
   Example: Luath (Labrador retriever; The Incredible Journey by Sheila Burnford)
   Silver Chief (half husky, half wolf; Silver Chief, Dog of the North by
   Jack O'Brien)

7. I Lived in. . . .
   Directions: What characters lived in the following places?
   Example: An icebox (the penguin in Mr. Popper's Penguins)
   A shoe (the old woman "who had so many children she didn't know
   what to do")

8. The Wrong Word
   Directions: Strike out the word that does not appear in the rhyme about each of
   these Mother Goose characters.
   Example: Humpty Dumpty: wall, men, boy, horses *(boy)*
   Georgie Porgie: ant, pudding, play, pie *(ant)*

9. Fix the Rhyme

Directions: Arrange the words in this nursery rhyme so that the rhyme makes sense. The words in each line are not in proper order.

Example: Hickety hen my pickety black,
Gentlemen for she eggs lays;
Sometimes sometimes nine ten and,
Hickety black my pickety hen.
(Answer: Hickety, pickety, my black hen,
She lays eggs for gentlemen;
Sometimes nine and sometimes ten,
Hickety, pickety, my black hen.)

10. Cryptographic Nursery Rhyme*

Directions: Each letter in the following nursery rhyme stands for the letter that ordinarily follows it in the alphabet. In the case of the letter "z," use the letter "a." Now, unlock the secret of the rhyme.

Example: Izbj Roqzs bntkc dzs mn ezs,
Ghr vhed bntkc dzs mn kdzm,
Zmc rn adsvhws sgdl ansg, xnt rdd,
Sgdx khhjdc sgd okzssdq bkdzm.
(Answer: Jack Sprat could eat no fat,
His wife could eat no lean,
And so betwixt them both, you see,
They licked the platter clean.)

11. Guess the Author

Directions: Each student prepares a biographical sketch of a favorite author, making the four clues progressively easier for his classmates to decipher.

Example: Clue 1: He was born in Springfield, Massachusetts.
Clue 2: His pen name is taken from his mother's maiden name, Suess.
Clue 3: His first published children's book was entitled And to Think That I Saw It on Mulberry Street.
Clue 4: This famous "doctor" also wrote The 500 Hats of Bartholomew Cubbins, Horton Hears a Who, and Fox in Sox.
(Theodore Geisel or Dr. Suess)

12. The Author's Name

Directions: Each word or phrase below is another way of saying an author's last name. How many do you know?

Example: What you find on a tree   (Leaf, Munro)
Two or a pair   (Twain, Mark)
A place where corn is planted   (Field, Rachel)

13. Rebus in Literature

Directions: Write a short book review or poem of no more than four sentences. Then substitute pictures, numbers, or other meaningful symbols whenever possible in the place of syllables or entire words. Or, write the name of a famous book character in rebus (picture-writing) style.

*Note: This is an excellent game to combine with the preceding game, Fix the Rhyme.

Example:

T + ☁ (PIN) + 🔫 (GUN) − 🥥 (NUT) = | P | I | N | G |

(from The Story about Ping by Marjorie Flack)

14. **Book Laddergram**

Directions: Think of a definition for each word in the first column. Fill in the blanks above the words. Remove one letter from the new word in the first column and rearrange the remaining letters to form a word that meets the definition in the second column. Remove another letter from the new word in the second column and rearrange the letters still remaining to form the word defined in the third column. Put the first letter removed in the blank at the left. Put the second letter removed in the blank at the right. The letters taken away will spell the name of a famous author and one of his books.

Example:

T	TRAMP _ _ _ Drifter	PRAM _ _ _ _ Baby carriage	RAP _ _ _ _ _ Knock	M
O	OBLATE _ _ _ Dedicated	TABLE _ _ _ _ Slab on legs	BELT _ _ _ _ _ Strap	A
M	STORM _ _ _ Tempest	ROTS _ _ _ _ Decays	SOT _ _ _ _ _ Drunkard	R
S	SKATE _ _ _ _ Glide on ice	TAKE _ _ _ _ Seize	EAT _ _ _ _ _ Consume	K
A	STAIN _ _ _ _ To discolor	TINS _ _ _ _ Containers	SIN _ _ _ _ _ To do wrong	T
W	WAWL _ _ _ _ Wail (Scottish)	LAW _ _ _ _ Rule	LA _ _ _ _ _ Music note	W
Y	DELAY _ _ _ _ Hold back	DEAL _ _ _ _ Sort out	LED _ _ _ _ _ Guided	A
E	MALICE _ _ _ _ Evil intent	CLAIM _ _ _ _ Assertion	CALM _ _ _ _ _ Placid	I
R	SPURN _ _ _ _ Reject	PUNS _ _ _ _ Play on words	SUP _ _ _ _ _ To dine	N

15. **Add-a-Mad Title**

 Directions: Write the name of a different book in each of the blank spaces. Then read your "Mad Title" story to your classmates.

 Example: When I was 1.................... , my father gave me 2.................... and two long 3.................. . My 4................... gave me a deerskin coat and a blanket. The chief gave me a 5. .... and a good-luck bag. I was asked to go and live in 6................... for three moons. I camped by a 7................... and caught a 8................... for dinner. The second day I was 9. .... By sundown I had a 10................... and two deer. The third day I went back to 11..................... That night we had a 12................. and I got my name which is 13................ .

 (Possible answers: 1. Going Barefoot; 2. Hailstones and Halibut Bones; 3. Circus Shoes; 4. Choo Choo; 5. Man Who Sang the Sillies; 6. The House of Sixty Fathers; 7. Steadfast Tin Soldier; 8. Wonder Clock; 9. Going Barefoot; 10. Kildee House; 11. Jingle Jangle; 12. Calico Bush; 13. Crow Boy.)

16. **Books I Know**

 Directions: Write the letters in a word such as Book, Story, Plot, Poem or other across the top of a sheet of paper. In the blank spaces fill in the words, starting with these letters, that are asked for in the column at the left. Some have been done to help you get started.

 Example:

	B	O	O	K
Name of a Famous Book Character: Male			Onion, John	
Name of a Famous Book				
Name of a Famous Author				Knight, Eric
Name of a Famous Book Character: Female				
Name of a Famous Book Character: Animal	Blaze			

17. **Scrambled Books**

 Directions: Unscramble the names of famous books, authors, and book characters in the lists below.

 Example:

Famous Books		Famous Authors		Famous Characters	
pyolo	(Loopy)	linem	(Milne)	siln	(Nils)
		ilopit		zubese	

A BANG-UP idea for a game. Each child receives one *Crazy Book Review* mimeographed form, with five headings, shown in parentheses as on the left below. Each child writes in a real or imaginary book title. When each has written a title, he folds his paper so that the title he has written is not visible. He passes the paper to the player on his right, receiving another paper from the player on his left. The person receiving the paper now writes the name of an author, imaginary or real. This procedure is repeated until there is a full set of facts on each paper. The papers are then opened and read for results.

Example: (Book title:)   Speaking of Cows
             (Author:)   Hickle Hogboom

             (Two sentences about the funniest part of the book:)
               They chased the cook around the stove.
               She fell into the pie dough.

             (Two sentences about the saddest part of the book:)
               He had hurt his side with the pitchfork.
               The monkey fell dead.

             (Name the main character:)   The Garbage Man

SELECTED LIST OF MATERIALS AND RESOURCES FOR THE TEACHER

Games—Books

Harshaw, Ruth, WHAT BOOK IS THAT? FUN WITH BOOKS AT HOME, AT SCHOOL. New York: The Macmillan Company, 1948.

Games—Related Materials

Judy Company, Minneapolis.
Folk Tale Puzzle Inlays. Series of seven. Each 9″ x 12″. For grades K–1.
Mother Goose Puzzle Inlays. Series of thirteen. Each 9″ x 12″. For grades K–1.

G. W. School Supply Specialists, Fresno, Calif.
Uncle Wiggly. A card game. For grades 3–5.
Fiberboard Inlay Puzzle. Set of 48 different puzzles based upon Mother Goose characters and scenes. For grades K–1.

Appendices

APPENDIX A

EVALUATION OF A PROGRAM IN CHILDREN'S LITERATURE

Evaluation of a program in children's literature is concerned specifically with examining a child's sense of appreciation and enjoyment of what they have read. Changes in children's attitudes and understandings are the primary objectives of the literature program. The acquisition of information and skills is secondary and results as a by-product of the total process.

Evaluation of the literature program must be made in terms of the personal development of each child. Signs of growth will be reflected in the maturing literature interests, goals, and tastes of children. A carefully conceived and developed program in children's literature always considers carefully the individual differences of youngsters and includes many different types of methods and materials. And any appraisal of the program that is undertaken must attempt to ascertain whether possibilities existed in the program for both independent work and group activity.

Evaluation is effective to the extent that it is planned, understood, and used by all who are concerned with the literature program: the children, the teacher, the librarian, the principal, and other specialists. To assist in planning the literature program, the teacher, with the aid of the children, must make a survey and analysis of the children's own needs, using information from many sources:

. . . from children, who can give suggestions relative to their own interests and who can contribute to an ongoing evaluation of available literature materials and methods;

. . . from the teacher, with her knowledge of children's reading abilities, interests, needs, and levels of maturation;

... from librarians, who can supply information on currently available materials and book selection tools;

... from the principal, who can give coordination to any schoolwide activities in literature;

... from specialists and supervisors, who can point the teacher and the children in those special directions through which literature experiences may be brought to a more fruitful conclusion.

Evaluating children as individuals, and judging their development in literature on the basis of such intangibles as appreciation and enjoyment, is not an easy task. Therefore, the teacher and her children must halt periodically and judge the success of what they are accomplishing and what growth is taking place through a consideration of the following:

... The recurring frequency with which a child uses his leisure time, in and out of school, to read books for fun and relaxation.

... The quality of books, stories, poems, and other reading matter the child selects independent of the help of a teacher or librarian.

... The ability to distinguish between desirable and undesirable qualities of literature: in themes, in plots, in characters portrayed.

... The achievement of a broader base of information, involving the acquisition and use of new words and phrases, which is used in the various subject matter areas in class studies.

... The eagerness with which well-liked stories and poems are shared with classmates, particularly through discussions and oral and written reports.

... The desire to reflect an interest in literature through creative expression: dramatizing, storytelling, writing, discussing, playing games, singing, constructing, painting, and otherwise demonstrating a developing and continuing interest in the fine arts.

... The recognition that books are precious things, to be acquired, if possible, but always to be cared for and cherished.

... The ability to work with other children in planning book fairs, in developing units and unit activities, in participating as members of book clubs, and in contributing to similar group activities.

... The extending of an individual child's special interest in an area of literature.

... The movement along the road toward a lifetime habit of reading.

... The acquisition of an understanding of people of different religious, racial, and socio-economic backgrounds, but—most important of all— the attainment of an understanding of self.

The results of evaluation will be evident in the nature of school life and in the life of each child. The school program, including the literature portion of that program, is judged by the changes it makes in the behavior of individual children. If a literature program teaches the aggressive child to share, the shy child to assert, the indifferent child to seek out, and all children to turn to books for enjoyment and knowledge, the program in children's literature has been successful.

APPENDIX B

GENERAL BIBLIOGRAPHY

The following list suggests a variety of general books, films, and pamphlets that may be used to locate materials related to the field of children's literature. None of these titles has been listed in the "Selected List of Materials and Resources for the Teacher" at the ends of the chapters. A brief annotation describes the subject of each reference.

Allen, Patricia H., compiler, BEST BOOKS FOR CHILDREN. New York: R.R. Bowker Co., annual. Bibliographic review of selected books.

American Library Association, WE READ: SELECTED LISTS OF CHILDREN'S BOOKS AND RECORDINGS. Washington, D.C.: Office of Economic Opportunity, 1966. Lists of books and recordings.

Anderson, Marian P., BOOKS TO GROW ON. New York: The American Jewish Committee, 1961. Books treating various races, religions, and cultures.

Arbuthnot, May Hill, CHILDREN AND BOOKS (3rd ed.). Chicago: Scott, Foresman & Company, 1964. Excellent source book on literature for children.

———, et al., CHILDREN'S BOOKS TOO GOOD TO MISS. Cleveland: Western Reserve University Press, 1966 (revised periodically). Annotated list of classics, old and new.

The Asia Society, BOOKS ON ASIA FOR CHILDREN. New York: The Society, 1961. As title states, with annotations.

A BIBLIOGRAPHY OF BOOKS FOR CHILDREN. Washington, D.C.: Association for Childhood Education, revised biannually. An annotated list of 1500–1700 books.

Blanck, Jacob, PETER PARLEY TO PENROD. New York: R.R. Bowker Co., 1956. Description of best juvenile literature.

BOOKLIST AND SUBSCRIPTION BOOKS BULLETIN. Chicago: American Library Association, revised semimonthly. Reviews books and reference books critically.

Books for the Teen Age. New York: New York Public Library, 1963. List of 1,500 popular titles.

Books of the Year for Children. New York: Child Study Association of America, published annually. Guide to new books for children.

Bulletin of the Center for Children's Books. Chicago: University of Chicago Press, published monthly. Reviews books through junior high level.

Carlsen, G. Robert, Books and the Teen-age Reader: A Guide for Teachers, Librarians and Parents. New York: Harper & Row, Publisher, 1967. Excellent book about adolescents and what they read.

Children, Books and Reading. Newark, Del.: International Reading Association, 1964. Ten articles on children and books.

Children's Book Council, Aids to Choosing Books for Children. New York: The Council, n.d., revised periodically. Select bibliography of booklists and review media.

———, How to Write to Publishers for Promotional Material or Information. New York: The Council, n.d. As title states, with publishers' addresses attached.

Children's Book Shelf. New York: Child Study Association of America, 1965. Articles, and lists of good books.

Children's Catalog. New York: The H.W. Wilson, Company, 1966 (supplements; revised every 4–6 years). A basic selection guide to about 3,300 books.

Colby, Jean P., Writing, Illustrating and Editing Children's Books. New York: Hastings House, 1967. The title describes the contents.

Committee on Junior Booklist, Current Books—Junior Booklist. Boston: National Association of Independent Schools, annual. Books of preceding year reviewed.

Contemporary Authors. Detroit: Gale Research, 1400 Book Tower, 1963 (supplemented twice annually). Bio-bibliographical facts about 4,000 writers, including authors of juvenile books.

Crosby, Muriel, editor, Reading Ladders for Human Relations. Washington, D.C.: American Council on Education, 1964. List of 1,000 titles.

Cundiff, Ruby, 101 Plus Magazines for Schools: Grades 1–12. Nashville, Tenn.: Tennessee Book Co., 1964. Evaluative information on children's magazines.

Dalphin, Marcia, Light the Candles! A List for Christmas Reading. Boston: The Horn Book, 1960. As title states.

Dawson, Mildred, and Louise Pfeiffer, Treasury of Books for the Primary Grades. San Francisco: Chandler Publishing Co., 1961. Has 300 titles for young readers.

Deason, Hilary J., compiler, AAAS Science Book List for Children. Washington, D.C.: American Association for the Advancement of Science, 1963. Annotated list of books in mathematics and science.

———, editor, A GUIDE TO SCIENCE READING. Washington, D.C.: American Association for the Advancement of Science, annual. List of 900 paperback science books.

Dobler, Lavinia, DOBLER INTERNATIONAL LIST OF PERIODICALS FOR BOYS AND GIRLS. New York: Grand Central Station, Box 193, 1960. List of 350 magazines, foreign and domestic.

DOORS TO MATURE READING. Chicago: American Library Asosciation, 1964. List of books accepted by young adults.

Duff, Annis, BEQUEST OF WINGS: A FAMILY'S PLEASURE WITH BOOKS. New York: The Viking Press, Inc., 1956. Promotes family enjoyment of books.

———, LONGER FLIGHT: A FAMILY GROWS UP WITH BOOKS. New York: The Viking Press, Inc., 1956. Pleasant discussion of a family's experience with books.

Dunn, Anita, FARE FOR THE RELUCTANT READER. Albany, N.Y.: Argus-Greenwood, Inc., 1964. List of books for reluctant teenage readers.

EAKIN, MARY K., GOOD BOOKS FOR CHILDREN. Chicago: University of Chicago Press, 1962. Reviews good books of years 1956–1961.

———, compiler, SUBJECT INDEX TO BOOKS FOR INTERMEDIATE GRADES. Chicago: American Library Association, 1963. As title states.

———, et al., compilers. SUBJECT INDEX TO BOOKS FOR PRIMARY GRADES. Chicago: American Library Association, 1961. As title states.

———, compiler, SUBJECT INDEX TO SHORT STORIES FOR CHILDREN. Chicago: American Library Association, 1955. As title states.

Eaton, Anne T., READING WITH CHILDREN. New York: The Viking Press, INC., 1952. Comments on children and literature.

———, TREASURE FOR THE TAKING. New York: The Viking Press, Inc., 1957. Annotated bibliography of good books.

Fenner, Phyllis, PROOF OF THE PUDDING: WHAT CHILDREN READ. New York: The John Day Company, Inc., 1957. Articles and bibliography on children's books.

———, SOMETHING SHARED: CHILDREN AND BOOKS. New York: The John Day Company, Inc., 1959. Stories and articles about literature.

FILMS FOR CHILDREN. New York: Educational Film Library Association, 1961 (1965 supplement). Annotated list of 272 films for children.

Fisher, Margery, INTENT UPON READING. New York: Franklin Watts, 1961. Critique of modern English fiction for children.

Frank, Josette, YOUR CHILD'S READING TODAY. Garden City, N.Y.: Doubleday & Company, Inc., 1960. Values of reading discussed; books reviewed.

Fuller, Muriel, MORE JUNIOR AUTHORS. New York: The H.W. Wilson Company, 1963. Short biographical sketches.

Gaver, Mary V., et al., editors, THE ELEMENTARY SCHOOL LIBRARY COLLECTION PHASES 1-2-3. Newark, N.J.: Bro-Dart Foundation, 1965. Order in which books and audio-visual materials should be purchased.

Gillespie, John T., and Diana L. Lembo, JUNIOR PLOTS: A BOOK TALK

MANUAL FOR TEACHERS AND LIBRARIANS. New York: R.R. Bowker Co., 1967. Plot summaries of 80 books for young readers aged 9–16.

GROWING UP WITH BOOKS: 250 BOOKS EVERY CHILD SHOULD HAVE A CHANCE TO ENJOY. New York: R.R. Bowker Co., annual. Bibliography of good books for children.

GROWING UP WITH SCIENCE BOOKS. New York: R.R. Bowker Co., annual. List of 250 best books in science.

Guilfoile, Elizabeth, editor, AVENTURING WITH BOOKS: A BOOK LIST FOR ELEMENTARY SCHOOLS. Champaign, Ill.: National Council of Teachers of English, 1965 (revised periodically). Annotated reviews of books in 12 categories.

———, editor, BOOKS FOR BEGINNING READERS. Champaign, Ill.: National Council of Teachers of English, 1964 (and supplements). Discussion about, and lists of, books for beginning readers.

Haman, Albert C., and Mary K. Eakin, LIBRARY MATERIALS FOR ELEMENTARY SCIENCE. Cedar Falls, Iowa: State College of Iowa, 1964. Reliable books in science are listed.

Hanna, Geneva, et al., BOOKS, YOUNG PEOPLE, AND READING GUIDANCE. New York: Harper & Row, Publishers, 1960. Lists books and methods to use with adolescents.

Hardgrove, Clarence E., MATHEMATICS LIBRARY: ELEMENTARY AND JUNIOR HIGH SCHOOL. Washington, D.C.: National Council of Teachers of Mathematics, 1960. List of books to enrich mathematics.

Haviland, Virginia, CHILDREN'S LITERATURE: A GUIDE TO REFERENCE SOURCES. Washington, D.C.: Library of Congress, 1966. List of 1,073 sources.

———, and Lois Watt, CHILDREN'S BOOKS 1967. Washington, D.C.: Government Printing Office, Supt. of Documents, 1968. List of 200 books, preschool through junior high.

Hazard, Paul, BOOKS, CHILDREN AND MEN. Boston: The Horn Book, 1960. Broad historical survey (multinational) of field of children's literature.

Heller, Frieda M., I CAN READ IT MYSELF! SOME BOOKS FOR INDEPENDENT READING IN THE PRIMARY GRADES. Columbus, Ohio: Ohio State University, 1965. Books for beginning readers.

Horn, Thomas D., and Dorothy W. Ebert, BOOKS FOR THE PARTIALLY SIGHTED CHILD. Champaign, Ill.: National Council of Teachers of English, 1965. An 80-page bibliography.

Huck, Charlotte, and Doris Young, CHILDREN'S LITERATURE IN THE ELEMENTARY SCHOOL. New York: Holt, Rinehart & Winston, Inc., 1961. A text on all phases of children's literature.

Huus, Helen, CHILDREN'S BOOKS TO ENRICH THE SOCIAL STUDIES FOR THE ELEMENTARY GRADES. Washington, D.C.: National Council for the Social Studies, 1966. Five-part annotated listing of subjects related to world history, etc.

International Institute for Children's, Juvenile and Popular Literature,

BOOKBIRD. New York: Package Library of Foreign Children's Books, Inc. A quarterly journal about children's literature from around the world.

Jacobs, Leland B., editor, USING LITERATURE WITH YOUNG CHILDREN. New York: Teachers College Press, Columbia University, 1965. Booklet (63 pages). Covers twelve aspects of methodology.

Johnson, Siddie J., et al., CHILDREN'S BOOKS FOR $1.25 OR LESS. Washington, D.C.: Association for Childhood Education, 1965. A guide to inexpensive books.

Jordan, Alice M., CHILDREN'S CLASSICS. Boston: The Horn Book, 1960. Discussion and list of recommended classics.

Kingman, Lee, editor, NEWBERY AND CALDECOTT MEDAL BOOKS: 1956–1965. Boston: The Horn Book, 1965. Acceptance papers, biographies, and related materials.

Kircher, Clara J., compiler, BEHAVIOR PATTERNS IN CHILDREN'S BOOKS: A BIBLIOGRAPHY. Washington, D.C.: Catholic University Press of America, 1966. Annotated, 507-title bibliography on character formation through books.

Klemin, Diana, THE ART OF ART FOR CHILDREN'S BOOKS: A CONTEMPORARY SURVEY. New York: Clarkson N. Potter, Inc., 1966. Analysis of illustrations of well-known illustrators.

Koblitz, Minnie W., THE NEGRO IN SCHOOLROOM LITERATURE: RESOURCE MATERIAL FOR THE TEACHER OF KINDERGARTEN THROUGH THE SIXTH GRADE. New York: Center for Urban Education, 1967. Annotated bibliography of books portraying interethnic situations.

Kunitz, S. J., editor, THE JUNIOR BOOK OF AUTHORS. New York: The H. W. Wilson Company, 1951. Biographical sketches of authors and illustrators.

Ladley, Winifred C., SOURCES OF GOOD BOOKS AND MAGAZINES FOR CHILDREN: AN ANNOTATED BIBLIOGRAPHY. Newark, Del.: International Reading Association, 1965. Eight-page pamphlet on 67 sources in print 1960–1964.

Larrick, Nancy, A PARENT'S GUIDE TO CHILDREN'S READING. Garden City, N.Y.: Doubleday & Company, Inc., 1964. About reading and about books for the home.

———, A TEACHER'S GUIDE TO CHILDREN'S BOOKS. Columbus, Ohio: Charles E. Merrill Books, Inc., 1960. How to bring books and children together.

Library Education Department, IF I HAD A HUNDRED DOLLARS TO SPEND . . . . OR MAYBE A LITTLE MORE. . . . Stillwater, Okla.: Oklahoma State University, 1963. Books for primary-grade children.

Library Journal, RECOMMENDED CHILDREN'S BOOKS. New York: R.R. Bowker Co., annual. List of about 1,000 titles evaluated in a given year.

LIVELY ART OF PICTURE BOOKS. Weston, Conn.: Weston Woods. Fifty-six minute film on picture books.

McWhirter, Mary E., editor, BOOKS FOR FRIENDSHIP: A LIST OF BOOKS RECOMMENDED FOR CHILDREN. Philadelphia: American Friends Service, 1962. Books to use with study units.

Mathes, Miriam, et al., compilers, A BASIC BOOK COLLECTION FOR ELEMENTARY SCHOOLS. Chicago: American Library Association, 1960 (revised periodically). Annotated list of essential books and magazines.

MAURICE SENDAK. Weston, Conn.: Weston Woods. Fourteen-minute film on this well-known author-illustrator.

Meigs, Cornelia, et al., CRITICAL HISTORY OF CHILDREN'S LITERATURE. New York: The Macmillan Company, 1953. Critical history of children's literature.

Millender, Dharathula H., CHILDREN'S AND YOUNG PEOPLE'S BOOKS ABOUT NEGRO LIFE AND HISTORY. Chicago: American Federation of Teachers, AFL-CIO, 1967. Selected bibliography of juvenile books on Negro life.

Miller, Bertha M., CALDECOTT MEDAL BOOKS: 1938–1957. Boston: The Horn Book. Information on the books and their illustrators.

———, NEWBERY MEDAL BOOKS: 1922–1955. Boston: The Horn Book, 1955. About Newbery books and authors.

Munson, Amelia, AN AMPLE FIELD. Chicago: American Library Association, 1950. Discussion of book topics and activities.

NOTABLE CHILDREN'S BOOKS OF 1967. Chicago: American Library Association, annual. Brief listing of the year's best books.

Nunnally, Nancy, GUIDE TO CHILDREN'S MAGAZINES, NEWSPAPERS, REFERENCE BOOKS. Washington, D.C.: Association for Childhood Education, 1965. Eight-page annotated listing.

PAPERBACK GOES TO SCHOOL. New York: Bureau of Independent Publishers and Distributors, annual. List of paperbacks for schools.

PAPERBOUND BOOK GUIDE FOR ELEMENTARY SCHOOLS. New York: R.R. Bowker Co., 1967. Subject guide to inexpensive paperback reprints.

Perkins, Ralph, BOOK SELECTION MEDIA: A DESCRIPTIVE GUIDE TO 175 AIDS FOR SELECTING LIBRARY MATERIALS. Champaign, Ill.: National Council of Teachers of English, 1966. Excellent guide to literature materials.

Pitz, Henry C., ILLUSTRATING CHILDREN'S BOOKS. New York: Watson-Guptill, 1963. Discussion of the history and techniques of illustrating.

PLEASURE IS MUTUAL: HOW TO CONDUCT EFFECTIVE PICTURE BOOK PROGRAMS. New York: Children's Book Council. Twenty-four minute film on 10 picture-book programs.

Quinnam, Barbara, compiler, FABLES FROM INCUNABULA TO MODERN PICTURE BOOKS. Washington, D.C.: Library of Congress, 1966. A selected bibliography, with annotations.

Rasmussen, Margaret, editor, LITERATURE WITH CHILDREN. Washington, D.C.: Association for Childhood Education, 1961. Pamphlet on 12 aspects of literature methods.

Reading and Language Arts Center, A PLACE TO START: A GRADED BIBLIOGRAPHY FOR CHILDREN WITH READING DIFFICULTIES. Syracuse, N.Y.: The Center, 1963. As title states.

ROBERT MCCLOSKEY. Weston, Conn.: Weston Woods. Eighteen-minute film on this well-known author-illustrator.

Robinson, Evelyn R., editor, READINGS ABOUT CHILDREN'S LITERATURE. New York: David McKay Company, Inc., 1966. Collection of 61 articles about children's literature.

Roos, Jean C., PATTERNS IN READING: AN ANNOTATED BOOK LIST FOR YOUNG ADULTS. Chicago: American Library Association, 1961. Fiction and nonfiction for young adults.

Sayers, Frances C., A BOUNTY OF BOOKS. Chicago: F. E. Compton, Co., 1964. Books for six age groups; annotated.

Schreiber, Morris, et al., AN ANNOTATED LIST OF RECORDINGS IN THE LANGUAGE ARTS. Champaign, Ill.: National Council of Teachers of English, 1964. As title states.

Smith, Dora V., FIFTY YEARS OF CHILDREN'S BOOKS, 1910–1960. Champaign, Ill.: National Council of Teachers of English, 1963. Historical review of children's literature.

Smith, Irene, A HISTORY OF THE NEWBERY AND CALDECOTT MEDALS. New York: The Viking Press, Inc., 1957. As title states.

Smith, James A., CREATIVE TEACHING OF READING AND LITERATURE IN THE ELEMENTARY SCHOOL. Boston: Allyn and Bacon, Inc., 1967. Helps build appreciations and standards.

Smith, James S., A CRITICAL APPROACH TO CHILDREN'S LITERATURE. New York: McGraw-Hill Book Company, 1967. Critical text on subject of children's literature.

Smith, Lillian H., UNRELUCTANT YEARS. Chicago: American Library Association, 1953. Criteria of book selection for children's reading.

Spache, George, GOOD READING FOR POOR READERS. Champaign, Ill.: Garrard Press, 1966. Books and other materials to use with problem readers.

———, SOURCES OF GOOD BOOKS FOR POOR READERS. Newark, Del.: International Reading Association, 1966. Annotated listing of 73 titles.

Spengler, Margaret Y., A BASIC BOOK COLLECTION FOR JUNIOR HIGH SCHOOLS. Chicago: American Library Association, 1960. As title states.

Spierl, Dorothy T., GUIDE TO CHILDREN'S MAGAZINES, NEWSPAPERS, AND REFERENCE MATERIALS. Washington, D.C.: Association for Childhood Education, 1962. Eight-page annotated listing.

Stolzer, L.R., YOUNG READER'S REVIEW. New York: Box 137, Wall Street Station. Book reviewing booklet, published 10 times a year.

Strang, Ruth, et al., editors, GATEWAYS TO READABLE BOOKS. New York: The H.W. Wilson Company, 1966. A bibliography for retarded readers.

Sullivan, Helen B., and Lorraine E. Tolman, HIGH INTEREST–LOW VOCABULARY READING MATERIALS. Boston: Boston University School of Education, 1964. 1,100 books for grades K-7.

Thomas, Della, AND MORE TO GROW! . . . . MATHEMATICS AND THE SCHOOL

LIBRARY. Stillwater, Okla.: Oklahoma State University, 1963. Books for the mathematics program.

Tooze, Ruth, and Beatrice Krone, LITERATURE AND MUSIC AS RESOURCES FOR SOCIAL STUDIES. Englewoods Cliffs, N.J.: Prentice-Hall, Inc., 1955. Legends and stories to use in social studies.

TRANSLATED CHILDREN'S BOOKS OFFERED BY PUBLISHERS IN THE U.S.A. Locust Valley, N.Y.: Storybooks International, Box 11, 1963. A catalog of books translated into English.

Walker, Elinor, BOOK BAIT. Chicago: American Library Association, 1957. Collection of 350 best books for adolescents.

Walsh, Frances, THAT EAGER ZEST. New York: J.B. Lippincott, 1961. Readings about children's literature.

Ward, Martha E., and Dorothy A. Marquardt, AUTHORS OF BOOKS FOR YOUNG PEOPLE. New York: Scarecrow Press, 1964. Biographical sketches of authors.

Willard, Charles B., YOUR READING: A BOOKLIST FOR JUNIOR HIGH SCHOOLS. Champaign, Ill.: National Council of Teachers of English, 1965. List of books for junior high pupils.

Index